THE HOLY SPIRIT WILL DELIVER YOU

Your Freedom Lies within These Pages

Patricia L. Loranger

THE HOLY SPIRIT WILL DELIVER YOU
YOUR FREEDOM LIES WITHIN THESE PAGES

Unless otherwise indicated, all scripture quotations are from The Holy Bible, English Standard Version® (ESV®). Copyright ©2001 by Crossway Bibles, a division of Good News Publishers. Used by permission. All rights reserved.

Scripture quotations marked KJV are from the Holy Bible, King James Version (Authorized Version). First published in 1611. Quoted from the KJV Classic Reference Bible, Copyright © 1983 by The Zondervan Corporation.

Scripture quotations marked NLT are taken from the Holy Bible, New Living Translation, copyright © 1996, 2004, 2007. Used by permission of Tyndale House Publishers, Inc. Carol Stream, Illinois 60188. All rights reserved. Website

iUniverse books may be ordered through booksellers or by contacting:

iUniverse
1663 Liberty Drive
Bloomington, IN 47403
www.iuniverse.com
1-800-Authors (1-800-288-4677)

ISBN: 978-1-5320-4976-7 (sc)
ISBN: 978-1-5320-4978-1 (hc)
ISBN: 978-1-5320-4977-4 (e)

Library of Congress Control Number: 2018906424

Print information available on the last page.

iUniverse rev. date: 08/21/2018

Contents

Book 2: Receiving Freedom

Author's Note

Dear Friend,

It is possible you had a great deal of trouble obtaining this book. My book is easy reading, but you might discover you are having a difficult time reading it. You might be easily distracted or easily lose your interest. If you discover this to be true, then demons do not want you to be set free. If this pertains to you, then you need to read this book. Not only that, but you also need the freedom that only the Holy Spirit can give you (Psalm 50:15). The devil does not want you set free. As long as you are not free, these evil spirits will have a great influence over the choices you make. They have your reins in their hands, and the bit is in your mouth. In my autobiography, *Child of Woe, Child of Sorrow*, I told of my devastating childhood and my dreadfully messed-up adult life. Then I told of my conversion in Christ, when the Holy Spirit set me free from legions of demons. In this book, I will take you through a complete guide on how to receive the same freedom I received through the Holy Spirit working in me and how to retain your new freedom. In this book, you will find the way to freedom from your sins that you find difficult to overcome and control. In being set free, you will find it much easier to resist the devil. When you do resist him and command the evil spirits to leave, they will flee. The spirits will no longer be inside of you but instead on the outside. The King James Version is the most reliable Bible from which to learn the truth; therefore, I will be using the King James Version for more basic truths. All other versions have been derived from the King James Version and lack some important details. For this reason, my preferred version I read at home is the King James Bible. I do, however, understand that *thee, thine, thou* and other words can be confusing for many readers. May the Lord bless you. May you find freedom through Christ, and may the Holy Spirit work through you as you read these words, which I received from my best friend, our Holy Spirit.

Yours truly,
Patricia L. Loranger

Prologue

Ye shall receive power, after that the Holy Ghost is come upon you:
—Acts 1:8

At its widest point, the King's Highway 401, also known as MacDonald-Cartier Freeway, in Canada has 18 lanes in the main line and an additional 4 lanes as connecting ramps, a total of 22 lanes. Every one of these lanes measures 15 feet across, thus making the Ontario Highway 401 the widest road in the world. Now, let us take a deeper look. The width of every lane (15 feet) multiplied by the number of lanes (22) equals 330 feet. The King's Highway is 330 feet wide. If our imaginations could enlarge this highway's width by 16,000 times, it would then equal 5,280,000 feet, making its width 1,000 miles across. That is a lot of road! Let us now say this is the wide road the Bible refers to that leads to destruction. We know there are billions upon billions who travel this road to destruction, so my imagination tells me this road to destruction is a wide road. In the year of 2017, the world population was 7,494,320,452 people, of which, let us assume, 1,000,000 were Christians. That means 7,493,320,452 people are all walking on this road to destruction.

For all of my early life, I walked on this wide and well-trod road to destruction, not knowing there was a pathway that led to everlasting peace, tranquility and eternity with God. This road to destruction is popular. People of every nationality, young and old, follow this great and mighty road. They see in the far distance, at the end of this road, a great and glowing amber in the sky. It stretches across the entire highway of destruction, and as it fills the sky, it resembles gold. The lust and greed in the human soul draws them to this mighty pot of gold at the end of this highway. Humankind walks this great road, and all are heading in the same direction as they move closer, hoping in their greed to reach out and take hold of the gold.

There is plenty to do as they travel this highway. They lust after immorality. The sins of the flesh feed their souls. They can see, as they travel along, many attractions on the roadside to feed the sinful lust of their flesh. All these side-road attractions are well posted and clearly pleasant to their sensual drive. Although I was often sad and often considered suicide, just the same, I found great pleasure in fulfilling the lust of my flesh. I enjoyed this road of destruction enough that I did not desire to leave it. I was greatly disheartened yet drawn to the false hope this road promised me.

As I walked this road, I saw an attractive man. His outward beauty appealed to my sensual drive, and we then made a connection. After some time, his lust for me went dry, leaving me in a deeper despair than before. I fell down to my knees; I was helpless as I dragged myself along this mighty road. My only goal then was to make it to the end of the road and rest eternally in peace as I died and went into the grave. I then saw in the brush by the road a person who looked kind and warm-hearted. I could see that He was motioning with His hand for me to come near. I got up off my knees and, uncertain and fearful, started walking closer to the edge of the road. As I stood before Him, I could see that He was a Spirit, and I could feel radiating from Him a love I had never felt before. He reached out and took me by my hands, pulling me off the road onto a narrow pathway. As I observed the path, I saw that it had not been often travelled on. With gentleness, He held my hand and led me along the path. I asked Him, "Does this path have a name?"

The Spirit answered, "This is the Narrow Path, which leads to life; many are called, yet few will follow." As He led me, I could feel on the inside that He was gently scraping and removing the dirt from within my soul. Like a potter with a lump of clay, He was moulding me into a new woman. On the inside, He was making me into something beautiful! I was falling deeper and deeper in love with Him. I did not intend to ever leave this pathway to go back to the road to destruction.

Many years passed. Anguish was flooding my soul as never before. My heart was breaking. Tears stained my face. I had lost all hope. This burden was more than my soul could endure. I then found myself back on the mighty road to destruction. I stood on the curb, bent over with my hands clasped on my knees. I was gasping for air. I thought if only I stood on this road for a few moments, I would catch my breath and then continue back on the Narrow Path. A spirit spoke to me. As I looked up into his face, I could see he had a name across his forehead. His name was Unforgiveness. He said, "He's not worthy; don't forgive him." Another spirit was standing next to him. His name was Bitterness. This spirit said, "Punish him. Get even. Make that man pay for his wicked deeds."

I then looked to the horizon of this great highway. To my amazement, I saw that the amber glow on the horizon was not at all what I had thought it was. The sight of it filled my heart with horror. What I'd thought was a pot of gold was a pit of fire the entire width of the highway.

As the people drew closer to the pit, it was like a magnet that pulled them in with a great force. The people were screaming as they were forced into this relentless, blazing pit of hell. I saw on both sides of this pit of fire two horrid spirits that held deadly spears in their hands. They forced the people into the flaming pit while uttering blasphemous words and cursing the name of God and our Lord, Jesus Christ. Suddenly, I heard a voice calling me back to the Narrow Path. As I turned to look, I saw that the Holy Spirit had never left my side. He had been there all along in the brush next to the road. He reached out, took my hands in His and gently led me back onto the path that led to life.

Psalm 34

I will bless the Lord at all times:
His praise shall continually be in my mouth.
My soul shall make her boast in the Lord:
The humble shall hear thereof, and be glad.
O magnify the Lord with me,
And let us exalt His name together.
I sought the Lord, and He heard me,
And delivered me from all my fears.
They looked unto Him, and were lightened:
And their faces were not ashamed.
This poor man cried, and the Lord heard him,
And saved him out of all his troubles.
The angel of the Lord encampeth round about them that fear Him,
And delivereth them.
O taste and see that the Lord is good:
Blessed is the man that trusteth in Him.
O fear the Lord, ye His saints:
For there is no want to them that fear Him.
The young lions do lack, and suffer hunger:
But they that seek the Lord shall not want any good thing.
Come, ye children, hearken unto Me:
I will teach you the fear of the Lord.
What man is he that desireth life,
And loveth many days, that he may see good?
Keep thy tongue from evil,
And thy lips from speaking guile.
Depart from evil, and do good;
Seek peace, and pursue it.

The eyes of the Lord are upon the righteous,
And His ears are open unto their cry.
The face of the Lord is against them that do evil,
To cut off the remembrance of them from the earth.
The righteous cry, and the Lord heareth,
And delivereth them out of all their troubles.
The Lord is nigh unto them that are of a broken heart;
And saveth such as be of a contrite spirit.
Many are the afflictions of the righteous:
But the Lord delivereth him out of them all.
He keepeth all his bones:
Not one of them is broken.
Evil shall slay the wicked:
And they that hate the righteous shall be desolate.
The Lord redeemeth the soul of His servants:
And none of them that trust in Him shall be desolate.

BOOK 1

Preparation for Deliverance

ONE

Not I That Do It, but Sin That Dwelleth in Me (Romans 7:17)

Stephen King said, "Monsters are real, and ghosts are real too. They live inside us, and sometimes they win."[1] Churches commonly teach that Christians cannot have evil spirits dwelling inside them. I am going to prove that myth to be wrong.

Through the aid of the Holy Spirit, I did two massive deliverances on myself, by which I cast large masses of evil spirits out of myself. Through my own deliverance, I learned that our human bodies can house large amounts of evil spirits.

The spirit called Highest-Ranking Captain in Charge, just before he came out of me, told me, "It is possible for one human body to house more than a billion spirits at one time—although this makes living quarters quite cramped." Evil spirits dwell in people, animals and small objects. Demons are a great deal larger than evil spirits; they dwell in buildings. All are unclean spirits. Throughout this book, I will be referring to these unclean spirits as evil spirits and demons.

Jesus cast a legion of spirits out of a man, and there were so many of them that when they came out and entered a herd of many pigs, the greatness of the spirits drove the pigs violently down a steep cliff to their deaths (Luke 8:30–33). Demon possession can be mistaken for mental disorders. Many of the characteristics of schizophrenia and bipolar disorder can be evident in a person suffering from extreme demon possession, which can occur with large amounts of evil spirits or extremely powerful evil spirits. Through my times of sufferings, I have learned that evil spirits have different levels

---

[1] Goodreads, accessed June 30, 2017, http://www.goodreads.com/audible.

of strength. Depending on their level of strength and on how many are possessing the person, they can make the possessed person appear to be extremely mentally challenged. Schizophrenia and bipolar disorder are real mental disorders that affect the brain. The problems I encountered when I had more than 8,000,000 evil spirits in me—before my first massive deliverance in 1999—closely resembled bipolar disorder. The evil spirits in me were giving me a disordered outer appearance.

The Holy Spirit assisted me through two massive spiritual deliverances. The first one occurred in 1999, when He cast a modest amount of a few thousand spirits out of me. The last one, in 2016, was a greater deliverance. He then assisted me in casting the remaining spirits out of me, more than 6,000,000. In total, I'd had up to 8,000,000 evil spirits living inside of me. The first deliverance was to set me free from a great bondage that was making it impossible for me to live a normal life. The second deliverance was to prepare me to write this book. Read 2 Timothy 4:18.

I suffered in many different ways. From when I was 18 years old to the year the Holy Spirit cast the first large mass of spirits out of me, I suffered from insomnia. I had great difficulties in falling asleep, and then once I was asleep, I would wake not long after, usually near three o'clock in the morning. This happened every night. Then I would have great difficulties in going back to sleep. Many nights, I would not fall back to sleep. For the last three and a half years before the Holy Spirit set me free from the massive amount of spirits that possessed me, I slept no more than 15 minutes on my good nights. Most nights, I did not sleep at all.

I heard voices all the time. They would talk often among themselves. I would hear full conversations back and forth between the spirits within me. They would also speak to me. They would often give me orders to kill people. This usually happened if someone was getting under my skin. When I did manage to sleep, I would have out-of-body experiences. Sometimes the spirit would lift my soul above my bed so I could look down at myself, and he would send my soul spinning at a massive speed, as if I were a wheel on an axle. Other times, he would take me into another room, where he would rape me and then bring me back into my body. Although I was asleep, I could remember everything that took place. I would always wake up as he was placing me back in my body.

I could not pray in my head. I could only pray out loud. When I tried to pray in my head, I would become confused and badly disoriented. I often felt the presence of something brushing over my skin. I could not lift my hands to worship the Lord in church without the spirits gripping my hands. I had an unnatural ability to foretell a person's future both through dreams and by looking at the person's face. While in a room with a person, I'd suddenly see a vision of the person getting into a fatal car accident and dying. Within a few hours or, at the latest, two weeks, the accident would occur, and the person would die in the accident.

These spirits could pick up my body and throw me across the room. They would also force me to the floor, where they would again rape me. In Mark 9:20–22, the spirit Jesus cast out of the young man would often throw him into the fire. I would later find out that one spirit's name was Spirit Guide. He gave me a numbing pain in the lower part of my spine; this was to indicate to me that a person was thinking sexual thoughts about me, angry at me, or wishing to do me an injustice. When sitting in church, while looking up at whoever was speaking at the altar, I would suddenly envision the speaker fully naked.

I suffered all the characteristics of extreme bipolar disorder. Praise the Lord that in 1999 came my first deliverance. After the Holy Ghost assisted me in casting these spirits out of myself I never suffered this affliction again. Everything came to an end, and all the dreadful bipolar symptoms never again happened to me. I was totally set free. More than a few of the spirits that left me called themselves legions. As I said, I was likely loaded with more than 8,000,000 spirits. I have no way of knowing how many spirits the Holy Spirit cast out of me with my first deliverance. However, in my second deliverance in 2016, the Holy Spirit assisted me in casting out of myself more than 6,000,000 evil spirits. I do know this: the word *legion* refers to a number from 3,000 to as many as 6,000. Many of the spirits that left me with my first deliverance called themselves legions.

The Lord God is our deliverer (Psalm 144:2). My first spiritual deliverance took place by the working of the Holy Spirit in February 1999. I had been a born-again Christian for 15 years when the Holy Spirit performed the first of my two deliverance by casting these legions of evil spirits out of me. Although my brothers and sisters in the Lord saw what looked like a healthy and well-functioning Christian on the outside, I battled inside my soul and mind the desire to do evil. I had long since learned that adultery and fornication were sins worthy of death, but I was possessed by a large amount of spirits of a sexual nature. The vast amount of spirits of this kind made it almost impossible for me to live righteously according to what God's law requires of us. This was a difficult battle for me to fight. I always felt the desire to commit adultery and sexually sin in every imaginable way possible. I even had, along with the many sexual spirits, two lesbian spirits that came out of me as a pair and some spirits of incest. It was out of fear of God's great wrath that I did not sin in those ways. However, although I did not sin in my physical body, I did battle the constant and overwhelming desire to do so. For this reason, I struggled against myself to live a righteous lifestyle. The Bible scripture (Romans 7:19–25) was very real in my life. Before my first deliverance, having this massive amount of sexual-natured spirits in me made it difficult for me to live a righteous life. My first deliverance made my Christian life a peaceful breeze compared to the dreadful horror I'd gone through before the evil spirits were cast out.

You need to know that with my first deliverance, only a few thousand evil spirits were cast out; therefore, more than 6,000,000 spirits still dwelt inside of me to later come out with my second deliverance. I did not pile in more than 6,000,000 spirits between 1999 and 2016.

The trinity of God exists as the Father, the Son and the Holy Spirit. I have come to believe that God created man also in three parts: the earthly tent, the spirit, and the spiritual heart. I will be referring to the spirit as the soul throughout this book. This is so you will not confuse the spirit of man with the spiritual heart of man. The soul of man is his intellect, emotions, feelings and thoughts. Our souls will either go to hell if we do not have the Holy Spirit in our spiritual hearts or, if we are Christians, go to heaven. I believe our spiritual heart is a fragment of our heavenly Father's heart, which is fully intended to give us life through Christ Jesus; the Holy Spirit lives in this part of the Christian believer, and no matter our destiny, whether we go to hell or enter heaven, our spiritual hearts always go back to God's spiritual heart (Ecclesiastes 12:7). Our earthly tent is the part of us that goes into the grave and rots. I want you to understand that just because the spiritual heart goes back to the heavenly Father does not mean the heathen goes to heaven. If you are not born again and washed in Christ's blood with your sins forgiven, then your intellect, the part of you that lives on, which is your spiritual body (your soul), will go to everlasting hell, where the flame is not quenched.

I have come to understand through my evil spirits being cast out that all our sicknesses are caused by the spirits that dwell in our souls and bodies. Bipolar disorder and schizophrenia could result from legions of evil spirits or fewer but much more powerful evil spirits. It is also possible it is an evil spirit of that name. The evil spirit's name could be Bipolar Disorder, or the spirit's name could be Schizophrenia. The name of the spirit will depend on the name of your disorder. Then the spirit's name is the name of your sickness. Nevertheless, you can be set free from your illness by having these spirits cast out. Since you can be set free from such a negative disorder, then why not?

This is in extreme cases of demon possession. These are the traits to look for if you believe you or someone you know is suffering from legions of evil spirits or extremely powerful evil spirits:

1. You often feel the presence of something brushing across your body.
2. You feel that someone is touching you.
3. You are not able to pray in your head. You become confused when you pray in silence.
4. When you are lifting your hands to worship God, you have the unmistakable feeling that someone is grabbing at your hands and will not release them.
5. You suffer from insomnia. You have trouble getting to sleep and are disturbed from your sleep, waking usually around three o'clock in the morning. You find it difficult, if not impossible, to get back to sleep.
6. You experience mood swings. Often, without anyone or anything provoking you, your behaviour can become violent.
7. You possess supernatural abilities. You have strange dreams in which your soul is removed from your body for short intervals of time. This can also happen when you are awake.
8. You are able to see into the future and tell a person's future.
9. You hear voices in your head.
10. You have blackouts, when you lose a period of time. You do not remember, or you are not aware of what has taken place. This happens when the evil spirit within you fully exposes himself. In some cases the spirit possessing you will manifest himself in order to intimidate a person who is helping you in dealing with this spirit. When you have one or more characters manifesting themselves at separate times the spirit can also reveal itself in a split personality. When your altered personality displays itself, you will

be unaware of that period of time when your altered personality is manifested.

11. When looking at a fully dressed person, you suddenly, in your imagination, see his or her nakedness.

Mind reading is real. It is done through the communication of evil spirits within one person and involves sharing that person's secret thoughts with the evil spirits in another person. Thus, a person receives the secret thoughts of another person. Spirit Guide was the name of the spirit that would give me the secret thoughts of another person. As you can believe, some people were uncomfortable with my ability, so I seldom would come clean about this. Some mind readers can read one's thoughts of words, but I would get a numb feeling in the lower part of my spine if someone had a thought that was sexual toward me, felt anger toward me, or desired to do some kind of harm to me. For me, it was a warning to stay clear of that person.

This is a list of symptoms of milder evil-spirit activity:

1. A bad temper
2. Gluttony
3. Lying

Anything you are in the habit of doing that is contrary to God's Word is the activity of a spirit in you. Remember, if it looks like a duck and quacks like a duck, then it is a duck.

Contrary to what some Christians believe, spirits should not be cast out of an unsaved person, because without the Holy Spirit dwelling in his or her heart, the person has no protection to stop the cast-out spirit from making its way back in. Furthermore, if the spirit were to be cast out, that spirit would come back in bringing with himself seven more spirits into the person that is not a Christian. Matthew 12:43–45 tells us,

> When the unclean spirit is gone out of a man, he walketh through dry places, seeking rest, and findeth none. Then he saith, "I will return into my house from whence I came out; and when he come, he findeth it empty, swept, and garnished." Then goeth he, and taketh with himself seven other spirits more wicked than himself, and they enter

in and dwell there; and the last state of that man is worse than the first. Even so shall it be also unto this wicked generation.

(Matthew 12:44) puts it this way: "The spirit finds the house empty, swept clean, and put in order." When an evil spirit is cast out, it is important that the Holy Spirit enter the empty space the spirit left. If the Holy Spirit does not enter the space the spirit was cast from, then, as in (Matthew 12:43-45), the evil spirit will find the space empty and bring in with him seven more spirits worse than himself, and they will all dwell in the person. The evil spirit will come back, and yes, if he finds the space is not housing the Holy Spirit, he will reenter, bringing in with him spirits much worse than himself. Without the Holy Spirit filling this empty space, the space is left unprotected so that the cast-out spirit can and will come right back into the place he was cast out from. The Holy Spirit only dwells in a born-again Christian; therefore, the Holy Spirit cannot fill the space of an unsaved person.

When you cast demons out of a house, you place the blood of Jesus over the window and door lintels. You also place the blood of Jesus over each and every wall. Then you plead the hedge of protection around every door, window and wall. The blood of Jesus and the hedge put a protective barrier around the house so that the cast-out demons cannot come back in. It is the same with people: they need the blood of Jesus and God's protecting hedge so that evil spirits cannot come back in. After an evil spirit has been cast out, if the person who had the spirit cast out is not a Christian, then he or she will not be protected from the spirit, because the person is not covered by Christ's blood and God's protective hedge. The person must be a Christian in order to be protected. Only a Christian is protected by Christ's blood, and God only places His hedge of protection around a Christian.

Job was a man who honoured God, and for this reason, God protected Job with His hedge. Job 1:1 tells us, "There was a man in the land of Uz, whose name was Job; and that man was perfect and upright, and one that feared God, and eschewed evil." For this reason, God kept a protective hedge around Job, his household and all that he had (Job 1:10). Only after God removed that hedge from Job's property and children could Satan destroy the blessings God had given Job (Job 1:13–22). After God removed the protective hedge surrounding Job, Satan caused painful boils to break out from the soles of Job's feet to the crown of his head (Job 2:3–7). Today it is no different: in order for us to be protected from Satan, we must be protected by God's hedge.

In (Psalm 139), King David mentioned this protective hedge: "Thou hast beset me behind and before, and laid Thine hand upon me" (Psalm 139:5). The Bible tells us in (Acts 13:22) that David was a man after God's heart: "I have found David the son of Jesse, a man after Mine own heart, which shall fulfil all My will." As with righteous Job and King David, God only puts His protective hedge around the born-again saint. Like Job, in order to have God's protective hedge, we must be blameless and upright.

David was still only human. Like us, he made mistakes, but when he sinned, he would fully repent and ask God's forgiveness, and he did so with an upright heart. The fact that David repented with an upright heart made him a man after God's own heart, and he really meant it when he acknowledged his own sins before God. For this reason, David was protected by God's hedge.

If we are not Christians, our most righteous deeds are like filthy rags (Isaiah 64:6). Because of what Christ did on the cross, all who believe in Christ and accept Him as their Lord will be given the right to be called sons of God (John 1:12) and be forgiven of their sins. God's grace washes over the saved so that our sins are as far forgotten as the east is from the west (Psalm 103:12).

In the same way the ozone layer protects us from harmful UV rays by keeping them from reaching the earth, our hedge protects us from evil spirits so they cannot enter our souls. In the same way aerosols and car pollution break down our protective ozone layer, the sins we commit break down our protective hedge. God will not remove our hedge, but when we sin, our hedge develops tiny pores. Our own actions weaken and destroy our hedge. I have seen that our protective hedge is like a glass dome that covers all around and over us.

I saw this hedge one night when I stayed overnight at my sister-in-law's home. She rents rooms out but lives on her own. She is a fine Christian woman, upright in every way. She rents the rooms out to men to make ends meet. She would have no way of protecting herself if one of these men were to attack her. I slept that night in her bedroom. She slept that night in another bedroom with her mother. The first thing I noticed as I entered her room was the hedge that fully enveloped her room. I saw this hedge in my spirit. It was invisible to the naked eye. It looked like a glass dome fully enveloping the entire room. In other words, the upright Christian is fully enveloped in God's protective hedge. Our sins break this hedge down so it crumbles. When we resist evil and do our best not to sin, then our hedge remains strong and protects us from everything evil. This hedge of protection covers the soul, mind, earthly tent and spiritual heart. It prevents evil spirits from entering our souls. In this case, God was using His hedge to protect my sister-in-law from the possibility of one of the men in the house doing her harm. "I sought for a man among them, that should make up the hedge, and stand in the gap before Me for the land, that I should not destroy it: but I found none" (Ezekiel 22:30).

I have searched the Internet, and I cannot find anything to prove my theory, but from personal experience, I have come to this conclusion. I believe it is possible that if a person is not enveloped in God's protective hedge and covered with Christ's blood, then demons can take that person's life. I am not talking about suicide. I am talking about murder. In the book of Job, Satan first attacked Job's children and all his livestock, only leaving a few servants and his wife living. Then Satan went after Job's body, attacking his health and leaving boils all over his body. In (Job 2:6), God told Satan he could attack Job's body to cause him to suffer, but he could not take Job's life. God would not have told Satan to spare Job's life if there were no possible way a demon could take the life of a person. God told Satan to spare Job's life because it was possible for Satan to kill Job's physical body.

I have had experiences that can prove my theory. The first occurred two months before I gave my heart to Jesus and started attending a Christian church. I had been stalking a man whom I was physically drawn to. One night, close to midnight, after I had walked to his house with the plan of slashing his tires, I was standing alone at the tracks, waiting for a freight train to go through. I was standing a safe distance from the train tracks, about 20 feet away. I repeat: I was alone. There was no one there with me. Suddenly, I could feel someone pushing on my back, trying to push me into and under the freight train. I was terrified. It was all I could do to stop this spirit from pushing me under the train.

Later, after I had been a Christian for 15 years, one night, I had a dream. In this dream, I was lying on an altar, which I was bound to by ropes. There were six fallen angels standing around the altar. They were dressed in black. Their hair was dark. They looked Greek. Some of them were dressed like women, wearing skirts, and they had long hair, although it was fully apparent to me that they were crossdressers. It was as if I were surrounded by the Mafia. At that point, a young man with golden streaks through his dark hair came into the room. He came to the altar and stood before me, staring into my face. His beauty was amazing. However, his eyes, as beautiful as they were, had no life in them. His eyes were as cold as ice. I had never seen anything as evil as what I saw in his eyes. I knew then that he was Lucifer. Satan himself was standing before me. As he stood over me, he had a wooden stake in his hands, which he lifted and placed on my chest to plunge into my heart. Amazingly enough, I felt at peace as I stared into his cold and ruthless yet astonishingly beautiful eyes. At that moment, Jesus entered the room and told him to let me go. As suddenly as Jesus spoke, Satan and every one of the angels who had fallen from grace fled from me, and I woke up from my dream. To this day, I believe that had Lucifer plunged that stake into my chest, I would have died that night of heart failure, and I would not be alive today to tell my story.

I tell you all this to make it clear to you how important it is that you keep your protective hedge around you in good shape.

When you spiritually clean a house, you must remove everything in the house that will draw the demons back into the house they were cast out from and, if possible, destroy it by fire. If these things are not removed and destroyed, then the demons will reenter the house. In the same manner, if a person who had a spirit cast out continues to do the things the evil spirit cast from him or her represents, then the evil spirit will reenter the person. I have learned through experience that for people set free to be protected, they must never again do the sin the cast-out spirit represented; they must not habitually sin.

I have had Christians tell me they believe it is not possible for an evil spirit to dwell in the same place as the Holy Spirit; therefore, it is their theory that Christians can't have evil spirits. Through my own experience, I know that Christians do have evil spirits in them. This is why I have come to believe that in addition to our hedge of protection, God has also given us a shield that protects our spiritual hearts. I believe that Christians have an invisible shield that surrounds their spiritual hearts. Furthermore, I believe that evil spirits cannot cross past this shield to enter into our spiritual hearts, because this shield surrounds the spiritual heart of the Christian. Therefore, that is what makes it possible for evil spirits to dwell in a Christian. Until we become Christians, our spiritual hearts are dead.

Speaking of the tree of knowledge of good and evil, in (Genesis 2:17), God told Adam, "The day you eat of it you shall die." However, Adam and Eve did not die in the physical sense when they ate the forbidden fruit. God cannot lie, so what death was God speaking of? He spoke of the death of their spiritual hearts, which happened when their eyes were opened. But once we receive the Holy Spirit, He enters our spiritual heart and gives our spiritual heart life (Romans 8:10). I believe that when our spiritual hearts receive life, the invisible shield encircles our spiritual hearts. I have come to believe that when you receive Christ as your Lord and the Holy Spirit enters into your spiritual heart, then your spiritual heart becomes the Holy of Holies, also known as the Most Holy Place. In Leviticus, only the high priest could enter the Most Holy Place. When we ask Jesus into our heart, the Holy Spirit enters into our spiritual hearts. Just as the common people of the Leviticus time could not enter into the Most Holy Place, the evil spirits dwelling in man cannot enter into our spiritual hearts. To these evil spirits, the spiritual heart is off-limits. Once your body houses the Holy Spirit, making your spiritual heart the Most Holy Place, your body, soul and spiritual heart become the temple of God (1 Corinthians 6:19). Our soul radiates around and throughout our fleshly body. Our soul is fused to our spiritual heart. Although our soul is attached to our spiritual heart, it cannot enter our spiritual heart. Like the Old Testament temple, our new heavenly temple, which is oneself, has a veil fully enveloped around our spiritual heart. This is so nothing unrighteous can enter the Christian's spiritual heart, which has now become the Most Holy Place, and nothing contrary to God can enter it. Evil spirits cannot pass into the spiritual heart of a Christian. Just as back in the old law, nothing common could enter the Most Holy Place, nothing unclean can enter our spiritual heart, which is our Most Holy Place. The evil spirits dwelling in Christians dwell in the Christians' souls and bodies, not in their spiritual hearts. However, because these evil spirits are inside the person, the spirits are, at all times, able to be close to the spiritual heart. Weeds, if you do not keep them pulled out of your garden, will choke a healthy plant; in the same way, it is these evil spirits' main plan, and they are always at work to choke out your spiritual heart.

With my second spiritual deliverance in the winter of 2016, the Holy Spirit assisted me in casting out of myself 75 evil spirits with the name Boa of the Bowels. Your spiritual heart—which is a spirit, so it is invisible—is located in your bowels. "Therefore My bowels are troubled for him; I will surely have mercy upon him, saith the Lord" (Jeremiah 31:20). Other Bible versions translate the bowels in (Jeremiah 31:20) as "My heart yearns for him." These spirits were coiled inside my bowels; however, they were not living inside my spiritual heart. They were encircled around my spiritual heart. There was no time when the Holy Spirit cast a spirit out of my spiritual heart. These spirits told me that their purpose was to tighten their coils around the spiritual heart to choke it and, if possible, even cause spiritual death—that is, cause the Christian to lose his or her salvation.

Through my deliverances, I have come to know that all sickness are caused by evil spirits. All diseases are spirits in you; their names are the names of your diseases. If you have cancer, if you are an alcoholic, or if you are suffering from any other disease, these are all caused by spirits dwelling in you. If you have cancer, then you have a spirit with the name Cancer living in you. If you are an alcoholic, then you will have a spirit named Alcoholism dwelling in you. Your soul surrounds and radiates through your body. All sicknesses you have in your body and mind are caused by spirits inside of your soul. Because your soul radiates around your body and throughout it, diseases you have are caused by spirits dwelling in you. Because they live inside of your soul, they are attached to and living in the body parts they are negatively affecting with pain and disease. Only by the deliverance of the Holy Spirit can we have these spirits cast out of us (2 Timothy 4:18). When you receive a healing from cancer or it has gone into remission, the only sure way to know the cancer will never recur is to remove the spirit of cancer that is in you. Just the same, if you had a wart on your finger and chose to remove it by digging the outer edge of your wart away with a knife or other sharp instrument so that it was no longer noticeable, the core of your wart would still be under the skin. No matter how many times you try to remove that wart, until you remove the core, it will continue to come back. Once you have removed that core, then your wart will never come back. In the same way, you can pray, the church family can pray, and you can receive a healing of the cancer, but as long as the spirit of cancer remains in you, there will always be the possibility of your cancer coming back. You need to remove the core of the problem; you need to remove the evil spirit whose name is Cancer. Only then have you removed the actual problem at hand.

Bad tempers, mental illnesses, trouble serving God, and bad thoughts are all spirits living in you. "The thief cometh not, but for to steal, and to kill, and to destroy" (John 10:10). However, through Christ, we destroy the works of the devil. (First John 3:8) says, "The Son of God was manifested, that He might destroy the works of the devil," and (Mark 7:21–23) tells us, "For from within, out of the heart of men, proceed evil thoughts, adulteries, fornications, murders, thefts, covetousness, wickedness, deceit, lasciviousness, an evil eye, blasphemy, pride, foolishness: All these evil things come from within and defile the man." All these are names of evil spirits, and all can be within a man. The apostle Paul said,

> For that which I do I allow not: for what I would, that do I not; but what I hate, that do I. If then I do that which I would not, I consent unto the law that it is good. Now then it is no more I that do it, but sin that dwelleth in me. For I know that in me [that is, in my flesh,] dwelleth no good thing: for to will is present with me; but how to perform that which is good I find not. For the good that I would I do not: but the evil which I would not, that I do. Now if I do that I would not, it is no more I that do it, but sin that dwelleth in me. (Romans 7:15–20)

Notice that Paul said he had sin dwelling within him. Paul also came to the understanding that something evil was dwelling inside of him. He said in (Romans 7:21–24),

> I find then a law, that, when I would do good, evil is present with me. For I delight in the law of God after the inward man: But I see another law in my members, warring against the law of my mind, and bringing me into captivity to the law of sin which is in my members. O wretched man that I am!

We serve the law of our flesh: "but with the flesh the law of sin" (Romans 7:25).

With my first deliverance, I discovered that the evil the apostle Paul spoke of referred to spirits dwelling in our souls and throughout our bodies. When, in 1999, the Holy Spirit cast the legions of spirits out of me, I found myself set free from the evil within me. I discovered that if it is possible to be fully cleaned of all evil spirits dwelling within a person, then this Bible reference would no longer refer to that person, and that person would have full deliverance from the law of sin that once dwelt in him or her.

The reason the Holy Spirit will not clean us of our evil spirits when He first enters into our spiritual hearts is because our spiritual growth is a slow process. We do not become perfect at the very moment of our convergence in Christ. Yes, the Bible does tell us our sins are forgiven (Colossians 2:13), and we are referred to as His saints (1 Corinthian 1:2), but this does not mean we are not capable of sinning. The Holy Spirit is slowly moulding us into better Christians. Just as a newborn infant is born helpless and without an understanding of the law, not knowing right from wrong, the new Christian lacks an understanding of God's law and therefore does not understand right from wrong. Therefore, since we are still, in many ways, living as our old carnal selves, the evil spirits are free to come back into the new Christians they were cast from and bring in with them spirits much worse than themselves. Because of God's love for us, when we first initially receive Christ, He will not at the time of our convergence, cast out from us the evil spirits already residing in us. If God were to cast these spirits out so early in our Christian walk, our lives would be in a terrible mess. Evil spirits will enter a person for something as purely innocent as smoking cigarettes. I am an alcoholic. For the first seven years after I received Christ and started attending church, my drinking was out of control. My preference was white wine. I would drink until there was no alcohol left in the house, or I simply barfed it up and passed out. If the spirits that possessed me had been cast out at the time of my conversion in Christ, then I would have been in a horrendous mess. With the way I was behaving, in no time flat, the spirits would have been back in with seven more spirits much worse than themselves. God loved me enough to leave my spirits in me until the time when I could handle being set free from them. Through God's amazing grace, He did not cast my evil spirits out until much later on. Praise be to God, who has mercy on us.

Some Christians have told me they believe that the moment a person becomes a Christian and the Holy Spirit enters into him or her, all evil spirits are cast out of the newborn believer. I think their logic comes from the fact that when we cast an evil spirit out of a person, we need the Holy Spirit to fill this empty space. Their belief is that with our conversion in Christ, the Holy Spirit fills our total body from head to toe. It is true that when you're casting out an evil spirit, asking the Holy Spirit to fill the room the spirit left protects you from an evil spirit entering this vacant room (Matthew 12:44–45). However, in my theory, the Holy Spirit dwells in the believer's spiritual heart, and when we cast a spirit out from within a Christian, we ask the Holy Spirit to enter the empty room so no other evil spirit can enter that room. I understand how strange this might sound, but I have cast many spirits out of myself and other Christians, and every time I have done this, I've asked the Holy Spirit to fill that room. This is for our own protection. It seems to me that our bodies have many rooms that house these evil spirits.

I was inexperienced the first time I did the spiritual cleaning of a house. A friend was frantic when she called me. Her house was in an uproar. Spirits were tormenting her whole family. She cried out over the phone, "Pat, get over here now! I don't know what to do." I wasted no time in getting to her home. When I walked into the house, I had to admit I did not have any clue what to do. As I walked in the door, the Holy Spirit took over. It was as though I had done this many times before. But the truth was, I had never cast a demon out of anything. I went from room to room, following the guidance of the Holy Spirit (Romans 8:14). I cast the demons out from every room. I placed the blood of Jesus over every door and window lintel and on every wall. I also put the protective hedge around every door, window and wall. The Holy Spirit showed me in my spirit every room that was not clean. He also showed me what was drawing the demons into her house. As I went through every room, I removed the objects that would draw the demons in and placed them outside the house to later burn them. In the final room, I cast the demons out of the house through an open door. After I was finished spiritually cleaning the house, in that room, I could see the most hideous-looking creatures crawling up her picture window. They looked like black cats trying to claw their way through a screen window. I knew in my spirit that these were demons and that there was still something in the house drawing them back in. Through the Holy Spirit, I knew that the thing drawing them back into the house was in the closest in that room. My friend insisted there was nothing in that closet that could be drawing the demons into her home. Therefore, there was no more I could do, and I went home.

Within the hour, the demons had made their way back into her home, and she was calling me to come back and start again the spiritual cleaning. The point here is this: when we place the blood of Jesus over the lintels and put the protective hedge around the windows, doors and walls, that is not good enough to keep the cast-out demons from coming back into the building. The things drawing them into the house must be destroyed. Just the same, although we are washed in Christ's blood and protected by God's hedge around us, still, the things drawing the spirits back into us must be destroyed as well. We destroy the things drawing the spirits back by not continuing to do the things these spirits represent through their names and by not habitually sinning.

As newborn babes in Christ, we are not ready to live such a perfect lifestyle as to prevent these spirits from coming back in. However, you can bind any spirit that is in an unsaved person. Sometimes we need to bind the spirits that dwell inside an unsaved person we are trying to lead to Christ. We often come across people whose spirits are hindering them from receiving Christ as their Lord. There are many reasons you might want to bind an evil spirit in an unsaved person. Although you should not cast the non-Christian's spirits out, you can always bind their spirits. Keep in mind however, Christians will still go to heaven without their deliverance. Not casting your spirits out does not mean that you won't go to heaven. I am just saying, "our daily walk with Jesus would be much more easy if we were to have our spirits cast out."

As you read this book, you will learn how to live in such a way as to stop the evil spirits from coming back into you after they have been cast out. I will introduce you to the Holy Spirit. He will become your best friend. He will assist you in setting yourself free from the spirits that bind you. I will give you a full lesson on how to do a spiritual house cleaning. You will learn how to break curses and how easy it is to cause a curse. You will learn how to love one another as God loves you. You will also learn how to keep your protective hedge in good shape, without any decay, and how to receive your physical deliverance.

You will find that much of my biblical information comes from the Old Testament scripture pertaining to curses, blessings, binding, losing and breaking. The Old Testament would not be included in the Bible if we were not expected to use it in our everyday walk with the Lord. The Old Testament is for us today. The Old Testament was not written for Abraham alone but for everyone who is born again in Christ. "Now it was not written for his sake alone, that it was imputed to him; but for us also, to whom it shall be imputed, if we believe on Him that raised up Christ our Lord from the dead." (Romans 4:23–24).

If you do not know Christ as your Lord and have not accepted Him as the Son of God as of now, then before you go any further in this book, you will need to know Jesus Christ in a personal way, or what you are about to read will be of no good to you. This is the time to make a sincere decision to accept Jesus Christ and start living the rest of your life for Him. If this is you and you truly want deliverance from the evil spirits that have for so long held you captive, then pray this prayer, and read on.

The Salvation Prayer

Dear Lord God, I come to you in Jesus Christ's name as a sinner unworthy of you. I am unworthy, dear Jesus, to untie your sandals. I am truly sorry for my sins, and I ask you, dear God, to forgive me of all my sins, both past and present. I thank you, Jesus, for shedding your blood for me at Calvary, and I ask you, dear Jesus, to now enter into my heart and take up residence in there. Holy Spirit, come into my heart, and dwell in me. Teach me the Father's ways, lead me into all righteousness and prepare me for the Father's kingdom so that I will dwell with Jesus eternally in His kingdom. Heavenly Father, I declare myself now your child, washed in the blood of Christ and sanctified as your saint, humble and true. Thank you, heavenly Father, for accepting my humble prayer. Thank you, Holy Spirit, for taking residence up in me, and thank you, Jesus, for accepting me into your kingdom. Amen!

Now, if you have said this prayer and meant it in your heart, then congratulations. There is a new name written down in heaven, and it's yours. The angels in heaven are rejoicing for your salvation. You can now move on to the next chapter.

TWO

Getting to Know Your Best Friend

I learned that I needed to personally know the Holy Spirit, or I was not going to get my freedom that I dreadfully needed. In order to make this book work for you, you need to know the Holy Spirit. He needs to become your dearest and best friend. You need to walk and talk with Him. You need to talk with Him every day. From my personal experience, I tell you that only then can He guide you to your complete, ultimate freedom.

The Garden of Eden was a perfect paradise that God created to place His most prized creation in:

> And out of the ground made the Lord God to grow every tree that is pleasant to the sight, and good for food; the tree of life also in the midst of the garden, and the tree of knowledge of good and evil. And a river went out of Eden to water the garden; and from thence it was parted, and became into four heads. The name of the first is Pison: that is it which compasseth the whole land of Havilah, where there is gold; and the gold of that land is good: there is bdellium and onyx stone. And the name of the second river is Gihon: the same is it that compasseth the whole land of Ethiopia. And the name of the third river is Hiddekel: that is it which goeth toward the east of Assyria. And the fourth river is Euphrates. And the Lord God took the man, and put him into the garden of Eden to dress it and to keep it. (Genesis 2:9–15)

God looked at Adam, and He was pleased. God's perfect plan was that of friendship with humans. Before the fall of mankind, God would meet with Adam and Eve in the cool of the day, and He would walk and talk with them.

> They heard the voice of the Lord God walking in the garden in the cool of the day: and Adam and his wife hid themselves from the presence of the Lord God amongst the trees of the garden. And the Lord God called unto Adam, and said unto him, Where are thou? And he [Adam] said, I heard thy voice in the garden, and I was afraid, because I was naked; and I hid myself. And He said, Who told thee that thou wast naked? Hast thou eaten of the tree, whereof I commanded thee that thou shouldest not eat? (Genesis 3:8–11)

Adam, Eve and God would meet and talk in the garden. God was not a stranger to them. They knew His footsteps; they knew His voice. He would meet them in the garden in the cool of the day. It was God's intention in the beginning that He would have an intimate friendship with mankind in which they would commune together—that is, God would speak to Adam, and Adam would speak to God. God does not change; it is still today His perfect plan that He talks with His born-again saints, and they talk with Him. Only after the fall of mankind did this perfect communion come crashing down to a close, with the exception of a few, including Abraham, Moses and Jonah, whom God did actually speak with.

Jesus promised us the Holy Spirit (John 14:15-17). Then with the death and resurrection of God's Son, Jesus Christ, God sent us the Holy Spirit (John 14:15-17). The Holy Spirit is God's Spirit. He is God with us (Matthew 1:23). By sending the Holy Spirit to all who believe in Christ and accept Him as Lord, God has opened the door for the intimate one-on-one relationship He once had with Adam and Eve. For every Christian believer, God is no further away than in your heart, for it is His very Spirit that dwells in you. You can talk to the Holy Spirit as a friend, and He will talk to you. Believe me when I say that in order to make this book work for you, you need this intimate relationship with the Holy Spirit of God. Start talking to the Holy Spirit today. Note, however, that you should always test the spirit that speaks with you to make sure it is the Holy Spirit of God speaking. The devil masquerades as an angel of light (2 Corinthians 11:14); therefore, be always on your guard.

The Bible tells us to always test the spirits to make sure the words we receive come from God: "Beloved, believe not every spirit, but try the spirits whether they are of God: because many false prophets are gone out into the world" (1 John 4:1). Most of the time, I do this. However, there have been times when testing the Word of God was not going to give me the answer, and there have been many times when I simply did not have the opportunity or time to think it over.

Teenage kids can be a handful at the best of times. In the early years of my daughter's marriage, one afternoon, my husband, our son and I were just heading out to go home after enjoying a pleasant afternoon with my daughter and her husband. After leaving their apartment, we were coming down in the elevator, when a thought entered my head to take my 15-year-old son by his hand and walk him out of the doors in the front lobby. My immediate response to this impulse was *No Way*. I believed from my own past experiences with my teenage children that taking his hand and walking him through the door would end in my son being offended that his mother had treated him as a child. He would have pulled his hand from mine, and all the way home I would have heard about this stab to his ego, not to mention that my son-in-law and daughter would have playfully rubbed my wound with salt for a number of years to come. Therefore, I ignored the impulse to take my son by his hand.

My husband (Maurice), and I got off of the elevator and walked to the doors leading outside. My son had, however, taken the stairway down. He went directly from the stairs to the large one-pane window. Believing the window was an open door, he walked right into the window, which shattered.

He was stunned as he stood in the centre of the broken glass window. One eyelid and the skin under the eye had been sliced open, and he was in shock. There was a sharply pointed piece of glass about 13 inches long loosely hanging from the frame above his head ready to come down, and go through his scalp. Had it come down he would have been a dead man. I know the Spirit of God guided me because I calmly walked over and took his hand and then I was lead to take my son out of that dangerous situation. The second he stepped back, the pointed piece of glass came straight down, missing his nose by only a couple of inches.

In that case, as I was coming down in the elevator, I did not recognize where the thought to take my son's hand and guide him had come from.

I had believed that as his mother, I was simply having a mushy mom moment. I did not even think to question that the Spirit of God was telling me I could prevent a frightful calamity from occurring.

See, I had a choice. I could have taken the thought as a warning from God of danger ahead, I could have believed the thought was my own as a mom or I could have believed it to be the devil guiding me into an act of foolishness. In that case, I would never have found in the Bible my answer to the question, "Is this from God, my own thought or from the devil?" Neither did I have a Bible in my hand or time to look up a verse in God's divine Word to see whether this was the voice of God speaking to me or not.

I was lacking an intimate relationship with the Holy Spirit. If I would have known His still, small voice, the accident never would have taken place. To this day, I believe that had I obeyed, taking my child by his hand and walking him through the door, he would have calmly held my hand and walked out of the door with me. There will be times when we all need a special relationship with the Holy Spirit of God so that we know His quiet voice warning us of danger ahead. Read (John 16:13).

The best way to come to know someone's voice and body language is to become his or her intimate friend. Until then, this person is just another face on the street. Although the Bible does not give us a great deal of information on how our relationship with the Holy Spirit should be worked out, in the book of Acts and all through the New Testament, there is a great deal of information regarding how in tune the disciples and other believers were with the Holy Spirit of God.

Until I started taking the time to know the Holy Spirit, I often would not recognize His voice. The Holy Spirit is the Spirit of God. Man has a soul and spirit, and God also has the Holy Spirit. Read (2 Corinthians 3:3).

When Christ was preparing to go to the Father, He told His disciples that He would not leave them as orphans: "I will pray the Father, and He shall give you another Comforter, that He may abide with you forever; Even the Spirit of Truth; whom the world cannot receive, because it seeth Him not, neither knoweth Him: but ye know Him, for He dwelleth with you and shall be in you" (John 14:16–17).

Once our spirits are in full tune with the Holy Spirit of God, it will then be much easier for us to hear and know the voice of God when He speaks with us. We need to have a good relationship with the Holy Spirit, and with this closeness to Him, we will then be able to recognize whether the one interacting with us is our own thought, the Holy Spirit or an evil spirit trying to lead us into corruption. Read (1 Corinthians 2:11–14).

Sometimes the Holy Spirit speaks to me by using my own voice (the interpretation of tongues). Other times, He speaks to me through a soft voice that comes to me through a thought in my mind, and other times, He speaks to me through the Word of God. Ask the Holy Spirit to help you recognize and know His voice. Read (Jeremiah 33:3).

With our spouses, over the years, as we live together, we become more aware of what affects them, because we know them so well. The same is true with the Spirit of God; as we get to know Him better through our intimate relationship with Him, we will become more sensitive to His soft voice that speaks into our hearts. The better we are acquainted with the Holy Spirit, the easier it will be to pick up His emotions, feelings and voice. Scriptures to look up include (Romans 8:26–27; 1 Corinthians 2:13; 1 Corinthians 2:10–11; Ephesians 4:30; Acts 15:28; 1 Corinthians 12:11; Acts 16:6–11; Acts 10:19; Acts 13:2; Hebrews 3:7; Revelation 22:17; John 16:13; Matthew 10:20; Mark 13:11; Acts 10:19–21 and Acts 5:3).

Second Corinthians 13:14 shows clearly that the Christian believers in the time of the early church were experiencing an intimate relationship with the Holy Spirit unlike Christians are aware of today: "The grace of the Lord Jesus Christ, and the love of God, and the communion of the Holy Ghost, be with you all. Amen." It says here that they were in fellowship with the Holy Spirit. To fellowship is to share mutual interests, experiences and activities. It involves companionship and friendship. The early church was in fellowship with the Holy Spirit. They talked with Him, and He talked with them. Read (Acts 10:19 and 13:2).

The book of Acts shows clearly to me that today's church more than ever before needs the old-time Pentecostal revival due to Satan's attack on the church and the world in these end times. What we need most is that one-on-one relationship with the Holy Spirit, as the early believers and the apostles apparently had.

The disciples and the early Christians were experiencing an electrifying relationship with the Holy Spirit that has since been carelessly swept under the rug. Although I had joined an evangelistic church well in tune with all the gifts of the Spirit, no one had any idea who on earth the Holy Spirit was. The little I knew about Him for the first 16 years of my new life in Christ makes me believe that if anyone in the church did truly know the Holy Spirit, the percentage was low. I myself understood Him to be no more than a vapour in the sky, and I believe that more than 90 percent of all born-again believers don't know the beautiful Holy Spirit of God to be any more than that.

Do you know that the Holy Spirit has a personality? Do you know that He laughs at the funny things we say and do? Do you know that He can cry? I've heard Him cry. The Bible says not to grieve the Holy Spirit: "And grieve not the Holy Spirit of God, whereby ye are sealed unto the day of redemption" (Ephesians 4:30). Jesus said, "Verily I say unto you, All sins shall be forgiven unto the sons of men, and blasphemies wherewith soever they shall blaspheme: But he that shall blaspheme against the Holy Ghost hath never forgiveness, but is in danger of eternal damnation" (Mark 3:28–29). The Holy Spirit has a sweet and gentle heart. Have you ever taken the time to know His heart?

I first started speaking with the Holy Spirit out of exhausted desperation. I had gone through three years with fewer hours of sleep than I could count on two hands. My spiritual attack had cost me my job and my health. I was so severely burned out that I was left wheelchair-bound. Because of the danger of my exhausted body running the car off the road, it was no longer safe for me to drive a vehicle. Talking to the Holy Spirit as if He were a person in the room with me was my last possible hope, and I took that desperate leap. I've never looked back since. I can't live without Him. He is the very air that I breathe. He means more to me than any person I know, and there is no one else I love as much as I love Him. He is God with us. (1 Corinthians 3:16). I assure you that if you give Him the chance, He will prove to be your best friend.

The disciples and Christians of that day were well acquainted with God's Spirit. They knew Him well. This showed in every one of their actions. The helper whom Jesus sent was intended to be a friend to the disciples and believers. Jesus said in (John 10:27), "My sheep hear my voice, and I know them, and they follow me." We know we are to read our Bible to learn how to live for Christ in obedience, but notice that this scripture tells us that the true follower of Christ hears His voice and follows Him. To know Christ's voice, we need to be intimate with the Holy Spirit of God and know Him. So you see, knowing the Holy Spirit is every bit as important as knowing Christ Jesus and knowing the Father. If you haven't yet then I encourage you to take the first step and begin talking to the Holy Spirit of God as if He is a friend right in the same room with you. He couldn't be closer to you than He already is. He is in your heart. Read (1 Corinthians 3:16).

Receiving the Gift of the Holy Spirit
with Evidence of Tongues

We know that we receive the Holy Spirit when we accept Christ into our lives. However, the Baptism is something different. It is a gift He gives to the believer.

Truths leading to the Baptism in the Holy Spirit:

1. Believe on the Lord Jesus Christ and thou shalt be saved: with the heart man believes unto righteousness and with the mouth confession is made unto salvation. (Romans 10:9–13)
2. After accepting God as our Heavenly Father and Jesus Christ as our Lord and Saviour, we should always desire to walk in His ways and follow His commands. (Luke 6:46)
3. Believers in Christ are familiar with repentance, but also need to be baptized (immersed as Christ was) and to desire the baptism of the Holy Ghost with evidence of tongues. (Acts 2:38)
4. This gift of tongues is for every person who has repented of their sins and been baptized in the name of Christ for the remission of sins. (Acts 2:38-39)

Benefits of speaking in tongues:

1. Praying in the Spirit builds our faith. (Jude 20)
2. The Holy Spirit makes intercession for us with our Heavenly Father speaking on our behalf. (Romans 8:26–27)

Situations that strongly repel Satan's buffs in our Christian life:

1. Guarding our minds and thoughts, the renewing of our minds, (Romans 12:2), Obeying His two required laws. (Matthew 22:37-39).
2. Guarding our hearts. (Proverbs 4:23).
3. Guarding our faith. (Hebrews 11:6, Hebrews 10:23).
4. Let the peace of God rule in your heart. Peace is a Kingdom Power. The God of Peace crushes Satan. "Thou wilt keep him in perfect peace whose mind is stayed on thee." (Isaiah 26:3)
5. Read the Bible (God's Word to us) daily. (Acts 17:11, Joshua 1:8)

6. Pray daily. A healthy relationship is built by spending time in close and open communication with the Father, Son and Holy Spirit. (1 Thessalonians 5:17)

7. Be a soul winner. Lead others to Christ. (Mark 16:15, Matthew 28:19)

8. Don't forsake gathering together for worship. Make it a habit if possible to weekly attend a Bible believing church. Jesus made it a habit to go to the temple (church) and He is to be our example. (Luke 21:37)

9. Give to God what is His, (a) tithing 10 percent of your gross income to the place you worship at, (b) additional offerings and gifts e.g. to those in need and outside ministries. (Malachi 3:10, Acts 4:35)

10. Completely trust in God and do not lean on your own understanding. (Proverbs 3:5-6)

11. Rejoice always in Christ, again I say rejoice. (1 Thessalonians 5:16-18)

12. Weapons we are to use against Satan are: (a) the blood of Christ; (b) the words of our testimony; and (c) surrendered and sacrificial lives. (Revelation 12:11)

13. Put on the whole armour of God so that we can stand against the wiles of the devil. (Ephesians 6:10-18)

To remain victorious:

1. Live a life of worship and praise every day. (Psalm 146:2)
2. Live a life of agape love, and forgiveness. (Colossians 3:12-14)
3. Obey Jesus, and do His will in your life. (John 14:23)
4. Be quick to deal with your disappointments.
5. Never let the sun go down on your wrath (anger, unforgiveness and bitterness). (Ephesians 4:26)

I have found the gift of tongues necessary and valuable in my everyday life with the Lord. As I got deeper involved in spiritual warfare, I found myself using it on a more regular daily basis. It is through His voice that the Holy Spirit uses me to cast the evil spirits out. He is my best friend, and I totally depend on Him. I cannot express enough how much every believer needs the gift of tongues. Read (Romans 8:26).

1. You need to first ask for this gift. He who asks will receive: "Ask, and it shall be given you" (Luke 11:9).

2. In order to receive the baptism of the Holy Spirit with signs of speaking in tongues, you need to be fully submissive to the Holy Spirit. You will need a prayer room and at least two hours of quiet time with the Holy Spirit—no phone, no TV. You will want no interruptions. First, bring before Him your request. Ask the Holy Spirit to fill you with the gift of speaking in tongues. Then just sit quietly, and be patient. Relax your tongue, holding your mouth slightly open. Do not pray, praise or worship. Do not speak. Let the Holy Spirit have total control of your vocal cords. When you start speaking in tongues, the sound will come from your spiritual heart. The Holy Spirit will use your vocal cords. For me, speaking in tongues started as a shallow whisper. As weeks went by, my speaking in tongues became louder and clearer. After a few months, I was speaking with a complete vocabulary. What was now coming off of my tongue, although the language was foreign to me, sounded like intelligible and complete sentences.

   Now you need to ask for the gift to interpret your tongues. The Bible tells us it is a must that we have this ability. A great deal of the Holy Spirit working with me through my deliverance consisted of Him speaking through me with the interpretation of my own tongues. This gift will be highly valuable in your own deliverance. It will be one of the main ingredients both in your own personal deliverance and in the spiritual house cleaning of your home. (Read 1 Corinthians 14) to see how essential this gift is in our everyday spiritual lives.

3. After you have received this gift, you need to use it, or it will not develop and expand. In order to receive the full extent of what I received in such a short time, you need to practice speaking in tongues each and every day.

You will often find yourself praying for other believers. Unless they choose to share with you their problems, you do not need to pry into their private needs. The Holy Spirit knows what their need is, and He knows what to pray. He can pray through you in tongues (Romans 8:26), and the Father will know what the Holy Spirit has prayed. That is all that is needed. I have often prayed for women in church who desperately needed prayer.

However, they did not want to share all of the details with me. I prayed in the Spirit for one woman, and she wrapped her arms around me and gave me a hug. Three months later, she came to me and shared her joy with me: her need had been answered in full. To top this off nicely, Satan and his evil spirits don't understand this heavenly language, this makes it private between God and yourself.

THREE

Sin That Dwells in Man

> No more I that do it, but sin that dwelleth in me.
> —Romans 7:17

I admit that at one time, I believed the same as 90 percent of Christians today believe. I believed that Christians could not possibly have demons in them and that only extremely mentally disturbed psychopaths would be infiltrated with demons. However, over the past 20 years, I have become aware of the ugly, sinister world that not only surrounds us but also dwells in every human being.

Demonization

Paul was a chosen apostle of Christ, yet he spoke of an evil that was inside of him. Paul asked that the thorn in his flesh would be removed, but the Lord did not remove it. Instead, God told him, "My grace is sufficient for thee." Paul says in (2 Corinthians 12:7–9).

> "Lest I should be exalted above measure through the abundance of the revelations, there was given to me a thorn in the flesh, the messenger of Satan to buffet me, lest I should be exalted above measure. For this thing I besought the Lord thrice, that it might depart from me. And He said unto me, My grace is sufficient for thee: for My strength is made perfect in weakness."

God left this thorn in Paul to keep him humble. Paul also mentioned an evil that dwelt in him. This evil made it difficult for him to keep from sinning (Romans 7:16–20). Battling this evil force would have kept Paul humble.

The Holy Spirit told me that in order for me to write this book, He had to cast out my evil spirits; otherwise, they would interfere and influence what was written. Every word of this book was to be inspired by and written from the Spirit of God.

Jesus cast legions of evil spirits out of some people, but He would cast out of many only one or two evil spirits at a time. It is my personal belief that Jesus never would have cast out all of anyone's evil spirits. This is because it is God's intention to use these evil spirits to keep in us a contrite and humble heart. (2 Corinthians 12:7–10), (James 1:2–4) and (Romans 5:3–4)

When the Holy Spirit cast legions at a time out of me, they came out through my open mouth like water from a spray nozzle on the end of a watering hose. I believe that in (Matthew 8:28–34), the two men would have sprayed these evil spirits out of their mouths. Depending on how many evil spirits there were, it could have taken two or more hours to cast these legions out. We do know, however, that there were enough evil spirits to drive a large herd of pigs to madness. Before my deliverance in 1999, the spirits within me drove me to madness, and if the Holy Spirit had not cast these spirits out, I know that this would have ended in my committing suicide. The large herd of pigs were driven to suicide; they were driven to their deaths.

Demoniacs have an inability to live normally. They have personality and behavioural problems, phenomena of transference of spirits, opposition to the things of God, gifts of clairvoyance, foreign languages and abnormal sex lives (sexual sins). They suffer from chronic fear and loneliness, and they exhibit superhuman strength and violence.

Demonizing and Infiltrating with Fragments of One's Soul

Working diligently at putting together this book has presented me with some wild hurdles to leap over, including three wizards: one from a Christian church, one who was an entertainer, and a man who came to our front door while impersonating an asphalt driveway sealer. There was also a priestess of the Church of Satan and a witch who were both from within a Christian church. All five cast spells on me, and all five filled me with their fragments.

The example I will use is the wizard who came after me and used my weakest point against me. He, like the other four, was trying to destroy the Lord's plans before I had even put a pen to paper. It took him no time at all to chant his spell against me. He would have had two methods to use to cast his spell: (a) chanting while gazing at the moon or (b) standing in the centre of a pentagram and summoning to himself demons and evil spirits.

This wizard, through the use of fragments of his soul and the families of evil spirits he had placed in me, made me into his human marionette; I was his puppet on a string. He could make me do whatever he wished. He was controlling and manipulating me, and I could not break free.

This wizard would astral-project out of his body and soul travel into my home. He did this numerous times over the period of six months. Every time he did this, he would rape me through what is called astral sex.

I suffered for some time under his spell before I became aware of the severe spiritual mess I was in. I prayed and asked the Holy Spirit to help me receive deliverance from this overwhelming dilemma. I could not find my way out on my own.

The best way to describe it is like this: I was in a room that measured four feet by four feet, with four solid 15-foot walls. There was no ladder, chair or anything to climb on to get out. I tried to jump; I tried to leap. But no matter how hard I tried, I could not get over the walls or find any way out of this trap. Without Christ, there would have been no way out for me. I started praying day after day, "Jesus, pick me up in your arms, and lift me over this wall. I can't get out on my own." I cried out to the Lord both day and night, until finally, on the third day of January 2016, the Holy Spirit started casting fragments of this man's soul which bore his first and last name out of me. The Holy Spirit also cast out of me many families of evil spirits this man had placed in me through chanting his spell.

Finally, Jesus did take me up into His arms, lift me over the wall and set me on the other side of the wall, giving me my freedom from the trap this man had me in.

As the Holy Spirit assisted me in casting this wizard's spirits and fragments out of myself He had me keep a record of the number and the names of the evil spirit's families the wizard had placed in me. The Holy

Spirit cast out of me 200,000 fragments of this wizard's soul. The fragments bore this man's full first and last name. One hundred thousand evil spirits bore the name Wizard; 300,000 evil spirits bore the name Romantic Love; 200,000 evil spirits bore the name I Will Care for You; and 300,000 evil spirits bore the name Good Sex. This added up in total to 1,100,000 evil spirits this man had placed in me when he chanted his love spell upon me.

Through experience, I came to know when evil spirits had entered me through a wizard's or witch's sorcery. Within the hour before I went to bed, I would start feeling in my lower abdomen a numbness and pressure. I became familiar with this feeling. When you cast these spirits out with the assistance of the Holy Spirit, you know who did the sorcery on you, because their fragments of their souls will always be left in you, and their fragments bear their full first and last name as though their calling card. They cannot cast a spell on a person without leaving their fragments. The fragments are a tattletale telling who did the dirty deed.

I was seven when my younger sisters and I started attending church services held in a small house in the village we lived in. That was when I first gave my heart to Jesus, which means that at the age of seven, I was old enough to make a decision to either follow or not follow Christ. I don't recall saying the sinner's prayer; however, I do remember falling deeply in love with Jesus.

My little brother was born when I was ten. Close to my 13th birthday, he tragically died, leaving my life in an emotional mess. This resulted in my giving up on God for what would be many years. At that point, I made a clear choice not to be a follower of Christ. Later, at the age of 33, I came back to the Lord, giving Him my complete life and holding nothing back from Him. As you can see, at the age of seven, I was fully ready to accept Christ as my Lord, and at the age of 12, I was fully able to choose not to accept Christ as my Lord.

I believe this to be true. Don't you kid yourself; the devil and his demons know the Bible, and I believe they also know when a child is at the age of accountability. Satan is not wasting any time in taking hold of our kids' souls. The sooner he can drag these children into his web, the more difficult it will be to get them saved. Jesus said in Matthew 18:3, "Unless we come as a child we cannot enter the kingdom of heaven." The tender, trusting heart of a child is easiest to lead to Christ. Satan knows that when a child has a sweet, tender heart, it is the easiest to lead him or her, so he goes after the children while they are young and incorrigible. He starts in the womb with the spirits that follow down the bloodline.

One demon cast out of me by the assistance of the Holy Spirit said that he had left my father as he was raping my mother, and then he'd entered me while I was yet in my mother's womb. He said that when my father was a small boy of six, the spirit would play a game with him in which he would give the illusion that clothing on top of the dresser would appear to be alive and moving. This evil spirit told the Holy Spirit and me that my father liked the game and was fascinated with the illusion, and the spirit was disappointed that I did not like the game but instead was afraid when he tried to play the same game with me.

The spirits that enter through the bloodline at conception are after the soul even before the baby is born. Many spirits that enter an unborn baby are spirits of health problems, such as cancer and diabetes. A large number of the spirits that left me through the command of the Holy Spirit told us that they had entered me while I was yet in my mother's womb. One of their names was Incest. Two lesbian spirits that came out of me as a pair holding hands told us they had entered me before my birth. There were more than a few evil spirits that said they had entered me while I was still in my mother's womb. There were many sexual spirits, and there were many spirits of witchcraft from both my father's and my mother's family lines.

The Bible tells us that if a child is trained up correctly in God's truth, then when the child is old, he or she will not fall away from it (Proverbs 22:6). The devil believes this scripture. He is busy training our children in his way as early as they can sit up and watch cartoons on TV.

When your child tells you that he or she has a boogeyman or monster in his or her bedroom closet and you can see that the child is sincerely terrified, then that should immediately give you a warning sign. I had a monster in my bedroom. He was on top of my dresser; when the lights were out, I could see his chest heaving up and down. I was frantic as I told my dad I could see him in the dimly lit room. My dad would just tell me that the monster was in my imagination. Years later, when the Holy Spirit was casting out my many spirits, a spirit came out confessing that he was the one that had terrorized me with this illusion of a monster. When a child says, "I have a monster in my bedroom [or closet]," it is time for Dad and Mom to start taking action.

As Christian parents, we are greatly responsible for the spiritual growth of our children. If we want to beat the devil at taking hold of our children, then we should be working on our kids as early as in the womb. This can start with playing Christian worship music and the mother singing Christian lullabies, such as "Jesus Loves Me," to her baby in her womb while she gently rubs her belly. You can also prepare the nursery with things that glorify God, such as a Baby's First Bible and putting Bible verses and clouds on the walls instead of unicorns and mythical creatures. Jesus tells us not to hold our children back from drawing near to Him and says that the kingdom of heaven belongs to such as them (Matthew 19:14). This is because He knew that the children would need to know Him as early as their understanding of good and evil. God also knew that in these later days, as Satan's days draw closer to the end, the devil would be that much harder at work to draw our children into his evil ways.

When they are ready to sit up and are starting to take interest in cartoons on TV, take control of what they are watching, and monitor the content closely. The world system is powerful, and you will be at war with the devil from every end, but we need to fight back. However, don't all together hide the evil world from your children. You should always be open to talking about worldly things that are outside of the safe place you have your child in. That way your child will be spiritually and emotionally prepared to be strong when the devil comes knocking at his or her door—and believe me, he will come after your kid's soul. He will come knocking through other children, TV, and school, and no matter how much we protect our children, he will come after them through the whole world at large. Satan will try to entice our children into his evil plans. There is no way of getting around this, but we can prepare our kids well and be always—through God's help—a hop, skip and jump ahead of Satan and his demons.

For a month, while I was preparing this book, I would wake three times a night, most often with this thought in my head: *Twenty minus one.* I told the Holy Spirit that I knew I was to place this text in this book. The next morning, I woke as the Holy Spirit was telling me, "A mother's smoking stunts the growth of a baby in her womb by one inch head to toe." He also told me, "A mother's smoking also places three evil spirits in the baby before it leaves her womb, (Nicotine, Asthma and Cancer)." Smoking cigarettes kills! It is a sin to smoke. Christians should not smoke.

FIVE

What Has God Got to Do with Sex?

"That every one of you should know how to
possess his vessel in sanctification
and honour not in the lust of concupiscence, even as the Gentiles
which know not God."
—1 Thessalonians 4:4–5

Sanctification of the Marriage Bed

Sex is a spiritual act: "Therefore shall a man leave his father and his mother, and shall cleave unto his wife: and they shall be one flesh" (Genesis 2:24). God said that the two would become one.

Through my deliverance of certain spirits and their names, I came to the understanding that at the time of a man's climax, several spiritual things take place.

1. If it is your first time with this sexual partner, then your soul tie with this person comes into existence. With his climax, the man releases 200 fragments of his soul into his sexual partner, and she releases 200 fragments of her soul into her sexual partner. These fragments' names are the full first and last names of the person you had sex with. This exchange is the creation of their soul tie; the two have now become one. His soul fragments are in his partner, and her soul fragments are in her partner, which causes them to be one person in spirit. This is why it is so important that we break all soul

ties with all other sexual partners we have had before or during our relationship with the person we are now married to, and we must cast out and send back all fragments of souls that came into us from all other sexual partners.

This is why it is important that you have only one sexual partner, and this partner is your marriage partner till death do you part. These fragments follow through the bloodline, which is how your children portray some of their mother's personality and some of their father's personality.

2. Every time two people are engaged in sex, at the time of the man's climax, the auras—that is, the souls—of the man and the woman become one, making them in the spirit form one person. Again, this happens with every sexual act. In the spiritual sense, the two become one (Genesis 2:24).

3. Then there are the transferring spirits. These families of spirits leave one partner and enter the other partner as well with the man's climax, and this again happens only the first time the partners engage in sex. There is the possibility that these could be large families of evil spirits that enter your partner. They are also known as our family curses. Each family has a name, and the name will be that of the sin or sickness that is following down the woman's and man's generational bloodlines. One family could have the name Cancer; another could have the name Bastard. If, with the climax of the man, the woman becomes pregnant, then these transferring spirits of both the woman and the man will enter the newly conceived baby while it is still in the mother's womb. This will take place with every child the couple conceives together. This is the way the sins follow down the bloodlines as curses to the 3rd, 4th (Exodus 34:7), and even 10th generations (Deuteronomy 23:2). Also, generational sickness, such as cancer, follow down through the generations via these transferring spirits.

God speaks us into existence (Romans 4:17). Through my own experience, I know our tiny souls receive their life in God's heart (Jeremiah 1:5). Our souls are created in His throne room, in His heart. At the moment the man's sperm comes in contact with the woman's egg, God releases one of these souls, combined with a single fragment of His spirit from His heart, and sends this tiny human to the mother's womb. There you see again the release of a fragment of a spirit combined with the climax of the male.

You might ask me, "How do you know our tiny souls begin in the heavenly Father's heart?" The answer to this is "I have a very rare long-term memory." As far back as I can remember, I knew that neither of my parents loved me, nor wanted me, even stating so. I was around three years old when, for the first time, I watched *The Wizard of Oz*. When Judy Garland, who played Dorothy, sang "Somewhere Over the Rainbow," I thought, *That place sounded familiar; that I came from there, and I wanted to return.* When she tapped the heels of her red shoes three times and said, "There's no place like home," I wanted a pair of red shoes so I could do the same and go home to that place over the rainbow. I was no more than a toddler, and I was so miserable with my present life that I wanted to die and leave this world. From as early as I can remember, for no apparent reason, a heaviness would come over me, and I would have uncontrollable crying fits in which I would wail at the top of my lungs. When I felt one of these uncontrollable situations approaching, I would hurry to a place out behind the barn, where I could cry alone. It happened often throughout my life until much later when the Holy Spirit took me through the following situation after which I no longer experienced any crying fits.

I was 62 years old when, one day, after one of these crying fits, while sitting in a chair in my office, I asked the Holy Spirit to take me back to where my pain had begun so I could deal with it. I then immediately started to wail as I collapsed from the chair onto the floor, where I rolled up into the fetal position. The Holy Spirit took me with Him back to the time of my conception and with this my full memory returned to me. I could hear and see from a distance my mother crying and trying to fight off a man as he was raping her. I did not want to become a part of this sorrowful life that I could see before me as a result of this sinful conception. I was at that moment in God's heart, where I was safe and comfortable, but He was letting me go. He was sending me to a place where I didn't want to go, (into my mother's womb).

I was crying out, "Don't send me! Please don't send me!" God told me I had to go because I was the only one strong enough to survive what was ahead of me and still come back home to Him. He told me that my own family would not love or want me, and I would be hated all my young years, but much later in my life, I would be an author of books. I was to remember my conception, my birth, and my mother's rape so that one day I could tell others what happens to a baby when it is aborted or when it comes into this world unwanted. Then He told me I would later return home (heaven) to Him.

As I travelled to her womb, I was wailing and screaming, "No! No!" I also remember wailing as I was swimming as an embryo in my mother's womb. All throughout the nine months she carried me, I knew she wanted me dead. I was also aware when she attempted to abort me. Coming out through the birth canal, I cried again, "No! No!"

Asking the Holy Spirit to take you back to a painful event you don't remember is the knowledge you need that leads to excellent healing therapy. When you remember the painful event, then ask Jesus where He was when that happened to you. Whether you were a Christian or not Jesus response will always be "I was there with you all that time". It's the knowledge of knowing that Jesus was there is the process that heals you.

Creating soul ties with your sex partner through the placing of 200 fragments of one's self into your partner is the equivalent of signing an agreement with God. This takes place when the man comes to his full climax. Thus, to have sex with any other person other than your spouse means you have broken your covenant with God. That is why Jesus said divorce is only acceptable on the basis of sexual sin. This is not giving you an excuse to divorce but instead warning you just how important it is that you keep sex within the marriage covenant only. "If a man vow a vow unto the Lord, or swear an oath to bind his soul with a bond; he shall not break his word; he shall do according to all that proceedeth out of his mouth" (Numbers 30:2). When you break an obligation made to God, you put a curse on yourself and your family generations to come. Marriage is a binding obligation. When you take an oath to bind yourself with the binding obligation of marriage, you have made a binding oath to God. All sex outside of marriage is a sin. "Thou shalt not lie with mankind, as with womankind: it is abomination" (Leviticus 18:22). Marriage between two men or two women is not, in God's sight, a marriage. It is a sin.

In the beginning, God designed the world to be perfect. In His perfect world, one man and one woman would be united together forever. They would only have sexual intercourse after they were married. Both of them would be virgins, and the tearing of the woman's hymen would develop a blood covenant. This blood covenant would be established between the two on their wedding night. God would knit the two together, creating a bond that would last for their lifetime. The offspring that came from this union would be blessed. Divorce would not ever be an option because the two would be one. Both the woman and the man would know there would never be the option of another marriage. The spiritual soul tie created in their union would allow the two people to grow together, nurture and love one another. Only in death would they be free from the law of marriage. (Romans 7:2–3).

Because in this imperfect world, most of us have had more than one sexual partner, it is important that we free ourselves from the ungodly soul ties and bonds created through our multiple sexual partners. Our Heavenly Father desires every part of us (1 Corinthians 6:19), and in having every part of us, God will defend and protect that which is His. Every part of us that we have not given to God leaves an opening for sin and evil to come in. The ungodly soul tie creates an opening in our armour. It is important that we overcome our own souls' wickedness. We should desire to live holy lives devoted to our Lord, Jesus Christ, and His kingdom, but the trouble is, these ungodly soul ties keep on drawing us back into our past sins. As I said in my autobiography, "You never forget your first sexual partner." The reason for this is because the tearing of the woman's hymen creates a blood covenant between you and your first sexual partner. In a case where your first partner is not the person you are now married to, you need to break the blood covenant formed with your first sexual partner. Even if your first sexual partner was only a one-night stand, still this ungodly soul tie has bound you to that person.

I declare that we are made by God; our physical and spiritual bodies are the works of His hands. God is our potter, and we are His clay. He gives us our breath and our spirit. While we are yet still in our mother's womb, He calls us by name. He carefully knits us together and forms us in the womb. God created man on this earth, and He mentions our name in the womb. We are God's workmanship, and He formed us. God knew us, and He sanctified and ordained us before conception. Before I entered my mother's womb, God planned that I would write this book. Jesus was conceived by the Holy Spirit. John the Baptist was filled with the Holy Spirit in the womb. (Genesis 1:27; Isaiah 42:5; Isaiah 49:1; Psalm 139:13 and Jeremiah 1:5).

(Psalm 139:13) in the English Standard Version tells us we are formed by God by being knitted together in our mothers' wombs.

Man's DNA is knitted together with tiny crosses. Looking at a picture of human DNA, you can see that DNA is woven together by crossing over each other. Every crossover forms the sign of the cross of Christ. Therefore, even before the fall of man in the Garden of Eden, God knitted man together by using the sign of the cross of Christ. God knew when He created Adam from the dust of the earth that we would someday need Jesus to sacrifice His life for us by dying on the cross.

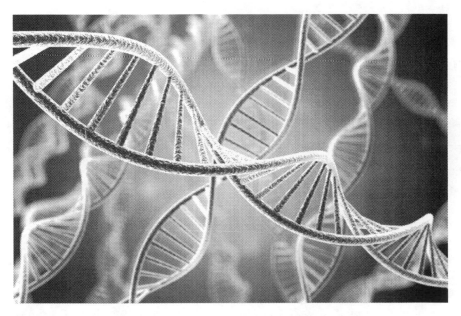

This is an actual photo of man's DNA. You can
see how the cross is carefully worked in.

When a woman decides to get rid of a baby she has conceived through her decision to sexually sin and aborts the unwanted infant, this human being is aborted while God is carefully knitting together this child's DNA. God is gently working on each tiny individual cross with His tender love.

When you sexually sin, you sin against your own body, which is the temple that houses the tender Holy Spirit of God. (1 Corinthians 6:18). This passage goes further to say, "Know ye not that your body is the temple of the Holy Ghost which is in you, which ye have of God, and ye are not your own? For ye are bought with a price: therefore glorify God in your body, and in your spirit, which are God's." (vs. 19–20).

Christians have various opinions of what the worst forgivable sin we could commit is. I believe if there were a worst forgivable sin that Christians would commit it would be of a sexual nature. This could be because the Holy Spirit convicted me so strongly about sexual sin. I do know that a good two-thirds of the spirits that came out of me with my second deliverance were evil spirits of a sexual nature. This might have a great deal to do with my opinion on sexual sin being the worst; however, you cannot deny that (1 Corinthians 6:18–20) makes it quite clear that sexual sin is done directly against the temple that houses the sweet and tender Holy Spirit of God. The Bible tells us not to grieve His Holy Spirit: "Grieve not the Holy Spirit of God, whereby ye are sealed unto the Day of Redemption" (Ephesians 4:30). Think about it: when you sexually sin, it is against the temple that is holding the sweet Spirit of God. I believe that when a Christian sexually sins, he or she grieves the tender, sweet Holy Spirit.

Through the assistance of the Holy Spirit of God, I cast out of myself seven families of curses related to being born outside of the marriage union. This has caused me to firmly believe that if any of your family members have created a bastard through fornication, adultery or have participated in incest, their family line is cursed: "Cursed shall be the fruit of thy body" (Deuteronomy 28:18). This will affect millions of family members for the next 10 generations and will continue after that unless all family members can avoid sexual sin for the next 10 generations, I can assure you that this is not going to happen!

Incest can lead to women hating men. By engaging in these sexual sins, we are actually worshipping Satan.

Incest is having sex with any blood relative, such as a father, brother, sister, mother etc. A bastard is a child conceived before the parents are married. Even if the parents get married after conception, the child remains a bastard. This is because the sin of fornication was committed before marriage.

Now, think about this: God has issued against the family line of those who worship man-made gods a three- to four- generation curse. (Exodus 20:5). However, He has issued a 10-generation curse on all those who conceive bastards and practice incest. (Deuteronomy 23:2).

Through my personal experience, I believe that people who have the *bastard curse* on them have problems with religious deception. They are more apt to cause strife in churches and church groupings. They are also more likely to become church vagabonds, travelling aimlessly from church to church.

As a result of my being conceived through the sexual sin of my mother being raped by an Italian hooker, I was born a bastard. For the reason that the hooker who fathered me was not married to my mother, although my mother and the man I grew up calling Dad were married at the time of my conception, still I was born a bastard. As a result of this, I had the *bastard curse* upon me. When I think of all the spiritual muck-ups I did from the night in August 1984 when I gave my total life to Jesus Christ, intending never to turn again back to my sinful life, to my first spiritual deliverance in February 1999, I realize that my birth as a bastard really took a crazy toll on my Christian life. I remember my daughter, son-in-law and son often speaking of my being a spiritual nut.

Just to mention one of my crazy acts, for a season in my life, I dressed like an Amish woman. I would wear my dresses loosely from my body so as not to attract anyone of the opposite sex. My dresses would cover my total body from my neck to my wrists and ankles. I wore no makeup whatsoever, wore no jewellery and always wore a hat in church. When I prayed in God's presence, I always covered my head with a hat or veil. My family told me I had turned into a spiritual nut. Then, in February 1999, the Holy Spirit cast thousands of spirits out of me, one of them being the *spirit* of *religion*. After this spiritual cleaning, the Holy Spirit told me, "If you continue to dress in this fashion, you will have the *spirit* of *religion* come back into you, bringing in with him seven more evil spirits even worse than he is and making your condition much worse than before. This will open the door to other spirits coming back in with seven more each, which will make it worse again." The Holy Spirit gave me a whole new dress code I had to stick with. As a result, I went from Amish-like clothing to short skirts, high heels, makeup, red nail polish and red lipstick. I could no longer wear a hat in church, except for the odd time of wearing a hat as a fashion accessory. If I were to continue with the Amish look and no makeup, I would draw the spirits of religion back into me; therefore, I went from looking like Mother Teresa to looking as if I had just stepped off of the front cover of *Vogue* magazine, which many complimentary women mentioned to me. Of course, my family as well as everyone else I knew saw this as another radical, earth-shaking leap in my out-of-sorts, crazy behaviours.

Pedophilia

The sexual assault of a child is a criminal offence that needs to be dealt with. Pedophilia is a disorder, not a crime. Pedophilia is the continual desire to sexually assault a child but does not carry out the actions to do so. However a pedophile does sexually assaults children. People who suffer from the dreadful urge to have sex with children are caught in a trap feeling no way of escape. See how Jesus feels about sexually assaulting children (Mark 9:42).

In my early years of being a Christian, I knew of a pedophile who attended a Christian church. He finally got caught and did time for his crime—he had raped more than 50 boys. Many of them were children who attended the church, and many times he raped them right inside the church building. This man, when caught, did two months of jail time in which he was under police protection so that no other inmates could get anywhere near him. He came out of jail a free man, with no follow-ups or counselling, and he received a full pardon for his crime. He moved to another town, where he was not known, and again started attending another Christian church, where he started to teach Sunday school. Unfortunately, he repeated the same crime attending that church, and three years later he once again got caught. This time, he had raped more than 200 boys. Again, many of the victims attended his church, and many of the rapes happened inside of the church building. This man then did two years for his crime.

I personally knew a man who, as a boy, loved the Lord. Even at the young age of seven, he had the gift to prophesy. He prophesied that his dad would come to know Jesus and, within the year, start attending church. His prediction did come to pass. This child had been baptized by immersion in water, and he was baptized in the Spirit with the evidence of speaking in tongues. This child was one of the man's sexual victims. Today, as a grown man, he won't step into the door of a church. He has children, whom he lovingly protects. Those kids mean the world to him, and for that reason, he will not take his kids to church and will not allow anyone else to take his children into a church. The pedophile who raped this man as a boy has the blood of this man and possibly his children's blood on his hands. Because of what this pedophile did to this young boy, the Bible passage (Mark 9:42) stands for this pedophile.

One does not make a choice to be a pedophilian whether they be a man or a woman. There is a misconception that pedophilia is the same as child molestation. Not every person who suffers the urge to sexually assault a child is going to do so. The inner conscience of some will kick in, telling them, "No, no, no! That is a bad thing to do!" Some people are spiritually strong enough to fight their urges and be victorious in their battle.

The law fails people who suffer from pedophilia. There is no help offered to people who suffer with thoughts of sexually assaulting a child. Actually, no one pays any attention to such a person until he or she has stepped over the line and started sexually assaulting children and gets caught and convicted for the crime. Even then, there is no help provided to pedophiles to free them from their sexual dysfunction. Therefore, another way of looking at this issue is that the law is not doing anything to prevent children from being sexually abused by pedophiles. The law is failing both the people who fight the urge every day to sexually assault a child and the children who fall into being sexual predators' victims.

If a person suffers these horrid, gripping feelings to sexually assault a child but has never done so, then that person is not guilty of the crime. However, the minute a person tells another that he suffers pedophilia, he is marked as a dangerous person. Speaking up in order to seek help can end in the pedophilian losing their education and their job and facing harassment and even violence. If people who suffer from this disorder have families, the Children's Aid Society will be contacted, and their children will be taken from them and placed in protective foster homes. There is no person or place that a person suffering from this horrid disorder can go to for help. However, I know a Great Healer (Jesus Christ) who can set the captive free. Families of evil spirits cause this disorder of pedophilia, and the Holy Spirit can, in the privacy of one's home, just between Him and the person suffering the disorder, cast out his or her spirits of a sexual nature and fully set that person free. How do I know? He did it for me. The pedophilian can find freedom in Christ, and he or she does not need to seek help outside his or her home. The great and mighty Healer dwells inside each born-again believer, and He is as close as the mention of His name.

If this is you, then there are prayers later in this book that can help. Here are some of the names of the families of evil spirits that will need to be cast out: Incest, Fear, Lust, Pedophilia and Pedophile. You will need to break the spirits' legal right to remain and then ask the Holy Spirit to assist you in casting them out.

By the way, sexually assaulting a child destroys the rest of the child's life. The only freedom from such an assault is through the freedom the

Holy Ghost provides the victim of sexual abuse. Later in this book, I have also included prayers for victims of sexual abuse.

Astral Sex and Sex with Demonic Spirits

I find it interesting to see that Satan uses the human sex drive that was created by God to pull off some of his most hideous crimes. These include astral sex, sex with demons, abortion, rape, homosexuality, lesbianism, pornography, child molestation, bestiality, adultery and fornication. It's interesting how many sexually transmitted diseases are out there. I have believed for some time that these diseases are curses that have fallen on the sexually immoral as a result of their corrupt actions. One of the sins that God detests is of the sexual nature. You see, "Every sin that a man doeth is without the body; but he that committeth fornication sinneth against his own body" (1 Corinthians 6:18). This Bible passage goes on to say, "Know ye not that your body is the temple of the Holy Ghost which is in you, which ye have of God, and ye are not your own? For ye are bought with a price: therefore glorify God in your body, and in your spirit, which are God's" (1 Corinthians 6:19-20). Various places throughout the Bible speak of how much God detests sexual immorality.

Through my own experience, I have learned that witches and wizards astral-project their souls from their physical bodies and soul-travel. They travel into houses, where they have sex (most often raping) with people while they sleep as well as while they are awake. They also have sex with one another while they soul-travel. These soul-travellers also have sex with demons while they travel. If you Google *astral projection* or *soul travel*, you will see that the web is full of pages on how to astral-project, soul-travel and have astral sex. I have learned that two soul-travellers can conceive spirits together. Furthermore, they travel into riverbeds and ocean beds, where the female traveller gives birth to evil spirits. These evil spirits then have an incubation period during which they grow and develop. These spirits conceived and birthed evil spirits.

SIX

Loving as God Loves Us

There are four types of love we are going to take a look at: eros, storge, phileo and agape. Let's first examine storge, eros and phileo.

Storge is the love that develops between family members and amongst friends. Storge love is a committed caring relationship. This type of love not only makes you feel secure, comfortable and safe but also builds a depth of honesty and integrity. An example of this love would be the friendship between King David and Jonathan. (1 Samuel 18:1–4).

Eros is a passionate and intense love that arouses our romantic feelings. This type of love triggers soaring feelings in a new relationship that cause you to say, "I'm in love." This is an emotional and sexual love. Eros love is important in the beginning of a relationship; however, if this type of love does not elevate to a higher notch, it will possibly not last. Eros love focuses more on self than on the other person. If something goes wrong, then this romantic love will die out, leaving no more than ashes. Simply said, the person stops loving his or her partner. Also, there is a fine line between this kind of love and sexual lust, which often can be mistaken for eros.

Phileo is an affectionate, warm and tender platonic love. This type of love makes you desire a friendship with a person. It helps to liven up the agape love. Although we love our enemies with agape love, we do not have phileo love for them. Phileo is love in the verb form. This is a committed and chosen love. You choose to love this way.

Agape love is what comes from the heart of our heavenly Father. This is an unconditional love. This type of love sees beyond the surface and accepts people as they are regardless of their many flaws, faults and shortcomings. This is the type of love that all Christians should be striving to have for all humankind. With agape love, although you might not like certain people, or they have hurt you multiple times with no remorse for their actions, still, you decide you are going to love them just the same. It is a sacrificial love. This love is all about giving without expecting anything in return. Agape love is our demonstrated behaviour toward another person. It is a committed and chosen love. This is the type of love God has for all humankind, and God expects all born-again believers to strive to love everyone with this agape-style love, including our enemies. Agape love makes it easier for us to forgive. Every Christian should be asking God to give him or her the ability to love the complete human race with this unconditional love. Also, having agape love for those we have never met causes us to desire to spread the gospel out into all the world. Jesus said, "Greater love hath no man than this, that a man lay down his life for his friends" (John 15:13). This agape love is what Jesus felt for the human race as He hung on the cross, suffered and died. This love is what God commands us to have for each other and for ourselves.

Because my rejection goes as far back as being conceived in my mother's womb, I came into this world without the ability to feel or express love of any kind. I grew up unable to learn how to give love or receive love, and then as an adult, I could not recognize love, nor was I able, no matter how dear a person was to me, to express myself in loving another. Although others loved me, I could not feel or recognize their affectionate feelings for me, and neither could I feel or recognize that I had any feelings of love for them. When I did at some point recognize my love for them, it was too late to regain their affection. Only after I had damaged the relationship between myself and the other to the point of no reconciliation would I finally know I had a deep emotional love for that person. Sadly, at that point, the relationship was so badly severed that there was no hope of reconciliation. Because of God's grace, I could come to Him, bringing my petitions, and know that my Heavenly Father was more than able to answer my prayers. I came to God crying out for the ability to feel the love my husband and children have for me and to be able to feel the love I have in my heart for them. God gave me the ability to love agape-style, which is His way of loving. When you cry out to God for such a need as to freely love, He will be quick to answer your request.

Part of not being wanted in our mother's womb is the curse of not being able to feel the love we have for others and the love they have for us. However, this curse can be broken. We can ask God to give us the ability to unconditionally love others as well as feel the love others have for us. If this is you, then ask God to teach you how to love all people with agape love just as He loves you and all people with His agape love.

Bitterness and Lack of Forgiveness

Since the Holy Spirit, being my guide and author to help prepare me to write this book, wanted no interference from any evil spirit, He put me through a lengthy spiritual deliverance on January 3, 2016.

On a Sunday morning in March 2016, an offence was committed against me that would have put a stumbling block in my way and oppose my deliverance. Because I right away saw the nature of the attack and what this spirit was after, I wasted no time in trying to undo the fresh new damage before it could put a hold on my spiritual deliverance and set God's plans back. I went right to the problem and took action to counterattack this spiritual attack.

First of all, you need to know that when someone hurts you so badly that you are left offended by his or her actions, an evil soul tie develops between you and your offender. When you are having problems forgiving a person who has offended you, you need to break the evil soul tie that has developed between you and this person through the offence he or she committed against you. It is important that you forgive your offender. You will need to break the legal rights and bind the spirits named Unforgiveness and Bitterness. Forgive the one who offended you, and then cast out from within yourself his or her soul fragments, and the evil spirit whose name is Bitterness and the evil spirit whose name is Unforgiveness.

When my lack of forgiveness from this offence first set into me—the person had only minutes before offended me—I had already lost the joy of the Spirit. The offence took place in church on a Sunday morning, just before the service. I went to my seat, and the service began, but I could not get into the heart of worship. I prayed, and then I became aware that a demon had followed me. This spirit was messing up for me what would have been otherwise a cheerful morning. I commanded this evil spirit to leave me and not return. Immediately, I was enjoying the morning worship service.

As soon as I was home, I broke the evil soul tie that had developed that morning between me and my offender. However, for the next two days, I battled feelings of a lack of forgiveness. I knew I was feeling offended. I tried to forgive this person, but I could not get rid of the feeling of bitterness.

The second night after the offence occurred, I spoke to the Holy Spirit, demanding that I receive the help I needed to forgive this person. I reminded the Holy Spirit that the reason this person had offended me was because I had been obedient to the Spirit of God in giving another lady some prayers on spiritual deliverance. This action had caused the spirits in my offender to verbally lash out at me. The Holy Spirit went right into action, and I received my freedom. I was relieved and set free from the bitterness and lack of forgiveness that had set in. I prayed this at eleven-thirty at night, and I woke in the night at two-thirty to the Holy Spirit commanding a spirit with the name of Unforgiveness to come out of me. This spirit had entered me on the evening of the day of my offence, and his entrance was on account of the struggle I was having with forgiving my offender. Because I had forgiven this person earlier that night and broken evil soul ties with her, this evil spirit no longer had the legal rights to remain. So with the command to come out, he had no other choice but to do so, and he came out of me (Psalm 18:1–3).

As I said, he had entered me on the evening of the day of my offence. This would have been sometime after the sunset that night. God's Word tells us never to let the sun go down on our anger (Ephesians 4:26). A good reason why the apostle Paul wrote to the Ephesians that they should never stay angry at anyone for even a short amount of time is because the lack of forgiveness breaks down our protective hedge. Then it takes little time— less than a 24-hour day—for the spirit named Unforgiveness to enter.

God has graciously, in His mercy and compassion, given the offended born-again believer until sundown on the day the offence occurs to forgive his or her offender. The spirit of Unforgiveness cannot enter the offended party until after the sun has set on his or her anger and bitterness. After the sun has set in the sky, the spirit named Unforgiveness has the legal right to enter the offended person. That is why Paul said, "Don't let the sun go down while you are still angry." After this person in church offended me, it only took until sundown that day for this spirit of Unforgiveness to gain his legal right and then enter me. This spirit did tell the Holy Spirit and me that his name was *Unforgiveness*.

"For if ye forgive men their trespasses, your Heavenly Father will also forgive you: But if ye forgive not men their trespasses, neither will your (Heavenly) Father forgive your trespasses" (Matthew 6:14–15). Because of our need every day for God's forgiveness and because God cannot forgive us if we do not forgive those who have sinned against us, it's possible for this spirit of Unforgiveness to forfeit us of our salvation.

In my early days as a Christian, I would get a lot of good advice from those in the church who held much wisdom. One of the things told to me was "Unforgiveness causes arthritis," which I later found out to be true. The spirit named Unforgiveness will bring in with him the spirits of Bitterness and Arthritis. Refusing to forgive is a sin that requires forgiveness. So the fact is, we need God to forgive us for harbouring this bitterness and lack of forgiveness toward our offender. Not only is it impossible for God to forgive the person who harbours unforgiveness in his or her heart, but also, without God's forgiving grace, the devil gets an upper hand over the person who is refusing to forgive and is harbouring bitterness toward an offender. This means that spirits of sickness that otherwise would not have been able to attack can now attack the physical body. That is how arthritis sets in. Many years ago, I harboured bitterness toward a certain person for a number of months and refused to forgive him—that was, until I developed the most dreadful pain in my right hand. I found out it was arthritis. I cried out for three months for God to heal me, but I did not receive my healing until one night, at the altar, I asked the Holy Spirit what was holding back my healing, and He told me I had not forgiven my offender. After I forgave my offender, I was healed of the arthritis.

As I've said, many Christians believe that a Christian cannot house evil spirits; however, the truth is, it takes only something as common as an offence to break down our protective hedge enough to allow the spirit named Unforgiveness to enter. I am living proof of this! Before the sun has the chance to set on the offence you have endured, break the soul ties that have developed between you and your offender, and pray for the Holy Spirit to help you forgive your offender.

To break soul ties with your offender, place the name of the offender in the prayer below:

> Almighty God, I break, renounce and denounce all evil soul ties I have with [offender's name]. Forgive me for developing evil soul ties with [offender's name]. I forgive [offender's name)] for controlling me. I renounce and denounce this evil soul tie. I break and wash this evil soul tie away with the shed blood of my Lord, Jesus Christ.

Prayer to Forgive Your Offender

Please, dear Jesus, forgive and love [offender's name] through me, and help me to forgive and love [offender's name]. Lord Jesus Christ, thank you for caring about how much my heart has been hurt. You know the pain I am feeling from [offender's name]. Right now, I release all that pain into your hands. Thank you, Lord, for dying on the cross for me and extending your forgiveness to me. As an act of my will, I choose to forgive [offender's name]. Right now, I release [offender's name] from my emotional snare, and I hand [offender's name] over to you. I refuse all thoughts of revenge. Thank you, Lord, for giving me your grace and power to forgive so I can be set free. It is in your precious name I pray this. Amen!

Praying a daily blessing over your offender will help set you free from your own bitterness and hurt. When you daily pray God's heaping of bountiful love over your offender, it will be natural that you will forgive and love him or her.

SEVEN

Today's Church

A number of years ago, the church I was attending was going through a dry spell, which had me concerned. At that time, I asked a number of my Christian friends who attended other Christian churches how their churches were coping. To my dismay, they told me that this overwhelming flow of dead Christian churches was nationwide across North America. Believers everywhere were losing their compassion for worship.

The Seven Demons That Attack the Christian Church

(Revelation 2:1) to (Revelation 3:22) describes seven demonic strongholds that can today be found in our Christian churches. Let us take a look at these seven demons who attack our churches.

1. *The Religious Spirit.* (Revelation 2:4–7) says, "Nevertheless I have somewhat against thee, because thou hast left thy first love. Remember therefore from whence thou art fallen, and repent, and do the first works; or else I will come unto thee quickly, and will remove thy candlestick out of his place, except thou repent. But this thou hast, that thou hatest the deeds of the Nicolaitans, which I also hate. He that hath an ear, let him hear what the Spirit saith unto the churches. To him that overcometh will I give to eat of the Tree of Life, which is in the midst of the Paradise of God." The Ephesus church was sound in doctrine but had lost their first love, their passion for the things of God. Religion, with its dull duty and traditionalism, had taken over. The power of the Holy Ghost

no longer was active, as it once had been. Demons had taken over; now being influential within the church. Speaking in tongues, and evidence of miracles would become no more than a memory. There was just a loveless routine of religious works in the place of what at one time had been the passion and power of the wonderful Holy Spirit. This Religious spirit is real today in our Christian churches and needs to be exposed and expelled.

2. *The Spirit of Intimidation.* (Revelation 2:10–11) says, "Fear none of those things which thou shalt suffer: behold, the devil shall cast some of you into prison, that ye may be tried; and ye shall have tribulation ten days: be thou faithful unto death, and I will give thee a crown of life. He that hath an ear, let him hear what the Spirit saith unto the churches; He that overcometh shall not be hurt of the second death." This church in Smyrna was enduring persecution, and many of their members had suffered as martyrs. Satan threatens us in order to try to strike fear into Christian believers' hearts. He does this by sending intimidations to frighten us away from being faithful to God and His Word. On the night Jesus was arrested, Peter was warming himself by the enemy's fire. He was intimidated by his surroundings and the voice of a little servant girl. Today's Christian church is silent in fear as it cowers down before the world and its governments. This demon of intimidation has got to be taken down and removed.

3. *The Spirit of Compromise.* (Revelation 2:15–17) says, "So hast thou also them that hold the doctrine of the Nicolaitans, which thing I hate. Repent; or else I will come unto thee quickly, and will fight against them with the sword of my mouth. He that hath an ear, let him hear what the Spirit saith unto the churches; To him that overcometh will I give to eat of the hidden manna, and will give him a white stone, and in the stone a new name written, which no man knoweth saving he that receiveth it." Pergamos was the capital city in the province of Asia. This city was historically rich. It had a library containing more than 200,000 volumes.

   This city had a god symbolized by a snake, which was their saviour. The people believed this god was embodied in snakes, so they would allow snakes to slither freely in the temple. People who were sick in their bodies would spend the night sleeping on the floor of the temple in hopes a snake would slither over their bodies, and they would then receive a healing. This city was the home of many deities. It is clear how this parallels many churches today. They operate under the control of Satan rather than God. What does the church do when ministry becomes overwhelming? Do we allow the snakes of humanism to slither through our congregations? Compromise is not our answer. Christians should not become comfortable with the sin that is around them. It is important that the Christian church take active steps to stand strong in this lost, dying world. We must recognize the conflict.

A church's permanent dwelling place is the city or town it is located in. It was not an option for the church in Pergamos to flee; instead, Jesus was advising them to settle into service and take up battle. Paul recognized the need to be ready in battle when he told of the armour of God in Ephesians 6. You need to be clothed in the armour of God to go into battle. The whole church body needs to go forward under the name and banner of Jesus Christ, never operating on its own, for it is in our flesh that the enemy can find our weakness. We need to repent of compromising. The church in Pergamos had weaknesses that had to be dwelt with. They would have had doctrinal problems as well as some problems with their deacons and leaders. They had a discipline problem. They tolerated the mess they were in by overlooking the sins in their own church. Jesus was calling them to repent.

Today the love of money has become the goal and a god of many individuals in the church body. Popular preaching has replaced prophetic preaching. The anointing has been reduced to the point that many Christians attending church get no more than a feel-good, candy-coated message. The church of Pergamos needed to turn their focus to Jesus, who would provide them with the sword of the Spirit. This is the weapon that Christians claim and use. We must cling to God's Word as our powerful war weapon. Our weapons are not carnal but are mighty in God (2 Corinthians 10:4). The devil will be defeated by the power of God's Word. Jesus promised this church of Pergamos they would eat hidden manna if they did not give into the sins that surrounded them or eat of the things offered to idols. This was His blessing to them. He promised them His presence when they were in the barren wilderness. He also promised a white stone. This white stone would most have likely been compared to the ancient Roman custom of awarding white stones to victors of athletic games. Jesus said, "To him who overcometh I will give hidden manna, and will give him a white stone with his name written on it." Jesus was giving the overcomer a white stone of victory. As long as we are overcomers, this promise is for us as well.

4. *Jezebel* Spirit *(Control).* (Revelation 2:19–28), "I know thy works, and charity, and service, and faith, and thy patience, and thy works; and the last to be more than the first. Notwithstanding I have a few things against thee, because thou sufferest that woman Jezebel, which calleth herself a prophetess, to teach and to seduce my servants to commit fornication, and to eat things sacrificed unto idols. And I gave her space to repent of her fornication; and she repented not. Behold, I will cast her into a bed, and them that commit adultery with her into great tribulation, except they repent of their deeds. And I will kill her children with death; and all the churches shall know that I am He which searcheth the reins and hearts, and I will give unto every one of you according to your works. But unto you I say, and unto the rest in Thyatira, as many as have not this doctrine, and which have not known the depth of Satan, as they speak; I will put upon you none other burden. But that which ye have already hold fast till I come. And he that overcometh, and keepeth my works unto the end, to him will I give power over the nations: and he shall rule then with a rod of iron; as the vessel of a potter shall they be broken to shivers: even as I received of my Father. And I will give him the morning star."

There is a war going on in today's church, and the battle line is drawn. The spirit of Jezebel is the most powerful at work in this ongoing battle, and it is a spirit of control. First Kings tells us about the woman this spirit is named after. She was the wife of King Ahab, and she was a follower of the false god Baal. The Bible tells us that Ahab's marriage to this woman was a terrible sin. Not only did he consider it okay to commit the sins of Jeroboam, son of Nebat, but he also married Jezebel, daughter of Ethbaal, king of the Sidonians, and began to serve Baal and worship him (1 Kings 16:31).

Jezebel ordered the murder of innocent Naboth so she could take ownership of his vineyard, which was his family inheritance. By her doing this, God's covenant with His people was broken.

In addition to the disrespect she had for the ordinary people and their property, she hated God's prophets. God's Word tells us that while Jezebel was killing off God's prophets, Obadiah hid 100 prophets in two caves and supplied them with water and food (1 Kings 18:4). Later, following the great contest in which God sent down fire from heaven to consume Elijah's burnt offering and defeat the prophets of Baal, Jezebel went after Elijah to kill him. She was relentless as she hunted after Elijah, forcing him into depression and thoughts of suicide. Jezebel's personality was evil; she was controlling, sexually immoral, murderous and demonic. This same strong and powerful spirit was still operating in (Revelation 2:20), and it still operates in today's Christian churches. You will find in every church congregation those who want to control, manipulate and subvert the women and men of God.

This is how you will recognize the Jezebel spirit: Jezebel is dominating and unwilling to mingle peacefully. This has nothing to do with women and liberation. This spirit can dwell in a man or in a woman. Many might think this spirit is identified with sexuality, believing a woman who looks a certain way is a Jezebel in her character, but that is not true.

The tool of the Jezebel spirit is using manipulation. First Kings 21 tells us that King Ahab would pout like a baby when he did not get what he wanted. He had seen Naboth's vineyard and greatly desired to have it, but Naboth would not give up his property, not even to the king. King Ahab lay on his bed, sulking like a spoiled child. Jezebel assured him she would indeed get him the property he wanted. This powerful woman not only introduced pagan worship into her kingdom but also thought nothing of killing the innocent to gain more power.

The seat of Jezebel appears in (Revelation 2:20). When the spirit of Jezebel begins to manifest itself in a church, it seeks a high seat, or a place of dominance in the church. It will most often manifest in someone who wishes to teach or lead and will lead him or her astray. In order for this Jezebel spirit to find a place of leadership, it must look and act in a spiritual manner.

These spirits were operating in biblical days. You will see the Jezebel spirit operating in Numbers 16, which tells us that Korah, the son of Izhar, the son of Kohath, the son of Levi, with Dathan and Abiram, the son of Eliab, and On, the son of Peleth, sons of Reuben, took men and rose up to Moses with some of the children of the camp, 250 leaders of the congregation, representatives of the congregation and men of renown. They gathered against Moses and Aaron and told them they were taking on too much. They said, "We are holy, every one of us, and the Lord is among us. Why then do you two exalt yourselves over and above the congregation of the Lord?" Korah was operating in the Jezebel spirit, Dathan and Abiram were operating as his power core and the 250 others were a structure under them. Moses immediately took action: he fell before God on his face and prayed. Right away after praying, he confronted the spirit, saying, "Is it a small thing to you that the God of Israel has separated you from the congregation of Israel, to bring you near to Himself, to do the work of the tabernacle of the Lord, and to stand before the congregation to serve them; and that He has brought you near to Himself, you and your brethren, the sons of Levi, with you? And are you seeking the priesthood also?" As a result, judgment came to the Jezebel spirit; an earthquake took the three evil leaders, and fire consumed the rest of them.

This controlling spirit wiggles its way into the church, bent on destroying the things that believers hold dear. Through manipulation, domination and control, this spirit starts its battle against the body of Christ. This spirit hates prophets, the true leadership of God. It cannot control them, and when it tries to win their approval and fails, then it will stop at nothing. If it is possible, it will even kill them. In addition to this, this spirit hates the preaching of the Word. It cannot cope with the gospel message. This spirit will try to reduce the messenger or the message. This controlling spirit also hates the praise service. Through the time of true and powerful worship, this spirit is exposed. The Jezebel spirit hates the preeminence of Christ Jesus. There is no way this spirit can compete against Him. The first time preeminence is mentioned is in (Colossians 1:18). The second time we find this word, the Jezebel spirit is trying to control the body of believers in (3 John 1:9). If you sense this spirit working in your church, then it is important that you see this enemy as spiritual, not fleshly. Don't hate the person who is controlling you and the church through the spirit of Jezebel. You need to recognize that this is a spiritual power, one that needs to be battled through spiritual warfare. Pray, "O our God, wilt Thou not judge them? For we have no might against this great company that cometh against us; neither know we what to do: but our eyes are upon thee" (2 Chronicles 20:12).

5. *The Spirit of Traditionalism.* (Revelation 3:1–6), "And unto the angel of the church in Sardis write; These things saith He that hath the seven Spirits of God, and the seven stars; I know thy works, that thou hast a name that thou livest, and art dead. Be watchful, and strengthen the things which remain, that are ready to die: for I have not found thy works perfect before God. Remember, therefore, how thou hast received and heard, and hold fast and repent. If, therefore, thou shalt not watch, I will come on thee as a thief, and thou shalt not know what hour I will come upon thee. Thou hast a few names even in Sardis which have not defiled their garments; and they shall walk with me in white for they are worthy. He that overcometh, the same shall be clothed in white raiment; and I will not blot out his name out of the book of life, but I will confess his name before My Father, and before His angels. He that hath an ear, let him hear what the Spirit saith unto the churches."

For centuries, the Church of Sardis has been the victim of rumours and hostility. Although churches do need to survive hostile environments, outward hostility is not the greatest threat to a church. Often, the greatest danger comes from within the church. The Sardis church had a fantastic reputation. However, Jesus ignored their human reputation. He told this church that they were listed in the obituary. Sardis was a wealthy city. King Croesus, born in 595 BC, found gold in the city's river. He issued the first gold coins in history. In the time of the New Testament, gold was commonly found along this riverside. This city was also known for its paganism. Their worship of pagan gods included sexual immorality. Remarkably enough, this community was at peace; they were comfortable in their self-sufficiency. This peaceful self-sufficiency made its way into the church, which became their spiritual death. Then all this church had left was its reputation.

What makes a church spiritually dead? If the Holy Spirit has gotten His walking papers, or if the Holy Spirit was simply never included, that makes a church as dead as a doornail. When we ignore the Holy Spirit—that is, when we do not embrace the complete work of God's Spirit in our church—the church body is headed for the cemetery. Jesus was telling this church that they had a spirit of religion, and they were missing the Spirit of God. You will not control the Holy Spirit with your religious traditions. What this church in Sardis needed was a pastor called by God who would serve God with his whole heart. The pastors who get voted in to shepherd the church flock are not always God's choice. When choosing a new pastor, our church body takes a vote. The congregation chooses our new leader. I believe if you were to take a census of the Christians in America, some would honestly say there has been at least one pastor who caused their church grief and pain. If the church board members choose a pastor simply by his reputation, his résumé, his physical appearance or a recommendation, they could find later they have made a mistake. The background information is important, but it is the fruit of this pastor's life and his walk with God that they should be investigating. It is the supernatural that matters, not the superficial. Hiring only on superficial grounds might later result in a blown-up mess and a short-term pastor for the church. In one local church, the congregation tried to remove a bad pastor and failed, and as a result, God had to take that pastor out through his physical death.

This church in Sardis was a hardworking church. They had a good name, but they were dead in the Spirit. They were an organization; however, they were not a living organism. They were so caught up in their reputation that they did not have any clue they had died. A dead church is a grave of uncompleted goals. These dead bones are evidence that a church walked part way and then stopped and started walking backward. The church that does this is doomed to the graveyard.

Now, how does such a church escape their spiritual death? They will need to eliminate this religious spirit from within their church. The leadership and the church family will need to gather in one accord and repent of their religious death. They will need to rebuke their religious pride that has strangled their church to spiritual death. They need to reject this spirit of religion, its reputation and its rules, and they need to fall in love with Jesus, the author of their lives. They should acknowledge the coming of Christ's kingdom and know that in that day, they will be held accountable for their accomplishments in Christ's name. They must determine for themselves to listen to the voice of the Holy Ghost. All their decision making regarding the church should come from the Holy Spirit. His glorified Word should rule, edify and reign from the pulpit. There will be, in most dead churches, a handful of believers who do live triumphantly and desire to be alive in Christ Jesus.

6. *The Spirit of Inferiority.* (Revelation 3:7–12), "And to the angel of the church in Philadelphia write; These things saith He that is holy, He that is true, He that hath the key of David, He that openeth, and no man shutteth; and shutteth, and no man openeth; I know thy works; behold, I have set before thee an open door, and no man can shut it: for thou hast a little strength, and hast kept My word, and hast not denied My name. Behold, I will make them of the synagogue of Satan, which say they are Jews, and are not, but do lie; behold, I will make them to come and worship before thy feet, and to know that I have loved thee. Because thou hast kept the word of My patience, I also will keep thee from the hour of temptation, which shall come upon all the world, to try them that dwell upon the earth. Behold, I come quickly: hold that fast which thou hast, that no man take thy crown. Him that overcometh will I make a pillar in the temple of My God, and he shall go no more out: and I will write upon him the name of My God, and the name of the city of My God, which is *New Jerusalem*, which cometh down out of heaven from My God: and I will write upon him My new name."

As much as Christ was pleased with this church, the fact still remains that this church was under a spirit of inferiority, which is a weakness. Far too many churches and individuals use their supposed weaknesses as their excuse for failing to move forward the cause of Christ Jesus. The New Testament church was anything but weak. When I read the book of Acts through to Revelation, I find it awesome the strength the believers had to stand strong through ridicule, prison and martyrdom in the name of Christ.

I often wonder how our North American Christians would stand up under such trials. I believe this attitude of weakness is false and demonic in its origin. This spirit has a stronghold of inferiority, self-pity and weakness. Satan deceives those who manifest this spirit by making them believe their attitude is that of meekness and humility. This is a counterfeit humility, and it is debilitating to God's kingdom. It cripples the advancement of the gospel, and it insults the precious Holy Ghost. The church of Philadelphia was at risk of being overtaken by this spirit. In order to become a pillar in the Lord's kingdom, they would need to overcome this spirit of inferiority.

The congregation of this church shows to be victorious. (Matthew 16:18) "The gates of hell shall not prevail against it." In his prayer for this church, Paul ends with this benediction: "Now unto Him that is able to do exceeding abundantly above all that we ask or think, according to the power that worketh in us, unto Him be glory in the church by Christ Jesus throughout all ages, without end. Amen" (Ephesians 3:20–21). It is within the church that Jesus's divine ability, energy and glory are lost. Christ's superiority is the answer to our inferiority. The church in Philadelphia had a little strength (Revelation 3:8). The Greek culture, international commerce and religious diversity were dominating over them. They worshipped the pagan god Dionysus, the ancient Greek god of wine, as the worship of Dionysus was thought to bring an end to their cares and worries. Plus, this city was the centre of Orthodox Jewish worship.

This tiny church could have given in to the pressure that surrounded it, but it did not. As a result of being faithful, it received wonderful encouragement in (Revelation 3:7–13), and for 140 years, this city remained a Christian city, even though it faced Muslim pressure. However, after centuries of courageous resistance, the unholy military alliance of Byzantine and Muslim forces overthrew the city.

This is what caused this church to overcome inferiority and have a ministry that would last for 1,400 years: it came to know the Lord (Revelation 3:7–8). Our obedience will always lead to our opportunity. God promised the key of David to this church. It had

God's favour, and was dependent on His superiority; therefore, nothing could stop this body of believers.

7. *The Spirit of Pride.* (Revelation 3:14–21), "And unto the angel of the church of the Laodiceans write; These things saith the Amen, the faithful and true witness, the beginning of the creation of God; I know thy works, that thou art neither cold nor hot: I would thou wert cold or hot. So then because thou art lukewarm and neither cold nor hot, I will spue thee out of my mouth. Because thou sayest, I am rich, and increased with goods, and have need of nothing; and knowest not that thou art wretched, and miserable, and poor, and blind, and naked: I counsel thee to buy of Me gold tried in the fire, that thou mayest be rich; and white raiment, that thou mayest be clothed, and that the shame of thy nakedness do not appear; and anoint thine eyes with eyesalve, that thou mayest see. As many as I love, I rebuke and chasten: be zealous therefore, and repent. Behold, I stand at the door, and knock: if any man hear my voice, and open the door, I will come in to him, and will sup with him, and he with me. To him that overcometh will I grant to sit with me in my throne even as I also overcame, and am set down with my Father in His throne."

In (Revelation 3), Jesus issues a charge to the church in Laodicea. This city was wealthy and prosperous. They had so much wealth that when an earthquake destroyed their city, they had no need for outside assistance to help them recover. The Roman historian Tacitus recorded that this city Laodicea arose from their ruins by their own strength and of their own resources. This city was famous for wool production; they were known for being the centre for fine wool in the ancient world. They had a famous medical school in which they produced two of the most popular medicines for the treatment of both eye and ear maladies. This city was full of pride. The Lord Jesus rendered His verdict on this church. He said, in effect, "This church makes me sick to my stomach. I could just barf it up."

This passage of scripture has always been a big eye-opener for me; it has always concerned me that Jesus could reject any of us to the point that He would barf us out of His mouth. It saddens me greatly that this church reflects the state of most of our American churches today. This church in Laodicea was just an ordinary church that was warm, but they had no fire. They lacked the Holy Ghost fire. If we are lacking the Holy Ghost fire, then the Holy Spirit has got no place in our church. In Acts, the Holy Spirit came down in tongues of fire (Acts 2:3). Warmth won't hack it; we need the fire. If they had been asked, they would have answered, "We are holding our own!" This made Jesus sick to His stomach. In God's work, there is no room for just getting by.

The complacent church is a disappointment to Jesus. This church had lost their love for Jesus and for souls. Their hot, burning love had turned to no more than smouldering smoke. It was the same old thing, week after week.

They had lost their faith. They had tried to become self-sufficient. They boasted of their wealth and their increase of material goods and felt there was nothing they were in need of, not even the Lord. They were cursed by their wealth. Sadly, this church did not see their true condition. Jesus called them "wretched, poor, blind, and naked." They were pitiful in God's sight. God saw them as without riches and spiritually blind. God saw this church as it truly was: no more than ashes and smoke.

They no longer had a righteous fear of God. This church no longer trembled in God's presence. They did not feel remorse for their failures. Jesus warned them, giving them these three motives to repent with: His love, His rebuke and His chastening rod which could have provided them with the motivation to set their church on the right track.

Jesus was standing and knocking at that church's door. He had been shut out and rejected; He was no longer the centre of that church. Jesus Christ is the common ground of fellowship amongst our churches. For this reason, when Jesus is not honoured in the church, the church has no base for fellowship with other churches. An example would be, a church without Christ can fellowship among themselves, but where there is no Christ, there is no unity: "That which we have seen and heard declare we unto you, that ye also may have fellowship with us. And truly our fellowship is with the Father, and with His Son Jesus Christ" (through the Holy Spirit) (1 John 1:3). "But if we walk in the light as He is in the light, we have fellowship one with another, and the blood of Jesus Christ His Son, cleanseth us from all sin" (1 John 1:7). Christ's presence is the common ground for all spiritual fellowship. Sadly, too many churches have shut Him out of this common bond.

Jesus is knocking at this church's door. Opening the door to Christ sets the stage for a revival, and then fellowship will be restored.

Do Not Believe Every Doctrine, but Test the Spirits

Many Christians run from church to church, searching for a spiritual high. They remind me of my rebellious days, back when I was bar hopping with my buddies and getting hammered to the point that we could not even stand up. It seems to me that these Christians are only truly happy when they're getting a Holy Ghost high. They need to be continually drunk in the Spirit, or they're not satisfied. They're not happy in their home church; it is never enough. These people are like waves tossed back and forth, blown here and there by every wind of teaching. Any Christians I have known who hopped from church to church to get their spiritual high of the week were not stable in their spirit, and as soon as trials came their way, they were walking out on the Lord. These Christians are babies. They're still feeding on milk. They need to grow up in Christ.

Now, what about holy laughter? This is my opinion: there is nothing holy about it. I am not saying it is not possible that the Holy Spirit, given permission by God, could grace a child of God with holy laughter. I had at one time suffered a deep feeling of depression that often brought me down to my knees wailing. Without any given reason, this depression would suddenly overtake me causing me to fall to my knees wailing at the top of my lungs. In a matter of 30 seconds this anxiety would always be lifted. Each time I would get back up and continue on with my daily routine as if that 30 seconds never happened.

When my daughter walked out of my life, I thought I would never feel the joy of the Lord again. There have been times when I could have used some divine cheering up; I could have used some holy laughter. Shortly after my daughter walked out of my life, one of my dear sisters in Christ knitted me a prayer shawl. With every stitch she put into the shawl, she prayed for me. She did this so that every time I felt the emptiness of my great loss, I could rap this shawl over my shoulders. Sure enough, every time I have put this shawl over my shoulders, the most beautiful peace envelops me.

I feel certain that this holy laughter is an outburst from the devil to disrupt church services. I don't feel right about this loud laughter. There is something about it that raises the hair on my back. I don't want anything to do with it. (First Corinthians 14:26-40) states everything should be done in a decently and in a fitting and orderly manner. As you read (vs. 26–40) you will see how this laughter does not fit in. According to (v.40) everything done in the church should be done in a fitting and orderly way. That means no uncontrollable outbursts of obnoxious behaviour.

In conducting our church service in a fitting and orderly way, we show respect not only to our speaker but also to our heavenly Father. If we are so busy laughing that we cannot hear what our speaker is saying, whose words the Holy Spirit anointed, then this outburst not only is disrespectful to God and our leader but also quenches the Holy Spirit and shows disrespect for Him as well.

It has annoyed me something bad when, at holiday dinners, when I was asked to give grace over our dinner, many of the younger family members carried on disrespectfully by loudly laughing and talking among themselves throughout the dinner prayer. I found that these outbursts from our younger family members showed no honour to God.

As I listened to this holy laughter on YouTube, I saw nothing holy about it. I heard no more than a rebellion, and I could feel the overwhelming presence of evil spirits as this laughter made a mockery of the wonderful gifts of the Holy Spirit of God. What I saw reminded me of (Exodus 32:17–18), when Moses came down from the mountain with the Ten Commandments and, upon coming into the camp, saw and heard the rebellion of the people. Remember, on account of this rebellion, God later struck these people with a plague. While listening to this laughter on YouTube, I heard no more than a rebellion led by the devil.

The Lord has often opened my spiritual eyes in church so I could see what was happening in the spirit realm. I have seen that when the service was dry and the congregation was simply sliding through the mere effort of singing the worship music, the sanctuary was loaded to its full capacity with demons. Five demons encircled every Christian in that congregation. When I commanded the spirits to leave, the whole congregation spontaneously went into the most beautiful flow of divine worship. My ears were filled with holy worship at its best. In today's society, many Christians believe they can get just as much out of church by watching evangelists on TV as by going to church on a Sunday morning. Demons are more faithful at attending the Christian church services than many believers are. Don't ever think for a moment that when spiritual excitement is happening in a Christian church, it must always be from God, from His Holy Spirit moving over the congregation. Always test the spirits, and ask the Holy Spirit to give you the discernment of these spirits.

The outbursts of laughter I saw on YouTube were in church settings, and every one of them occurred while the pastor was giving his sermon. During the message, the congregation suddenly went into an outburst of so-called holy laughter. In one video in particular, the pastor tried to continue to preach, but this disrespectful interruption drowned out his words, and the pastor gave up and started laughing with the congregation. My discernment of spirits set in, and I could see evil spirits covering my computer screen. There were so many of them that they resembled a dead carcass covered in maggots. I then saw two of the spirits leap out of the screen toward me, and I quickly closed the video. I strongly suggest you have nothing to do with this thing called holy laughter.

Gold-Dust Revival

One morning, I was reading the Lord's Word after doing my devotions, when I took notice of a light pale yellow dust that had appeared on the pages of my Bible. I had no idea what I was looking at, so I took my Bible to the garbage can and dusted the light-coloured powder into the garbage. Four years later, my sister-in-law excitedly asked me, "Pat, have you heard of the gold-dust revival?" She started to explain about gold dust landing on the pages of Christians' Bibles while they were reading God's Word and how excited it made these believers. Immediately, I remembered seeing the odd-looking yellow dust on my Bible pages and carelessly brushing it into a garbage can. I thought, *Oh! Did I carelessly brush gold dust from heaven into a garbage can?*

From 1999 to 2011, this gold-dust revival was strong, and many Christians were excited about it. Globally, it was the big talk of believers in Christ.

As for this gold-dust revival and other exciting things that draw in Christians nationally and globally like hotcakes, all I can say is this: the devil is a liar searching for whom he can devour, and if possible, he will deceive even Christ's elect. "Be not carried about with divers and strange doctrines. For it is a good thing that the heart be established with grace; not with meats, which have not profited them that have been occupied therein." (Hebrews 13:9). There are many deceivers who will mislead. I have never been to one of these gold-dust revivals. I can't honestly say if this is a deception from the devil or if gold was truly raining down from heaven. All I can say is this: be careful that you are not deceived. I don't go running after every strange new doctrine I hear about, and neither should you. I am comfortable enough in Christ that I don't need a gold rush or an uncontrollable outburst of laughter to have an amazing time with the Holy Spirit.

I am not saying it is not possible that God has rained down pure gold dust from heaven upon His believers. God's chosen race ate manna from heaven for the 40 years they wandered in the wilderness. It is possible this gold dust did come from heaven. With God, all things are possible. But remember that Jesus said, "For there shall arise false christs and false prophets and shall shew great signs and wonders, insomuch that, if it were possible, they shall deceive the very elect" (Matthew 24:24). For this reason, I suggest we should always test the spirits and see whether they are from God.

New Age Movement

We are now living in what is called the New Age, which was first mentioned in a popular song from my teen years. "The Age of Aquarius" claimed this age was a dawning of Aquarius. This dawning is the birthing of the New Age.

With the New Age, Satan has begun to attack the Christian church with more vigour than he has ever used since the beginning of mankind by using false prophets who will cause the elect to fall from glory, if it is possible. With this New Age, the devil has raised up people who have changed the Scriptures and translated the King James Version into less complicated versions for easier reading.

Many of these new Bible translations are being prompted by New Age cults and religions. The only Bible you can read while being sure you are not being misled is the good old KJV. All other Bibles are classified as what

I call "near Bibles and scripture." The new translations have disregarded some verses, including (Matthew 18:11): "For the Son of man is come to save that which was lost" (KJV). This verse was removed from the Bible with the writing of the New International Version. There are at least 26 verses that have been removed from the Word of God with the writing of the new versions, and these are in the New Testament alone. There are at least 28 New Age Bible translations in which biblical text is missing or mangled.

Our Bible tells us in (Luke 4:4) that man shall not live by bread alone but by every word of God. Because God's every word is not found in the newer Bible translations, when you read translations other than the KJV, you are not receiving every word of God.

I have been for some time now reading only the King James Version, and I know how difficult it is to understand and read this Bible version. However, I have found an easier way of reading and understanding the word of God. I read my King James Bible with another translation open before me online. The other translation is there only in case I get stuck; then I can check and see another interpretation of that verse. By the way, in doing this, I have found a heap of misinterpretations and missing Bible scriptures.

I mentioned in Chapter 2 that knowing the Holy Spirit and taking Him as your dearest friend will help you a great deal in finding your freedom from spiritual darkness. He will also open the Word of God to you and give you divine understanding. Jesus gave us the Holy Spirit as our teacher. It is the Holy Spirit that gives us understanding of the gospel (John 14:26). Every time I read my Bible, I ask the Holy Spirit and God to help me understand His Word and show me things I have not yet seen. I ask God to put His Word into my heart and mind so that the Holy Spirit can bring it back to the surface when needed. I also ask God to translate His Word to me in today's English. Not only does the Holy Spirit of God translate the KJV to me in today's English, but also, I have picked up on all of the mistakes and all of the Holy Scriptures that have been removed with the writing of the new translations.

Prayer

Dear Father in Heaven, I forgive my ancestors, descendants and any other people, I ask you, dear God, to forgive me, and I forgive myself for any involvement in New Age cults and Eastern religions and political, economic and social groups, including following leadership; believing in false Bibles, near Bibles, false teaching and false doctrines; ignoring and not following the Holy Bible and falling into the trap of occult practices and techniques. I ask this in the name of Jesus Christ my Lord and Saviour. I now break all New Age curses, soul ties and demonic holds. I pray for healing of damage done to my soul, mind, will, emotions and body by New Age influences. Thank you, Jesus, Father and Holy Spirit. Amen!

Buying and Selling in the Temple

In 2006, I opened my seamstress business out of my home. I did this with stern instructions from the Holy Spirit. He told me, "You will make baby quilts; to honour Me. You will give them to missions. You will write books; they also are to honour Me. You will write them to give glory to God. The seamstress business, however, is yours. The money you receive from this business is yours to spend. However, you can never buy, sell or advertise your business inside the church walls or any place of worship. If you disrespect me by buying, selling and advertising in any church or place of worship, God the Father will raise up an adversary against you, and you will suffer a great loss." The Holy Spirit also spoke these words to me. (John 2:14-16 "(Jesus) found in the temple those that sold oxen and sheep and doves, and the changers of money sitting: and when He had made a scourge of small cords, He drove them all out of the temple, and the sheep, and the oxen; and poured out the changers' money, and overthrew the tables; and said unto them that sold doves, *Take these things hence; make not My Father's house a house of merchandise*."

Many churches have bulletin boards on which those in the congregation who are self-employed can advertise their businesses. To the best of my knowledge, most Christian churches have a room in the lobby where you can buy Bibles and various things you would find in a Christian bookstore. They have dessert auctions. When a music group comes and graces the church family with an evening of worship music, their music CDs are sold in the church lobby. All churches, including the Christian churches, are comfortable with this. Because our churches have conformed to this buying and selling within their church walls, without even noticing it, I found myself slowly conforming to this system.

The enemy had concealed from me the trap I was stepping into. I didn't even see myself falling into the corrupt routine of advertising my business and dealing with customers within the church. I was dropping off and picking up their garments and making money exchanges even within the church sanctuary. I was doing everything the Holy Spirit had warned me not to do—buying, selling and even advertising within the church. For a time, everything was going smoothly, and then the wrecking ball came swinging at my seamstress business.

For the average business, it takes close to three years to start to build up their clientele and six years before the business starts to round off nicely. For me, clientele were building up at a slow pace. The Holy Spirit had told me this business was my income; therefore, I was taking every step while believing He would see me through this drought. I believed I would come out more than an achiever and victorious in Christ.

I had been running my seamstress business for one year, when another seamstress business opened on the main street. Because my tiny home-grown business was off of the main drag, the new business gave me a beating. At that time, my only line of advertisement was distributing my business cards. As fast as I could put my cards on store bulletin boards, someone was taking them down. I would load each of the boards in the downtown section with a dozen of my cards, and I would check up on them the next day—not one card would be remaining on the boards. Yet I had nearly no business coming in. Therefore, I strongly felt that whoever was taking down my calling cards was tossing them into the trash.

Many of my friends told me I was paranoid and should just wait for business to start coming in—that was, until the day when a friend of mine actually saw a woman taking down my cards and tossing them into a nearby trash can. This friend of mine followed the woman around town and observed as she went into every building that had bulletin boards, removed every one of my cards and threw them into the garbage. To top this off, when my friend witnessed this act, it had only been an hour before that I had pinned my cards to these bulletin boards.

My business went into a spiralling nosedive. My clientele was cut down to less than half. I cried out to the Holy Spirit, "You told me to open this business, and I trusted you! Why have you turned your back on me?"

He responded, "I told you not to buy, sell or advertise in the church, and if you did so God would raise up an adversary against you, and you would suffer a great loss." Again, the Holy Spirit repeated (John 2:16) to me. "You have made My Father's house into a common marketplace." I then repented, asked for forgiveness, stopped shopping in the church's bookstore and quit advertising and making monetary exchanges in the church. I told all church customers they needed to bring their sewing to my house and pick it up from my house, which again cost me the loss of some more customers. However, even with that most recent loss, I was now in God's grace.

The main-street competitive business that was devouring me alive remained for another three years. For those three years, I remained faithful to God as I struggled, barely seeing any improvement in my business clientele. Finally, the day came when the Holy Spirit told me, "God has seen in your heart that you have repented and that you have not sinned by buying, selling and advertising in His church. Within six months, the seamstress business on the main street is going to close their doors." Six months from that date, the business uptown did close their doors, and my seamstress business started building up clientele with leaps and bounds.

There are two Bible references that recall Jesus going into the temple and turning over the tables of the money changers. In (Luke 19:46 and Matthew 21:13), Jesus says, "You have made my Father's house a den of robbers." But in (John 2:16), Jesus said to stop turning the Father's house into a marketplace. I believe there were two separate times when Jesus went in and told the money changers to stop buying and selling within the temple. The one time, the money changers were charged with the offence of being common thieves, but the other time they were told not to use the house of God as a common marketplace.

For instance, let us look at divorce. Because of the stubborn, hard core of people's hearts in the Old Testament, God had permitted divorce (Deuteronomy 24:1–4). In (Matthew 19:8), however, Jesus said that Moses had permitted the people to divorce because their hearts were hard. Therefore, God overlooked it. Just because God overlooked the situation at hand did not mean He approved of their actions. Coming back to my situation, my three years of financial famine under the curse that the downtown business held over me cannot be just swept under the carpet as a mere coincidence. In the end, my final choice was to no longer make money exchanges in the church building. In the end, the final choice you make will be your own.

Most Christian believers will argue that Jesus was referring to the money changers charging too much and not giving people their proper change. However, no one can deny that in (John 2:16), Jesus did say, "Don't make my Father's house a marketplace." He meant, "Don't sell and buy within the church." To be fair, I have looked up this Bible scripture in every translation. Not one mentions robbing the people within the temple, but every translation does say not to make the Father's house into a marketplace. Stores today are open seven days a week. Therefore, there is no need for faithful believers to buy and sell within the church walls.

I once attended a Christmas tea where, upon walking into the church lobby, I saw several vendors selling their handcrafted gifts—it was a tiny Christmas bazaar. As I looked around at the vendors, I saw that various ladies were diligently trying to persuade people to buy their goods. There was a powerful scent of incense coming from one of the tables. This table had a dark cloud settled over it, and I could see with my spiritual eyes that the table was loaded with evil spirits. God never intended His church to be a common marketplace. All Christians should keep their buying, selling and monetary exchanges outside of God's house.

Did you know that in the 1980s, many Christian churches believed it to be a sin to buy and sell within the church and kept their books on a rack in the lobby for anyone who wished to take them home and later return them? From my own painful experience, I have come to believe that if all Christians would take heed of (John 2:14–16) and stop shopping in the church, and if all pastors would take heed and stop promoting shopping in the church, God would abundantly bless the Christian church.

Should a Man Remove His Hat When Entering a House of Worship?

The question is this: Is it disrespectful for a man to wear a hat in a house of worship? All who are sports fans should be familiar with national anthem etiquette. During the singing of the national anthem, all citizens should stand at attention, salute at the first note and hold the salute through till the last note. The salute is to be directed at the flag if one is displayed or, otherwise, to the music. All men in the crowd should, with their right hands, remove their hats and other headdresses and place them at their left shoulders over their hearts. At all football, baseball, hockey, basketball and soccer games, this rule stands. This is done out of respect for the flag and for the veterans who gave their lives for America in the First and Second World Wars as well as for all others who have since fought in wars.

If you were a man standing before a judge while being convicted of a crime and you were wearing a hat, having the hat on your head would automatically imply to the judge that you did not respect him. This could easily affect his final verdict; while determining the sentence he is handing down to you as your punishment, he might make your criminal charges worse.

Since it is an offensive act for a man not to remove his hat when the national anthem is being played or in a courtroom before a judge, it is my opinion that it is even more offensive for a man not to remove his hat in the Lord's house. Removing your hat for the national anthem is an act of respect for the veterans who gave their lives in the First and Second World Wars. Since Jesus gave up His life for all humanity when He suffered and died on the cross, every man should remove his hat in humble respect for Christ, who suffered and died for him. Everything on the earth is fleeting; it will not always be in existence. However, we should always greatly respect and hold in high regard the Father in heaven, Jesus Christ and the Holy Spirit. Therefore, a man removing his hat is the proper thing to do when he enters a church. In doing this, a man is showing honour and respect to his Lord. Many people see this today as a bygone tradition, However, for a man to wear a hat in church is showing that he is disrespectful and ignorant. To refuse to remove your hat is to act out of contempt and is much the same as refusing to shake a person's hand. If you don't remove your hat out of ignorance, then to many in the church, you have made yourself look foolish and uneducated. It is no different from not knowing what to do when someone reaches out to shake your hand.

These are the long-past rules of hat removal. A man should remove his hat outdoors

1. when he is being introduced to someone;
2. while talking with a woman, an elder or a person of prominence;
3. while the national anthem is being played or his country flag is passing and
4. at a funeral or during the passing of a funeral procession.

Indoors, a man should always remove his hat in a home, church or restaurant. Remember, it is considered a sign of contempt and is disrespectful not to remove your hat when it is proper for you to do so. Don't get me wrong: I do not care in the least if you remove your hat in my presence, but please show decent respect for the Lord by, if you are a man, young or old, removing your hat and keeping it off when you enter the Lord's house. Consider that the Word of God tells us, "Every man praying or prophesying having his head covered dishonoureth his head" (1 Corinthians 11:4). So yes, a man should remove his hat when he enters a church.

Should anyone want to argue this with me, read (1 Corinthians 11:6–15): a woman should have her head covered. Because a woman's hair is her covering, she should not shave her hair off as a man does; instead, she should wear her hair as her covering.

EIGHT

The Church, Prophecies and Myths

Today more than ever before, our men of the cloth are involved in sexual sin. Fornication, conception of babies with women within their congregations, sexual immoralities and perversion abide in our trusted churches. I have chosen to mention only a few of the occurrences. Sin is running rampant in our churches. The devil has gotten his hooks into all Christian churches, and a part of the problem is that we don't recognize the devil when he shoves the temptation to sin right into our faces. Many of our youth who grew up in good Christian homes and under the loving care of their Christian church family are following the call of God to attend Bible colleges but unfortunately, graduating college as homosexuals and lesbians. One young man just beginning his first pastoral job, got his girlfriend pregnant and had to rush into marriage so as to hide the sin. Some pastors and board members go as far as to rob God by scooping their hands into the offering plate and lining their own pockets. It is my opinion that the entire Christian culture of North America is under a black cloud of sin, and Satan has many of us in his hooks.

I believe Christians have become lazy to spiritual warfare, and to be honest, I am sick and tired of hearing, "You don't look for a demon under every rock. Don't talk too much about Satan. That puffs up his ego!" We, as the Christian church, need to become more aware that demons are hiding under every rock. If the thought comes into your head that Mrs. Brown sure does look good, then don't hesitate to wonder, *Is this my thought, or is it the devil?* Bind the spirit, and command the spirit to be silent. In (Matthew 16:23), Jesus didn't hesitate and ask, "Is this Satan, or is this Peter?" No,

Jesus spoke up boldly and said, "Get behind me, Satan." I have learned that silencing an evil spirit and driving him out of yourself is easy to do. When the temptation to lust after another person's spouse enters your head, driving out the spirit is as easy as saying, "In Jesus Christ's name, I bind, break, renounce and denounce the spirit named Adultery legal right to remain in me." Then, with a firm loud and demanding voice, say, "Spirit of Adultery, come out of me now." This procedure will work every time.

In my own experience, when temptation comes my way, it is always point-blank the devil. The Bible says sin comes from within the heart. Too many Christians don't believe Christians can have evil spirits dwelling in them; therefore, when sin attacks them from within their hearts, they think the sin is their thought and not a spirit tempting them. Once you realize that evil spirits do dwell within all humans, then you will know that when you are tempted, even when the temptation comes from within your heart, it is still an evil spirit tempting you. "Submit yourselves, therefore to God. Resist the Devil and he will flee from you" (James 4:7). Believe all temptation to be from the devil, and don't give in to temptation.

The Democratic Party is consistently on the wrong side of moral issues. This party led the way for abortion and homosexual legislation, including same-sex marriages. A culture of sin has fallen upon the Christian church. I can see that the entire Christian class is in denial. Immorality is running rampant.

Many churches are in need of help. You can rest assured that no matter how small the sin might be, it will be exposed when God reveals it in His own time. I believe these pastors and board members are aware of their sins. What does this all boil down to? The devil's lie is this: "Once born again, always born again. You can sin however you wish, and you will still go to heaven!" Give me a break. These pastors are living a lie. Spiritual darkness is everywhere. Some well-known TV evangelists are living a lie. There are homosexuals directing church choirs, and some are pastors and clergymen.

Church Prophecy and Myths

I have found that another aspect of Ahab and Jezebel's story is charismatic witchcraft. Witchcraft is the act of trying to control others for personal gain. Charismatic witchcraft involves leaders and others exercising control over other Christians within the congregation. There are many demons associated with control of others. This practice is mind control.

Through my second deliverance, I learned that we develop evil soul ties with those we submit our wills to. We can develop evil soul ties with leaders in the church as well as anyone in the occult whom we go to for guidance. The church leaders are cursed for trying to take God's place in our lives. The congregation is cursed for following man rather than God. Read (Galatians 3:10).

We have no right to control others. God gave every person a free will, and even He will not control us. For this reason, when we attempt to control others, we enter into agreement with Satan and his demons. By doing so, we practice witchcraft (1 Samuel 15:23).

Three years into my marriage, I started attending a faith-believing church, giving my whole life to Jesus. Six years later, my husband, Maurice, gave his heart to Jesus. My husband was bubbling with excitement as he started praying for our family, friends, neighbours and loved ones to find the same freedom in Christ we had found. You can imagine how excited he was when his best buddy was introduced to a fine Christian girl who led him to the Lord and later become his wife. He started attending church with her. However, just starting out in his Christian walk he was not strong in the Word and therefore was blown away by listening to strange doctrine.

I was as snug as a bug in my home church, so I was not easily caught up with every visiting evangelist who came to the surrounding churches to entertain believers who had too much curiosity for their own good. When my husband and his friends started chasing after prophets and healing evangelists, I continued to attend our home church while they ran from one church to another. Then, one Sunday night, Maurice came home bubbling with excitement as he proceeded to pull from his pocket a handful of cassette tapes that a visiting prophet had made up for his buddy, his wife and him. As he started to play the cassettes, my gift of discernment of spirits started to kick in. I told Maurice, "Smash the cassette tapes! They are from the devil. Furthermore, you had better warn both your friends not to take to heart what was prophesied to them tonight." I told Maurice, "It will end in a disaster." His friends were sure of the great fortune prophesied to them; therefore, they did not take heed of what I had said. However, Maurice took my warning and destroyed his cassette tapes.

When his friends saw that the prophecy was not coming into play as the false prophet had said it would, they decided to force the hand of God and make it come true. The prophecy was that Maurice's buddy would start his own business, and it would do well. In six months after they tried to make it on their own the business went under, causing them to lose everything. As a result they walked away from the faith, their business failed and also their marriage.

They were not the only Christians to attempt to make their own personal prophecy come true which ended in disastrous results. Charismatic witches use personal prophecy to control other Christians. (1 Samuel 15:23) "For rebellion is as the sin of witchcraft." Controlling others for one's personal gain is being rebellious. Prophecies can be a blessing or a curse. Since a true prophet allows the Holy Spirit to prophecy through him or her, the truth will always be spoken.

Many prophecies are soulish prophecies. This means they are made up in the person's mind. Most often, they will not line up with the Word of God. I immediately recognized that the prophecy given to Maurice's friends was done in such a way as to cause confusion in the church. It was not done in an orderly manner. (1 Corinthians 14:26–33) gives detailed instructions on how an orderly church service should be performed. (V. 27) indicates that "no more than two or three should speak in tongues." In the church setting in question, there were six prophets standing on the platform, all speaking in tongues at the same time. (V.29) "Only two or three at the most shall prophesy, and let one interpret". In this church setting, all six who stood on the platform prophesied. I picked up right away that the prophecy had not been carried out in an orderly manner. The Holy Spirit revealed to my heart that this prophecy, if followed through would end in disaster.

We as Christians have a responsibility to check out everything we read, see and hear to make sure it lines up with the Word of God. Otherwise, we will follow every wind of doctrine. Some prophecy is divination, which means it is a false gift of prophecy. Just as Maurice's friend and his wife's marriage was destroyed, these divinations have destroyed many churches and ministries. Diviners want to take over the pastors and the churches.

Remember, Satan has a counterfeit for everything God has created. Just because something is spiritual and happens in a charismatic gospel church does not mean it is from God. Demons come into our churches to do damage to the church body. I have often said that demons are more faithful at going to church than many Christians are.

The charismatic myth that irritates me something bad is "Once born again, always born again." This belief is Satan's tool to get every born-again believer into hell. The worst lie that far to many born-again Christians believe is the misunderstanding of (John 10:28-30). Some believe they can live like the devil all week and come into church on Sunday morning acting as perfect saints with no cares or worries, for they believe they're on their way to heaven. However, on Judgment Day, they will be disheartened when Jesus says, "I never knew you!"

Don't read only one or two lines of a Bible scripture. Read the complete passage. Otherwise, you could be reading into a lie from Satan. (John 10:27–30) Jesus said, "My sheep hear My voice; and I know them, and they follow Me. I give unto them eternal life; and they shall never perish; neither shall any man pluck them out of My hand. My Father; which gave them Me, is greater than all; and no man is able to pluck them out of My Father's hand. I and My Father are one."

For a short time, I attended a church in which the senior pastor believed the lie "Once born again, always born again." He was preaching this from the pulpit. He told his flock he did not like the Bible passage (Hebrews 6:4–6) because it proved his theory false. If you are one who believes "Once born again, always born again," does that mean you believe the Bible passage (Hebrews 6:4–6) is a misprint or should not even be in the Bible? The Bible contains God's words spoken to us. I suggest if you believe the lie from Satan that you cannot lose your salvation, you ask the Holy Spirit to reveal His Word to you, and then read (John 10:27–30). This passage is telling us, "As long as we live according to God's law, the devil cannot snatch us out of the Father's hand." However, this passage does not say we cannot snatch ourselves out of our Father's hand by our own choice to walk away from salvation.

The promise in (John 10:27–30) of us not losing our salvation is based on the condition that we listen to the Holy Spirit's voice and follow Christ—that is, live according to the standards the Bible lays out for us. I will give you an example: when I was suffering from Bipolar Disorder, the spirit that spoke to me told me that he was God and that I was to read the Bible only as he instructed me to, only a word or two at a time. He would take me often to (Exodus 1:16), where he would have me read, "Ye shall kill him." Then I was instructed to close my Bible. This spirit wanted me to commit murder. That was what he was instructing me to do. But when you read the passage properly as intended by God, it reads as follows: "And he said, 'When ye do the office of a midwife to the Hebrew women, and see them upon the birth-stool; if it be a son, then ye shall kill him; but if it be a daughter, then she shall live'" (Exodus 1:16), this was a command from Pharaoh to kill the Hebrew boys. You can see how easily a Bible passage can be taken out of context. (John 10:27–30) does not mean "Once born again, always born again." This scripture is intended to reassure you that if you are a born-again saint honouring God in everything you say and do, then no person, not even the devil himself, can pluck you out of God's protective hands.

Prayer

I forgive those who have controlled me with charismatic witchcraft. Please forgive me, dear Father, for practising witchcraft and trying to control other people's wills. I take authority over all these evil forces, I break all evil soul ties and I break all curses placed on me. In Jesus Christ's Name, Amen!

NINE

Weakness of the Pastors and the Church

I have noticed with various pastors over the years that some biblical topics are seldom, or never, taught. We need to hear more about spiritual warfare, deliverance and the gifts of the Holy Spirit. It saddens me that many areas of the Bible are not explored, taught and preached by the fivefold ministry. I have often thought that maybe some areas of the Bible make some pastors uncomfortable; maybe it hits too close to home. (Ouch!) It has become apparent to me that many pastors selfishly choose to preach not only what they are comfortable with but how they present it to further their ministry. They avoid areas they feel are controversial, unpopular or may cause them to lose some of their congregation or even offerings. Although they may justify themselves before man, on the Great Judgment Day they will answer to God.

Our home church has been blessed with good pastors. I had been a Christian for only one year when I chose to help another local church that was suffering in numbers. Through this choice to attend this new church, I also witnessed another weakness there: the pastor who says, "We must keep it simple so the baby Christians will understand." The problem with this is they are feeding the babies only milk (watered-down gospel) and not changing the babies over to solid food (the meat of the Word). These babies will never grow up into mature, strong Christians. When trials and tribulations come their way, many of them will fall away and go back into the world (2 Peter 2:22). My last year there, we got a new pastor. He did not believe in speaking in tongues, raising hands to worship or any gifts of the Holy Spirit. He was not charismatic. They say "You don't know how green your own grass is until you've crossed over the fence". I returned to my home church. They say "home is where the heart is", and my heart was in my home church. I have learned through my travels that the body of Christ does need the fivefold ministry, which consists of apostles, prophets, evangelists, pastors and teachers (Ephesians 4:11).

We need our pastors to cover and teach the whole Word of God in a systematic manner, not just what feels good but what stirs up the body of Christ to desire to put in action what they have heard. This aids people towards making positive choices in their lives.

I have spoken to many who say that, like me, they walk out of church and quickly forget the message. There is a clear difference between preaching and teaching. Preaching seizes the moment in the prophetic power of the Spirit were as teaching is for the future; it gets people to remember the message and apply it to their own lives. Teaching gives them a sound foundation to build on and then gives them the structure to build on the foundation. I am pleased with the pastors we have had over the last few years for their knowledge and for always providing us with plenty of choices of at-home Bible studies. Not only do you learn much more through this system, but also, the body of Christ gets to know each other better on a one-on-one basis.

Another weakness is catering to one's fleshly desires. One good example would be the desire to have money and possessions. I have, over the years, had little interest in TV evangelists. Many of them make themselves wealthy on the money Christians should be tithing to their home churches, and I see this as a great injustice.

Read (Philippians 4:19). As much as I don't believe in prosperity preaching, I do, however, know that God will provide us with as much as we need. We just need to learn how to apply God's Word to our everyday lives. If you have been tithing over and above your gross income to your home church, blessing others and giving to the needy, when you lay your hands on the Bible scripture (Malachi 3:10–12) and claim God's promise to yourself, then God will bless you exceedingly well, and you will be surprised at how God will cause your money to possibly even triple itself. I am speaking from experience.

I spoke with two Christians who told me they had done similar things. A lady told me that she and her husband were in such troubled need that they had only twenty dollars, and their next paycheck was two weeks away. In desperation, she put her last twenty dollars into the offering plate and then laid her hands on her Bible, which was open to (Malachi 3:10–12), and claimed this promise to herself and her husband. Before that day was out, a stranger came to her door with an envelope and told her, "I was told to give this to you." When she opened the envelope, two hundred dollars fell out onto her lap.

Similarly, a man told me that he and his wife were making ends meet week by week and were just barely squeaking by. One week, they had just three dollars and no groceries in their house but had four kids to feed. He laid his hands on his open Bible, on (Matthew 14:16–21), and claimed God's Word for his family. He then took his three dollars to a store; explained his situation to a cashier, who was understanding of his need; and bought a barrel of fried chicken with three dollars. They sat down to eat and noticed that the kids had all gone back into the barrel for a third helping. He and his wife saw that the barrel of chicken was not going down. The family ate their dinner, and the barrel kept refilling itself for four days.

After I repented of my sin of advertising and making monetary exchanges in the church, still, I was struggling under the pressure of the seamstress business that had opened on the main street. In desperation to make ends meet, I laid my hands on my Bible, which was open to (Malachi 3:10–12), and claimed God's promise to myself. The business uptown had not gone away, and I had not seen any improvements. Because I had sinned, I was still under God's chastisement; however, in moving in faith by claiming God's Word into my life, although I was not earning the money, miraculously enough, like the five loaves of bread and two fish in (Matthew 14:16--21), my money was multiplying itself.

You might wonder how this can be. It's a miracle! Just as five loaves of bread and two fish fed 5,000, God is still doing miracles like that today. However, keep in mind that Jesus said, "It is easier for a camel to go through a needle's eye, than for a rich man to enter into the kingdom of God" (Luke 18:25). God blesses us with as much as we need. Too much money will make a Christian greedy, and those who struggle to make ends meet are far more likely to learn to lean on Jesus. I personally know where I would rather be, and that is in Christ's bosom, all cozy and cuddled. 1 Timothy 6:10 puts it this way: "For the love of money is the root of all evil: which while some coveted after, they have erred from the faith, and pierced themselves through with many sorrows" (1 Timothy 6:10). Remember, Jesus, the Son of God, had no pillow to lay his head on, and Jesus is the example we are to follow. Read (Matthew 8:20). Jesus was born in a stinky barn. It gets no more humbling than that. Pastors, encourage your congregations to seek not possessions and prosperity but, rather, what they can do for God and His kingdom.

TEN

Putting On the Whole Armour of God

Put on the whole armour of God, that ye may be able to stand against the wiles of the devil. For we wrestle not against flesh and blood, but against principalities, against powers, against the rulers of the darkness of this world, against spiritual wickedness in high places. Wherefore, take unto you the whole armour of God, that ye may be able to withstand in the evil day, and having done all, to stand.

—Ephesians 6:11–13

I have come to believe through what I have seen in the small community I live in that today most Christians are forming their spiritual beliefs around the ideas and practices of our culture. With this, today's society is teaching them to be tolerant of the anti-Christian beliefs that surround them. It is important that we stay firm to our Lord's teachings and what He commands of us in His Word. You must be sure your belt of truth is firmly buckled around your waist. In this day of immoral teachings, sin and filth, we need to stand on the only truth, which is the Word of God and take our stand on His truth.

When Paul was writing (Ephesians 6:10-17), he was thinking about how the Roman soldiers dressed in their armour. He had firsthand knowledge of Roman weaponry because of how much time he spent in the Roman prison. He had seen many of the Roman soldiers fully equipped from head to toe. In that time people would have been fully aware of how soldiers dressed as they prepared for battle. As a matter of fact, the rise of the Roman Empire was due to how well equipped the Roman soldiers were in their training, weaponry, defence and understanding of their enemies. Paul used the Roman soldier's armour as an example to describe the armour of God in the book of (Ephesians), including weapons of both defence and offence.

Purpose of the armour:

To Fulfill And Obey God's Commands.

- To have complete protection against the fiery darts of the devil in our daily battles (Ephesians 6:16).

The following is not only a synopsis of the armour worn by Roman soldiers in Biblical Times as witnessed by Paul when in prison, but how it applies today to the Christian believer in Christ Jesus.

(1) Belt Of Truth:
    Description:

- A wide belt constructed of leather containing loops (holders) and was the first piece of armour applied daily to his body especially positioned around his waist.

Use:

- Held important equipment, different swords, ropes and darts, and a ration sack (their lunch kit) later emptied to hold jewels, gold and loot.
- When positioned properly it gave support to other pieces of armour making them more effective.

Our daily application:

- To pray, read the Word (the truth) and study. (1 Thessalonians 5:16-18).
- We gain knowledge of the Word. (2 Peter 3:18)
- We grow in our personal relationship and intimacy with the Three In One (God The Father, Son and Holy Spirit) (1 John 5:7).
- It gives guidance and direction for our daily lives (Psalm 119:105).

(2) Breastplate of Righteousness:
     Description:

- Was lightweight, allowing easy movement.
- Was the second piece of armour to put on.
- Was attached to the belt by leather thongs passed through the rings on the bottom which kept the breastplate firmly in place, well anchored to the belt and worn just above the belt.

Use:

- Protected the soldier's heart, an important organ responsible for sending the blood through the circulatory system to keep the soldier alive.

Our daily application:

- When we walk in righteousness of God, our breastplate of Righteousness is our defence against Satan's accusations and strategies.

(3) Feet Fitted With Readiness:
     Description:

- The Roman soldier's footwear was equipped with spikes on the soles.

Use:

- Provided strong balance, and sturdy footing.
- Superior posture when on hills and uneven ground.

Our daily application:

- Helps us keep our feet planted firmly on God's Word.
- Satan's threat and lies will not move us.
- Protects us when we walk through the rough places.

- Keeps us steady in the heat of the battle.
- Keeps demons and evil spirits where they belong: under our feet.

(4) Shield of Faith:
Description:

- The Roman Soldier's shields were long and rectangular covering from their knees to their chin.
- It was much larger than the circular Greek shield.

Use:

- Could kneel behind their shield for protection from both arrows and spears.
- Groups of soldiers under besiege could close in together and hold their shields over their heads to make a huge circle and protect their group from an arrow barrage.

Our daily application:

- The shield stands for our faith in God's promises.
- Knowing God's Word gives us even greater faith.
- God fights along with us, and this provides us with some powerful awesome protection.

(5) Helmet of Salvation:
Description:

- Romans had the best helmets of the ancient world.
- This helmet had a chinstrap and visor and came down to cover the back and sides of his neck.
- It had leather inside for comfort and good fit.
- The exterior of the helmet was made of bronze or iron, depending on the rank of the soldier or officer. The exterior would have been made of gold for parade use.
- Depending on the officer's rank, his helmet had a ridge of mounted plumage on top similar to the brush of a broom.

Use:

- Designed to protect from various angles of attack.

Our daily application:

- Protects our minds so fiery darts don't lodge in our thoughts.
- Destroy arguments and opinions raised against the knowledge of God.
- We take every thought captive to obey Christ.

(6) Sword of the Spirit:
Description:

- It had two edges, with the end turned upward.
- It cut in two directions.

Use:

- This sword was very deadly.
- It inflicted much more damage than other swords did.
- Not only was this sword intended to kill, but it would rip the enemy's insides to shreds.
- The soldier did not have to twist the sword in the enemy's flesh to inflict damage.
- Today it could be compared to aiming the most deadly machine gun and letting it rip.

Our daily application:

- Our sword of the spirit is the Word of God.
- Paul describes the Word of God as our awesome and powerful personal weapon. (Hebrews 4:12).

Every Christian needs to know how to battle evil. God's Word gives us detailed instructions on how to fight the evil forces of darkness.

1. We must put on the full armour of God (Ephesians 6:11–13).
2. We must wear the belt of truth (Ephesians 6:14). The belt of truth
    covers two places: our hearts and our minds. Truth keeps the
    Christian secure in Christ Jesus, and it makes effective all the other
    pieces of our armour. It is the belt of truth that holds our armour
    in place. It is important that we commit ourselves daily to walk
    in the light of God's truth. Make (Psalm 86:11) your daily prayer.
    "Teach me Thy way, O Lord; I will walk in Thy truth: unite my
    heart to fear Thy name."
3. We must wear the breastplate of righteousness (Ephesians 6:14).
    The soldier who wears the breastplate will go into battle boldly with
    perfect confidence. Satan is constantly attacking God's children
    with his lies; he accuses us and reminds us of our past sins. If we
    are not wearing our breastplate of righteousness, these darts will
    penetrate our spiritual heart. All Christians should be aware that
    they may come boldly into the Lord's presence: "Let us therefore
    come boldly unto the throne of grace, that we may obtain mercy,
    and find grace to help in time of need" (Hebrews 4:16).
4. We must wear the shoes of peace and preparation (Ephesians 6:15).
    The shoes of peace and preparation allow Christians to step freely
    and without any fear so they can turn their full attention to the
    battle at hand. These shoes aid in our movement and our defence.
    These shoes that God gives us propel us onward to proclaim true
    peace because Jesus Christ is our peace. It is important that we
    prepare ourselves to follow Jesus no matter what takes place.
    Putting on the shoes of peace is as simple as feeling at peace
    (Colossians 3:15-17). Anxiety and fear are the opposite of peace.
    There have been times when the Holy Spirit corrected me that I
    felt no peace. Yet when I have been in the most dreadful of valleys,
    it was the peace of Jesus that sustained me.
5. We must wear the shield of faith (Ephesians 6:16). This shield will
    defend not only our whole body but also our armour. The Bible
    does not say it quenches some of the fiery darts, but all of them.
    No matter what direction the attack comes from your shield will
    protect you.
6. We must wear the helmet of salvation (Ephesians 6:17). Satan's
    target is our mind. Satan's weapons are his lies. He wants to make
    us doubt God and our salvation. Our helmet protects our mind

from doubting God's truth that He has saved us through His loving grace; through Christ giving His life for us on Calvary as a sacrificial Lamb. "But let us, who are of the day, be sober, putting on the breastplate of faith and love; and for a helmet, the hope of salvation." (1 Thessalonians 5:8). "Be not conformed to this world: but be ye transformed by the renewing of your mind...(Romans 12:2).

7. We must wear the sword of the Spirit (Ephesians 6:17). The sword of the Spirit is our only weapon of offence that we have in our armour. The Word of God is our tool for our defence. Strongholds, arguments and our thoughts are all weapons that Satan uses against us. With the sword of the Spirit, which is God's Word, God's children are equipped to deal with everything Satan sends our way. It is important that Christians trust in the truth of God's Word. God's children need to have their confidence in the value of God's Word. We need to hunger for and desire the Word of God.

8. We must use prayer (Ephesians 6:18). We need to pray in the Spirit in all situations, through trials and through good times. In the dreadful valleys and on the pleasant mountaintops, we should never cease to pray (1 Thessalonians 5:16-18).

ELEVEN

What Is Hell? What Is Heaven?

What Is Hell?

Is there a Hell? Yes! Many believe there is no hell. Others believe that a loving God would never send anyone to hell. Still others believe hell is a party place where they will get drunk with their friends. Few truly know what hell is really like. I would like to start by telling you that God does not send anyone to hell. Man predetermines himself to hell when he chooses to reject Jesus Christ, the Son of God.

In the Old Testament the Abyss is the name of the watery depths of the earth. In the New Testament this place is referred to as Hades. This is the state the dead without Christ exist in, a person's disembodied existence, a place of great torment. Jesus was three days in Hades. Later Hades will give up its dead for the great judgment.

The Old Testament refers to Sheol as the abode of the dead. Throughout the Old Testament period it was believed that it was located in the depth of the earth, this is the holding place for both the wicked and the righteous, and that no one could avoid going to this place.

The New Testament indicates Sheol is the temporary holding place for both the souls of the righteous and those without Christ as they wait for the final resurrection. There are two parts to Sheol. One being that which holds those who have rejected Christ, this is the temporary place called Hades (Fiery Furnace). The other being that which holds the righteous in Christ known as Paradise or Abraham's bosom.

(Daniel 12:2) reveals later a resurrection of the dead when Sheol will give up it's dead. The righteous in Christ will be rewarded with everlasting life, and the corrupt will experience everlasting judgment.

Let's look at just some of what the Bible tells us about this horrible place called Hell (Hades):

- Hell was created for Satan and his angels (Matthew 25:41).
- In Hell the soul does not sleep; the dead are fully conscious.
- Hell is eternal.
- Hell is a place of wrath and sorrow. It is dreadfully frightful.
- It is fire that is not quenched, the worm never dies (Mark 9:48). The lake of fire and brimstone is in Hell.
- The body is not re-created, or exterminated. Perished, lost and destroyed does not mean demolished.
- In Hell people have full knowledge of events. They can remember their past life.
- There is nonstop destruction, pain and torment (Luke 16:23).
- Hell is damnation.
- A place of outer darkness (Matthew 22:13).
- The wicked, idolaters and all who are not with Christ are cast into Hell (1 Corinthians 6:9-10).

You'll notice in (Matthew 13:50), the evildoers are cast into the furnace of fire, but in (Revelation 20:14) with the second death they are cast into the lake of fire. The furnace is located in the centre of the earth; the lake of fire is a bottomless pit of fire in outer darkness (Revelation 9:2). "The devil that deceived them was cast into the lake of fire and brimstone, where the beast and the false prophet are, and shall be tormented day and night for ever and ever." (Revelation 20:10).

My Vision Of Hell

In my bedroom (that which the Holy Spirit called my Island of Patmos), I had a vision in which I went to hell. I felt the horrid heat; I heard the dreadful wailing and screaming. I was thirsty, but there was no water, and in my nostrils was a ghastly stench. Out of the seven visions of which I was prepared to write this book, this is my third vision.

We have five great bodies of water: the Pacific Ocean, the Atlantic Ocean, the Indian Ocean, the Arctic Ocean and the Southern Ocean. With this vision I travelled through deep water. (Job 26:5) tells us that the souls who have left their bodies are down underneath the ocean floor. The smoke from Hell's flames comes up through the black smokers in the bed of the ocean (Revelation 14:11). Scientists have found the centre of the earth to be a large iron ball, which they call the *inner core*. As you know, a furnace's outer layer must be made of a material that can withstand the heat. This large iron ball in the centre of our earth is the furnace that is mentioned in (Matthew 13:42). I have discovered that the souls who die without Christ travel this same route in their destiny to hell.

My soul left my body and began what is for the dead without Christ the trip of no return. I broke through the ocean's surface. I was travelling at a massive speed, heading for the ocean bed. Suddenly, although I was at the bottom of the ocean, the heat was becoming unbearable. Everything was happening so quickly. For a moment, I saw hydrothermal vents on the seabed; they were venting out hot black smoke. Then, just as suddenly, I was travelling into one of these incredibly hot smokers. The smoker was only wide enough for a human soul to travel through. I became aware that a great vacuum was pulling me through this chimney at a massive speed. At the end of the tunnel was a slight twist, and then, with great force, I was propelled out and landed on my bottom.

I was then in the centre of the earth—in other words, the core of the earth. The first thing I saw as I entered into hell was an enormous lake of fire. The heat was dreadful—unbelievable. Scientists have discovered the earth's inner core has a temperature of over 11,000 degrees Fahrenheit.

As I entered hell I could see people in the lake of fire—they were crying out for mercy, but there was no mercy given to them. As they would try to get out of the flames, the demons would force them back down into the flames with two-pronged pitchforks. As I looked up, I saw giant spirits chained to the wall by both their hands and their feet just above the burning lake of sulphur. They were struggling to get loose; however, they could not. I saw that the flames from the lake of fire were licking the bottoms of their feet. I believe these were the fallen angels (2 Peter 2:4).

I saw prison cells. They had three solid stone walls around them and bars in front of them. This was where demons were assigned to torment and torture people both day and night. Every soul in hell was naked. The demons were powerful, large and incredibly ugly. I saw in one prison cell a demon eating the flesh off of a man. When it was finished eating all of the man's flesh so that he had no flesh remaining on him, the man's flesh would grow back, and the demon would repeat the same procedure. I saw in another cell two demons holding a man down as another demon beat him up. In another cell, I saw a woman. Two demons held her arms and legs spread apart as a hideous, ugly demon raped her with an iron rod, which he shoved into her with great force. She was screaming and wailing. She cried out for mercy, but there was no mercy given to her.

I knew the Holy Spirit had allowed me to see these souls suffering in these cells so that I would have an account of what I had seen to bring back and place in this book. These souls were in outer darkness such as you would not believe. Unfortunately, these demons could not be detected as they approached in their attack.

Then I looked away from the fire. It was pitch black. There were billions of these prison cells, all of them holding people who were wailing, screaming, being tortured and tormented each by three demons assigned to them. All were crying out to God for His mercy, but no mercy was given to them.

Scientists have discovered cracks in the ocean floor, which allows water to seep deep down into the earth's crust. As the ocean water trickles over hot rocks and is forced back up through hot springs, it is heated. The water that gushes out of the hot springs, or hydrothermal vents, could possibly be more than three times the temperature of boiling water at sea level. However, at the bottom of the ocean, water cannot boil because the water pressure is too great for any gas bubbles to form and escape. This superheated water contains hydrogen sulphide, which is the stuff that makes rotten eggs smell bad.

In hell, the odor is like rotten eggs gone bad, rotten meat and sour milk—the putrid smell of burning flesh and sulphur. It's not the place for a person with a weak stomach. The water at the bottom of the sea looks like smoke, so scientists calls these vents smokers. Often, a chimney of rock forms around the vents. The tunnel I went through as I went into hell was like a hot chimney. Most living creatures would be killed by the high temperature and toxic mixture of chemicals. It is amazing that the soul of man could live in such a toxic place. I myself am a clean and picky person. It is shocking anyone could live through this horrid smell, the worst smell you could ever dream of. However, in the ocean floor, this horrendously hot water gushes from the vents teeming with microscopic life.

Some of these heat-loving microbes are bacteria. Others, however, are what is thought to be one of the oldest forms of life on earth. Both the bacteria and archaea have developed special proteins that help to keep these life-forms living under these harsh conditions. They are not like other forms of life that depend on sunlight for energy; these creatures depend on the chemicals in the water. Some of these microbes live in and around the hot vents. The smoker chimneys in the ocean are tall, and hot water pours out of them. This is home to some strange animals. Some of these animals are two-foot-long worms. The Bible tells us, "Where their worm dieth not, and the fire is not quenched" (Mark 9:48). These worms live with temperatures that would cook most other animals.

Scientists have also discovered a worm they have called the devil worm. It lives in the smouldering heat close to the centre of the earth. Its home is found at a depth of more than one kilometre into the earth's crust. That deep in the earth, it is so hot that it is impossible for any living thing to survive the heat. They have found evidence that this worm has been there for thousands of years. This devil worm has a high temperature tolerance and is believed to be able to live in 41 degrees Celsius (105.8 Fahrenheit). It lives in boiling-hot water. Therefore, could these be the worms mentioned in (Mark 9:48)?

You need to remember that in hell, it is so hot that the water would evaporate, there is no water, food or rest in hell. Although you are tremendously exhausted, you do not sleep. This horrendous suffering never stops! Outside of the great lake of fire, hell is a place of spirits: demons, human souls, evil spirits, fallen angels, and later with the second death Satan and the Antichrist.

There is eternal punishment for the confessing Christians who has left salvation. According to (2 Peter 2:20–21),

"For if, after they have escaped the pollutions of the world through the knowledge of the Lord and Savior Jesus Christ, they are again entangled therein, and overcome, the latter end is worse with them than the beginning. For it had been better for them not to have known the way of righteousness, than after they have known it, to turn from the Holy commandment delivered unto them".

The Christians who believed the saying "Once born again, always born again" and, although they received Christ and confessed with their tongues Jesus to be their Lord, were never circumcised in their hearts.

"Not everyone that saith unto me, 'Lord, Lord,' shall enter into the kingdom of heaven; but he that doeth the will of my Father which is in heaven. Many will say to me in that day, 'Lord, Lord, have we not prophesied in thy name? and in thy name have cast out devils? and in thy name done many wonderful works?' And then will I profess unto them, 'I never knew you; depart from me, ye that work iniquity." (Matthew 7:21–23)

Some Christians have gone to hell and come back to give accounts of what they saw. One of these was a woman who said she saw a pastor she had known who had passed away suffering in the burning lake of sulphur, and demons were using two-pronged pitchforks to push him back down into the flames as he cried for mercy. She told the Holy Spirit, "I know this man, he was a pastor. What is he doing here in hell?" The Spirit of God answered, "He was stealing out of the church offering plate and never repented of his sin." He was robbing God to line his own pockets, (Acts 5:2-4).

The Bible tells us that hell has different degrees of punishment, and I will tell you this: based on what I saw as I journeyed through hell, there are definitely different degrees of punishments. "Verily I say unto you, it shall be more tolerable for the land of Sodom and Gomorrah in the day of judgment than for that city" (Matthew 10:15). (Luke 12:47–48) says,

And that servant, which knew his Lord's will, and prepare not himself, neither did according to His will, shall be beaten with many strips. But he that knew not, and did commit things worthy of stripes, shall be beaten with few stripes. For unto whomsoever much is given of him shall be much required; and to whom men have committed much, of him they will ask the more.

And consider this verse: "Of how much sorer punishment, suppose ye, shall he be thought worthy, who hath trodden under foot the Son of God, and hath counted the Blood of the covenant, wherewith he was sanctified, an unholy thing, and hath done despite unto the Spirit of grace?" (Hebrews 10:29).

Remember that this hell is the first death. (Revelation 20:11–15) tells of the second death. This earth will no more be, and God will create the new heaven and new earth. This new place of judgment will be a lake of fire, and everyone who is in the first place of judgment (the belly of the earth) will enter the final place of judgment to suffer for eternity with Satan, his angels, the beast, the false prophet, demons and evil spirits.

What Is Heaven?

Here are some Bible passages that relate to heaven: (Revelation 21:4; 1 Corinthians 2:9; John 14:2; Revelation 22:1–5; Luke 23:43; Hebrews 11:16; Revelation 21:21–27; John 3:16; 2 Peter 3:13; Revelation 21:1; Luke 12:33; Hebrews 13:14 and Revelation 21:1–5).

My Vision of Heaven

In my bedroom (that which the Holy Spirit called my Island of Patmos), this was my seventh vision. In this vision, I went to heaven.

Outer space begins at 100 kilometres up from the earth. It takes the great speed of a rocket ship to travel into outer space—seven miles per second, or 25,000 miles per hour. Just to reach low Earth orbit, which is where shuttle astronauts travel, requires the modest speed of five miles per second—that is to reach the distance of 62 miles from the earth's surface.

At the time of our departure from this earth into eternal life, if we are Christians, a white chariot will immediately meet us at the place where we have passed away. If it is a hospital bed, the chariot will enter the hospital room we were in when we passed out of this life.

My Trip to Heaven

"And it came to pass, as they still went on, and talked, that, behold, there appeared a chariot of fire, and horses of fire, and parted them both asunder; and Elijah went up by a whirlwind into heaven" (2 King 2:11). My vision of heaven began, like my vision of hell, at the moment of my physical death. But in this case, a beautiful white chariot landed at my right side. The driver got out, came around and took my hand as I stepped up into the chariot. Maybe you have watched Christmas movies in which Santa, his sleigh and his reindeer whirl in the sky as he bids all a good night. In much the same fashion, my chariot driver took me on a guided tour of this spectacular universe. After that, we made a straight beeline for eternal paradise.

Travelling in outer space at an amazing speed that was almost unbelievable, I found myself at what today's scientists are calling the Whirlpool Galaxy. When I was directly in front of this astonishing spectacle, the white chariot I was travelling in picked up speed, leaving a streak behind it like that of a shooting star as we went shooting through the black hole, heading into a light with a perfect cross in the centre. This black hole at the centre of the nebula is 43,000 light years from our earth. This galaxy is 35 percent the size of the Milky Way. The mass of this galaxy has been estimated to be 160 billion solar masses. This bright light and cross are the entrance we take into heaven.

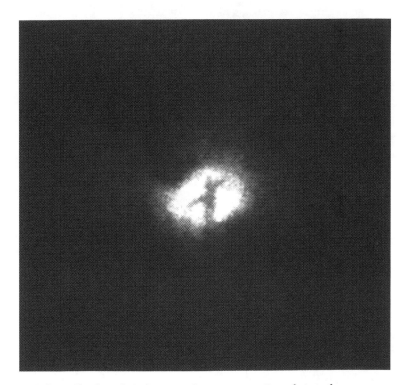

The Whirlpool Galaxy is the entrance I took into heaven.
Credit: H. Ford (JHU/STScl), the faint Object
Spectrograph IDT, and NASA/ESA

Upon entering heaven, I was greeted right at the entrance. It is not a boring place. There are many people, and they are all busy at one thing or another. No one is standing around bored. You might have heard, as I had, that everyone is in the sky, fluttering his or her wings with a harp in hand, as if this is all we will do for eternity. That is hogwash. This could not be further from the truth. There is so much to see and do. There is a crystal-clear sea of water, and there are trees. Birds fly in the sky, and there are fluffy clouds; however, there is no rain. Instead, at all times, there's a fresh, light mist in the air. There are meadows of pretty flowers.

I saw a city that was glowing. The beauty of this city took my breath away. The Bible describes this city like this:

> And he carried me away in the spirit to a great and high mountain, and shewed me that great city, the Holy Jerusalem, descending out of heaven from God, having the glory of God: and her light was like unto a stone most precious, even like a jasper stone, clear as crystal; and had a wall great and high, and had twelve gates, and at the gates twelve angels, and names written thereon, which are the names of the twelve tribes of the children of Israel: on the east three gates; on the north three gates; on the south three gates; and on the west three gates. And the wall of the city had twelve foundations, and in them the names of the twelve apostles of the Lamb. And he that talked with me had a golden reed to measure the city, and the gates thereof, and the wall thereof. And the city lieth foursquare, and the length is as large as the breadth: and he measured the city with the reed, twelve thousand furlongs. The length and the breadth and the height of it are equal. And he measured the wall thereof, an hundred and forty and four cubits, according to the measure of a man, that is, of the angel. And the building of the wall of it was of jasper: and the city was pure gold, like unto clear glass. And the foundations of the wall of the city were garnished with all manner of precious stones. The first foundation was jasper; the second, sapphire; the third, a chalcedony; the fourth, an emerald; the fifth, sardonyx; the sixth, sardius; the seventh, chrysolite; the eighth, beryl; the ninth, a topaz; the tenth, a chrysoprasus; the eleventh, a jacinth; the twelfth, an amethyst. And the twelve gates

were twelve pearls; every several gate was of one pearl; and the street of the city was pure gold, as it were transparent glass. And I saw no temple therein: for the Lord God Almighty and the Lamb are the temple of it. And the city had no need of the sun, neither of the moon, to shine in it: for the glory of God did lighten it, and the Lamb is the light thereof. And the nations of them which are saved shall walk in the light of it: and the kings of the earth do bring their glory and honor into it. And the gates of it shall not be shut at all by day: for there shall be no night there. And they shall bring the glory and honour of the nations into it. And there shall in no wise enter into it any thing that defileth, neither whatsoever worketh abomination, or maketh a lie: but they which are written in the Lamb's book of life. (Revelation 21:10–27)

I also saw many mansions; every one of God's precious children will have a mansion of his or her own.

In heaven, people don't age past 33 years old. If we go to heaven as an old man or old woman, then we are young in heaven. People can fly, and we can leap three stories high. There is no more death, and there are no more tears. We have a marvellous new body, and the most beautiful light radiates from us.

I entered my mansion. All of my pets that had died before me were in my mansion as I entered, waiting to greet me, among them was Dixie (my childhood pony). Every one of my babies I had miscarried and my baby I had aborted were all there and were all happy to see me. My baby I had aborted gave me the most beautiful smile. If I had carried this child, he would have been a boy. By the way, the babies we abort love us very much, and they hold no grudge against their moms and dads. I will share my mansion with all of them, and the same will be true for you. Even your pets you had before you received Christ will be in heaven with you. In my main room, above my fireplace mantel, hung a large painting of my first love, Danny Rivets.

Many of the mansions uniquely built for God's children slowly revolved in a circle, as if they were on an axle, giving a beautiful view of heaven from every angle. The mansions have large windows so the occupants can fully enjoy heaven's splendour. Our mansions and heaven will be everything we ever wanted. That is why it is called paradise. Just as my mansion is decorated for me, your mansion is especially decorated for you.

Then I climbed onto the back of my pony (Dixie), and rode through heaven. I saw in the distance an amusement park. There were exciting rides. I saw a huge roller coaster, and I could hear laughter and screams of delightful excitement coming from the amusement park. It was easy to tell that those inside were having fun.

Next, I walked on a street made of the purest gold while I ate a hamburger and french fries. Then I was sitting at a formal dinner table with my friends. A roast duck was centred on the table. We were eating and drinking wine. We were chatting as we fully enjoyed each other's companionship. The room was full of our laughter. In heaven, there are restaurants; we can eat and drink.

In heaven, there is a swimming pool and also a swimming hole with a waterfall you can jump off of into the water below. I saw in my mansion a three-story swimming pool with a water slide. If you can't swim here on this earth, in heaven, you will be able to swim. I went swimming in my third-story pool, and I glided down my water slide into my second-story pool. Then I glided down my water slide into my first-story pool. I should tell you that I can't even float, let alone swim. If you could never ice-skate, in heaven, you will ice-skate. God will have a skating rink just for you. God has a hockey rink for both the men and the women. I plan to play hockey!

I then rode on Dixie's back to a movie theatre. The screen of this theatre took up two whole side walls of the building. The screen was in the shape of a half circle, and there were seats to sit on. It was amazing how realistic the show was. You will be able to go to the movie theatre and watch movies.

Dixie and I road to another building, a museum and history building. In this building, you can watch on a lifelike screen the total creation as told in Genesis 1, and you can watch anything else you might have wondered about. This building has manna on display, as well as other historical things from the history of the Old Testament.

There is a library, which contains all the books that have been written by Christians. If you as a Christian have wrote a book, then it is in this library. You can take the books out to your mansion and read them at home.

I then rode my pony to one of the many portals located in heaven. A portal is a large hole you can look down through to see your loved ones who are still on earth.

As I stood looking through the portal, I felt someone place a tallit over my shoulders. Having this Jewish shawl placed on my shoulders gave me the same peaceful feeling a knitted prayer shawl does when it is placed over your shoulders. I turned to look and saw that it was Jesus, who had placed the tallit on me. Then I saw that my dad and mom, my grandpa and grandma Campbell, Ricky and many other friends and family who'd gone before me and had made it into heaven were gathered at the portal with me. I recognized every one of them. I looked down into the portal, and I could see my kids, my grandkids and everyone remaining on earth whom I knew. I give you my word: heaven is not boring, and heaven is for eternity. There will be no night there. There is no need for the sun, for the Lord God gives heaven its light (Revelation 22:5). Oh yes, there is a place to go dancing in heaven. Wow, the list of things to see and do just goes on and on.

It is my deepest wish that no one should suffer in hell. When they have taken their last breath and their days on this earth have come to an end, many so-called Christians will be surprised to find out that Jesus never knew them.

> "Not everyone that saith unto Me, 'Lord, Lord,' shall enter into the kingdom of heaven; but he that doeth the will of my Father which is in heaven. Many will say to Me in that day, 'Lord, Lord, have we not prophesied in Thy Name? and in Thy Name have cast out devils? and in Thy Name done many wonderful works?' And then will I profess unto them, 'I never knew you: depart from me, ye that work iniquity.'" (Matthew 7:21–23)

The ones who will be surprised at their dreadful outcome will be those who had all the other believers in church well fooled—that is, except for God. You can't fool God. Those unknown to Jesus will be those who were led astray by false teachers; those who, after accepting Christ, continued to sin wilfully; those who, when they heard the Word of God, did not obey it; those who trusted in their own righteousness; those who wilfully refused to forgive their debtors and those who did not persevere to the end.

In (Matthew 7:21–23), when this person says the name *Lord* for the second time, he is implying to the Lord, "I know you personally." When Jesus answers, "I never knew you," Jesus is saying, "I never had an intimate relationship with you." For many Christians, everything looks really good externally. They have all their fellow Christian brothers and sisters fooled regarding what is truly in their hearts, but they cannot fool God. The fact is, anyone who continues to practice lawlessness—that is, wilfully sins—will not enter heaven (Hebrews 10:26).

Maurice put it this way: "Hell is a place of great pestilence." In other words, hell is a plague against all who have rejected God's commandments and Christ Jesus as their Lord. If you fear large, scary, powerful monsters, then hell is the one place you do not want to go. I have had people tell me they want to go to hell because they are planning to party there with their departed friends. The point is this: there is no water in hell; therefore, there will be no beer in hell.

One vile heavy-metal rock band sings the lyric "Satan has their souls." The souls of the unsaved enter hell for eternity. The band's words could not be closer to the truth. If a person dies not a Christian, then Satan does have his or her soul, and the person will be tormented in hell.

I will tell you this with full honesty: 100 percent of the people who are now in hell believe there is a hell. Most of these people never believed they would go to hell. The point is, we either have Christ in our hearts, or we don't. We are either going to hell, or we are not.

I was never as terrified as the time I woke from a particular nightmare. I was covered in sweat, and my heart was racing. I had never been so glad to wake from my sleep and realize it had only been a bad dream. In this dream, I was driving a car, when suddenly, the brakes were totally gone. No matter how much I tried to push on the brakes, I could not stop the car. I was heading straight for a concrete wall, and my car was picking up speed at a tremendous rate. I hit the wall at 300 miles per hour; I was dead on impact. With that, I immediately went to hell. The heat was more than any human being could ever imagine. There was a lake of fire, and the flames were rising high. Demons started circling around and gathering in toward me. They were ugly, and I could see dreadful hate in their eyes. My whole body was in tremendous pain. My flesh was peeling off of my body. As a result of the tremendous pain, the fear I felt toward these ugly demons and the unbearable heat and fire, I was screaming at the top of my lungs. Just then, I woke up; thank God it was only a bad dream. However, it did give me a heart like I had never had before to win the unsaved to Christ and warn the lukewarm Christians that we need to be on fire for Jesus.

Dr. Azzacove, an atheist scientist, drilled a well deep into the earth. He broke through to hell. He witnessed the sounds of human voices screaming in pain. He also saw coming up through the drill site luminous gas, and a demon rose up through it and said, "I have conquered." You can find more about this discovery on the Internet at http://smokeys-trail.com/Jesus/dighell.ram. "The fool hath said in his heart, There is no God. Corrupt are they, and have done abominable iniquity" (Psalm 51:3).

In the year 1977, Dr. Maurice Rawlings, a heart surgeon, by the use of CPR, brought a man who was suffering in hell back to life. This is an amazing story I suggest you read of both a doctor and his patient becoming born-again saints. You can read his book *To Hell and Back* or, on the Internet, go to http://www.divinerevelations.info/border/home_truquoise_ball.png.

"They, and all that appertained to them, went down alive into the pit, and the earth closed upon them: and they perished from among the congregation" (Numbers 16:33). They went to hell, the centre of the earth. This great furnace would only need to be 100 miles or less in diameter to contain, with much room to spare, all of the 40 billion or so people who have ever lived on this earth (this is assuming their spiritual bodies are the same size as their physical bodies are here on the earth). The inner core located in the centre of the earth extends 900 miles (or 1,448.4096 kilometres)—plenty of room to hold the billions of people who have lived on this earth. The earth's inner core has a temperature of over 6,000 Celsius (or 10,800 degrees Fahrenheit)—as hot as the surface of the sun.

I do not deny that scientists have declared the centre core to be a solid ball; however, I know in my vision it was through a smoking vent in the ocean floor, I travelled to hell. I know what I saw! Jesus said that He would spend three days and three nights in the belly of the earth (Matthew 12:40). He went to hell and took the keys of death and Hades (Revelation 1:18). The Bible's description of hell as a place in the heart of the earth matches up with scientists' discoveries. Inside the heart of this earth are millions of lost, tormented souls burning, weeping and wailing without any hope whatsoever. This will happen to every person who dies without Christ. Our planet Earth is the crust that holds hell within it. Nothing on Earth—not movies or crime scenes filled with blood and gore—could ever begin to match the horror of hell. No human on the earth could ever imagine what hell is like. All souls in hell have abandoned all hope. The Bible does not tell us anywhere that there is hope for a person in hell. For a person who has entered hell, it is too late. Hell is forever. "For what shall it profit a man, if he shall gain the whole world, and lose his own soul?" (Mark 8:36).

Jesus has given us over and over again in the scriptures warnings about how horrid hell is. He took hell seriously, and so should we. Jesus said we should remove from our lives all things that keep us out of God's grace. Telling people to pluck out their own eyes or chop off their hand or foot is shocking to even think of, but Jesus saying this in Mark 9:43–47 just shows how serious He was and still is about hell and how seriously He wants us to take it. Jesus is telling us that we would be better off groping around for the rest of our lives with our eyes plucked out, blind, than having our sight and burning in hell. A friend of mine once introduced me to her elderly father. The man was diabetic. He had lost both of his arms at the shoulders, and he had lost both legs at the hips, leaving him with no more than his head and a stump for his body. Can you imagine living your life that way? For Jesus to say you would be better off living without your hands and feet than burning in hell proves just how serious Jesus was about this place of agony. Jesus said in (Mark 9:43–47),

> And if thy hand offend thee, cut it off: it is better for thee to enter into life maimed, than having two hands to go into hell, into the fire that never shall be quenched: Where their worm dieth not, and the fire is not quenched. And if thy foot offend thee, cut it off: it is better for thee to enter halt into life, than having two feet to be cast into hell, into the fire that never shall be quenched: Where their worm dieth not, and the fire is not quenched. And if thine eye offend thee, pluck it out: It is better for thee to enter into the kingdom of God with one eye, than having two eyes to be cast into hell fire.

Hell is real; Jesus could not be deceived. Judgment is for everyone who dies without Christ: "And as it is appointed unto men once to die, but after this the judgment" (Hebrews 9:27). This is one sure thing for all of humankind: we will all someday die. Three people die every second, which means 180 people die every minute.

Hell is right now in the centre of the earth. Later, after Judgment Day, hell and death will be cast into the lake of fire and then cast into outer darkness. (Revelation 20:11–15) tells us that this earth as we know it now, as well as heaven, will no longer exist. At the final destruction of this earth, the sea that I travelled through to enter hell, which is the fiery furnace in the centre of the earth, will give up the dead who are inside of it, and all who died without Christ will be judged and thrown into the lake of fire, which is the final judgment (Revelation 20:11–15).

Could this description be anyone of us?

> As I leave my body, I know something is going powerfully wrong. I don't like this. I hear a sound; it is getting louder and louder—screaming, weeping and wailing. Terror and fear beyond anything I could have imagined overtake me. "This can't be happening to me! Oh God, no! No!" I am screaming in terror. My nostrils are filling with the dreadful stench of burning flesh. My flesh sizzles and crackles. My flesh is peeling from my bones as I am engulfed in this pit of flames. Now I find I am madly thrashing and convulsing from the horrible pain. The agony does not stop. "Oh, why can't I die?" I scream, weep, wail and gnash at my tongue. "Oh God, how I thirst. Will this pain ever stop?" But I know it won't. I know it is forever. I am so afraid. The darkness engulfs me. I sense something moving in the darkness. "Dear God, no, this can't be happening." I cannot see them, but the monsters are huge; they tear my arms and legs off of my body as if I am no more than tissue paper. I curse the day I was born. "Oh my God, why did you not warn me?" Then I remember the pastor who gave me every opportunity to repent. I found such pleasure in my sin. I listened to the ones who told me, "It does not matter how we live our lives; no one can pluck us out of God's hand. Once born again, always born again." I thought I had lots of time to repent. I remember reading the gospel. "Dear God, don't you care? I prophesied in your name, I cast demons out in your name and I even performed many miracles in your name." How many times I read (John 3:16): 'For God so loved the world.' I thought a loving God would never send anyone to hell. I had believed that surely a loving God would never send anyone to a place like this. But then I remember (John 3:36): "He that believeth not the Son shall

not see life; but the wrath of God abideth on him." I realize I am here for eternity.

If you do not believe in hell, then you are calling Jesus a liar, because He said there is a hell. In hell, there is torment; you have a body of some sort that is in flames, but it does not get consumed. You have eyes to see and a mouth and tongue to speak; you thirst. You have ears to hear the continuous wailing and screaming that will never cease. Here is the question: Do you want to go to heaven or hell? You might want to go back to the last page of Chapter 1 and say the salvation prayer with a deeply repentant heart.

TWELVE

Fortune-Telling, Tattoos and Body Piercing

There shall not be found among you anyone that maketh his son or his daughter to pass through the fire, or that useth divination, or an observer of times, or an enchanter, or a witch. Or a charmer, or a consulter with familiar spirits, or a wizard, or a necromancer. For all that do these things are an abomination unto the Lord: and because of these abominations the Lord thy God doth drive them out from before thee.

—Deuteronomy 18:10–12

Fortune-Telling

Fortune-telling is an abomination, and born-again believers should not be practising in it. Neither should Christians consult mediums or fortune-tellers. Even cracking open a fortune cookie and reading the message inside is consulting with demons.

Fortune-telling requires advice or affirmation from a demon or evil spirit. The Bible forbids this. Various names given to a fortune-teller are crystal-gazer, spaewife, seer, soothsayer, sibyl, clairvoyant and prophet. Methods they use are astromancy, horary astrology, pendulum reading, spirit board reading, tasseography (reading tea leaves in a cup), cartomancy (fortune-telling with cards), tarot reading, crystallomancy (reading of a crystal sphere) and chiromancy (or palmistry, reading of the palms). Spiritual consultation is another form of fortune-telling in which the advice and prediction the practitioner gives the client come from evil spirits or a vision.

Today fortune-telling is a big money-making business that brings in the rich and powerful. Fortune-telling brings in bankers, lawyers, the police's criminal investigation department and more. For many people, fortune-telling is their full-time business. For others, it's a paying business on the side. In various states of United States of America, fortune-telling is illegal.

It is possible you have been to a fortune-teller who could give you an accurate reading of your future. My mother could. My mother was known for miles around to be accurate with her fortune-telling. Many came to her to have their futures read. Mom always had the future correct right down to the last detail. She was also correct the day she read my brother's death.

As a 12-year-old girl, I saw the dark and sinister side of fortune-telling as my family learned a painful lesson through the dreadful death of my baby brother of two years old. My mother practised fortune-telling by the use of a deck of playing cards as far back as I can remember. The death of my brother was foretold through both my mother's card reading and my psychic ability to read into dreams. I knew the night I woke from the dream of my brother's death that he was going to die. I sat up in my bed as I began wailing and screaming. Only days before, I had stood in the kitchen as my mother turned over the death card, and her face went as pale as a sheet. Dad asked her what card she had turned over, and she muttered, "The death card. It is one of the kids." In less than two weeks, Ricky was dead, and my mother and father were planning the funeral for their only son.

I will tell you how the psychic reading of my brother's death came to be true. My mother, while reading her own future, turned over the death card. Only days later, I dreamed that horrid dream. Then the spirits of fear and pride that dwelt in my mother for a short time manifested themselves and attacked my mother, momentarily modifying her maternal instinct of a sweet and loving mother and causing her to do the unthinkable— something she never would have even thought of doing. She panicked and, out of fear, murdered her little boy. She did love him. Because of her loss, she suffered for the rest of her life. There was not anything magical about Mom's fortune-telling or the tragic loss we went through with the death of my brother. Do you see how dangerous dabbling in the occult is?

I believe my baby brother possibly would have lived if my mother had never turned over the death card and had not so convincingly believed in the accuracy of her own fortune-telling, and if I had not believed in the accuracy of my reading into dreams he could possibly be alive today.

In Mom's later years in the nursing home, I remember watching my mother as she sat, and when she thought no one was watching, she would talk to herself. I know who she thought she was talking to: her dead son. How many times I envied her for those precious moments only she could enjoy. She loved her little boy. Back in 1999, I was going through a demon possession and had limited control. Although most of these spirits within people are tiny, they are powerful, especially when they are manipulating the brain. Later in my life, I came to know my mother as the most precious and sweet mother a woman could ever ask for. It was not my mother who killed my brother; the evil spirits in her did it.

It is offensive to God when a Christian goes around saying, "I'm a Gemini. What are you?" Believers should not be associating themselves with pagan astrology. I know Christians who enjoy reading the little fortunes they find in fortune cookies. In the checkout of the grocery stores, you will see little horoscope books. In the funnies section of the newspaper, you will always find the horoscopes. Christians should not be reading or listening to their fortunes and horoscopes. It is time for all Christians to stop dabbling in the dark, sinister world of Satan.

Satan wants all the attention. He is an attention grabber, and he will go to any length to get all the glory. People cannot tell the future. We have no way of knowing it; however, evil spirits can alter the future according to what the fortune-teller has predicted. In doing this, they give the devil the glory. Don't think for a moment that demons won't or can't bring two people together. Perhaps you had your fortune read and were told the name of the man you were going to marry, and it was accurate. Under the condition you received this foretelling of your future from a medium, a demon would have been your matchmaker who brought your spouse and you together.

Okay, let us say a Christian goes to a medium to seek her future. The evil spirits within this Christian see their lucky break. There is an attractive man she has spoken to on more than one occasion, and although she is unaware of it, he is smitten with her. A spirit whispers into the thoughts of the medium the name of this man, and the medium in turn gives her the name of this man as the first name of the man she is going to marry. Then the demons play matchmaker. In the bread section of the grocery store, she greets this man whose first name is the name the medium gave her in the reading. This man had, on a few occasions, spoken to her in the local coffee shop, and he found her quite appealing but had not yet gotten the nerve to ask her out on a date. The truth of the matter was, she did not even know his first name. The spirits in him knew that he found her desirable. The spirits in her knew that she liked his bubbly personality, and she hoped he would ask her out. The demons knew both of them and knew the name of the man would match the medium's foretold future event. He decided it was now or never, and while in the bread aisle, he asked her to dinner and the movies. She found out that his first name was the name of the man the medium had told her she would marry. He was charming and good looking. It was love at first sight, and six months later, they were married. What a lucky break for that demon. Talk about a feather in his hat. He had only one goal: to make this Christian embrace something that God hates—divination.

Back in the 1960s, they did not yet have the proper tools to detect how many babies were in a mother's womb or if there was more than one. If a woman was expecting a multiple birth, she would find out how many babies she carried when she gave birth to the babies. My mother went into a carnival fortune-teller's booth when she was pregnant with the twins. Although the fortune this medium read was a farce, the fortune-teller was accurate with one small detail: she told Mom she was carrying two babies.

How did the medium know? Evil spirits and demons communicate with each other. Before my massive deliverance in 2016, I would often hear the evil spirits within me bicker among themselves. At times, I was aware of a battle in which they were pushing and shoving each other. They do talk back and forth. When I use the box with spiritual deliverance, I put a gag in the spirit's mouth so that he cannot communicate with Satan and other demons and evil spirits. The medium's spirits, who were ether surrounding her or were within her, would have asked the spirits within my mother some details about Mom's pregnancy. My mother's evil spirit from within would have said, "I've got a good one: she's expecting twins, one of each. The boy is the weaker of the two." Then the evil spirit passed the message to the medium, and the medium told my mother, "You carry twins in your womb." Those were the very words she spoke to my mother and dad.

Many fortune-tellers are pranksters; they rely on information you give them through your body language to guide them through their predictions. A few are the real thing, as my mother was, but they get their accurate readings through communication with evil spirits. Satan and his vast army have been, from the fall of Adam and Eve in the Garden of Eden, manipulating the human race. Satan knows how to handle mankind. He is well practised in manipulating the human race.

Only God knows the future. Satan and his demons do not know what tomorrow holds. Satan can, however, alter the future when foolish people are naive enough to believe such trickery. If you show any interest in the area of horoscopes, divination or fortune-telling, the demons will without a doubt try to fan the flames. I know from my early childhood just from watching my mother's divinations and the curiosity it fanned in me and my siblings how powerfully the human race are drawn to the psychic world. The unsaved person does not understand why he or she is drawn to psychics and magic, but I believe one is drawn because deep in the subconscious mind, he or she is drawn back to his or her beginning. All people have spiritual hearts in them that remain dead until they give their spiritual hearts and lives to Jesus. That tiny spiritual heart, although it is dead in the heathen, still is drawing the unsaved person back to his or her ancestral beginning, which in this case is the heavenly Father's heart. Therefore, the human race, as confused as they might be, are drawn like a magnet to the spiritual world of psychics and magic, which is Satan's counterfeit for heaven, from which people were created and received their beginning.

Christians should be on guard about this. It is our subconscious mind that drives our desires for the glimpse into our future. It is because of God's great and unconditional love for us that demons are so hard at work to cause us to embrace the things God hates. These spirits want to cause enmity between us and God. The devil is hard at work, seeking something he can take to God and say, "Did you see what Emily did? She cracked open her fortune cookie and read her future."

As believing Christians, we need to stay away from this satanic farce. I say that horoscopes, fortune-telling and all other forms of divination are humbug. Next time someone tells you he or she is a Gemini, just politely smile and tell him or her, "I'm a Christian."

Now let us take a look at what the Bible tells us about fortune-telling, superstition, horoscopes and charms. Are Christians permitted to believe and indulge in such things? (Deuteronomy 17:2–5) says this:

> If there be found among you, within any of thy gates which the Lord thy God giveth thee, man or woman, that hath wrought wickedness in the sight of the Lord thy God, in transgressing his covenant, And hath gone and served other gods, and worshipped them, either the sun, or moon,

or any of the host of heaven, which I have not commanded; And it be told thee, and thou hast heard of it, and inquired diligently, and behold, it be true, and the thing certain, that such abomination is wrought in Israel: Then shalt thou bring forth that man or that woman, which have committed that wicked thing, unto thy gates, even that man or that woman, and shalt stone them with stones, till they die.

(Leviticus 20:6) tells us that God will no longer consider the person who goes to a diviner his child. Doing this is a test against your heart. Do you love God? (Deuteronomy 13:1–4) says,

If there arise among you a prophet, or a dreamer of dreams, and giveth thee a sign or a wonder, And the sign or the wonder come to pass, whereof he spake unto thee, saying, Let us go after other gods, which thou hast not known, and let us serve them; Thou shalt not hearken unto the words of that prophet, or that dreamer of dreams: for the Lord your God proveth you, to know whether ye love the Lord your God with all your heart and with all your soul. Ye shall walk after the Lord your God, and fear him, and keep his commandments, and obey his voice, and ye shall serve him, and cleave unto him.

Follow the Lord, and fear Him. Obey Him, and keep all His commands. Worship Him only, and be faithful to God and only God. We are not to worship the stars, moon and sun. Horoscope readings are done through astrology, which is reading the stars. By worshipping other gods or the sun, moon and stars, men and women alike sin against God and break His covenant. "Regard not them that have familiar spirits, neither seek after wizards, to be defiled by them: I am the Lord your God" (Leviticus 19:31). This scripture tells us not to go to people who consult the demons for our advice.

Read (2 Kings 21:6; 2 Chronicles 33:6 and 1 Samuel 28:3–25) to see how sinning against God by consulting a fortune-teller or medium stirred up God's anger. When a person suggests you seek fortune-tellers, you are to answer, "Don't listen to mediums. What they tell you will do you harm; it will do you no good at all." (Isaiah 44:25) says, "That frustrateth the tokens of the liars, and maketh diviners mad; that turneth wise men backward, and maketh their knowledge foolish." God makes foolish and frustrates the words of the fortune-tellers and the predictions of the astrologers. You don't need to go far to see this; just look at what happened with the death of my baby brother.

Read (Isaiah 47:10–15). Disaster will come upon you, and your magician will not be able to stop it. You will not have the power to stop this disaster. There will be no prediction that will help. The fortune-tellers and astrologers cannot help themselves, so how will they help you? Who was there to help my family as my mother took hold of the coffin my brother's lifeless body lay in and tried to yank it off its stand or as I stood helplessly staring into the casket at Ricky's dead body, hoping that if I could imagine hard enough, all the magic I had grown up believing in would put breath back into his tiny lungs and make him sit up? How I wished I could once again hear him call out my name: "Nana!" Calling on demons to learn your future will only lead to your calamity.

The book of Jeremiah tells us not to listen to the prophets or any other person who claims to predict the future, whether by dreams or by calling on the dead: "Therefore hearken not ye to your prophets, nor to your diviners, nor to your dreamers, nor to your enchanters, nor to your sorcerers" (Jeremiah 27:9). In (Jeremiah 29:8), God warns us not to seek mediums and fortune-tellers.

God tells us that curses won't come on us unless we deserve it: "As the bird wandering, as the swallow by flying, so the curse causeless shall not come" (Proverbs 26:2). God's good and perfect plan for His children is to bring prosperity, not disaster. His plan is to give us the future we hope for. He wants us to call upon Him, not upon fortune-tellers. He says to his children, "Pray to me, and I will answer you; seek me, and you will find me. And this is because you have sought after me with all your heart." (Jeremiah 29:11–13) says, "For I know the thoughts that I think toward you, saith the Lord, thoughts of peace and not of evil, to give you an expected end. Then shall ye call upon me, and ye shall go and pray unto me, and I will hearken unto you. And ye shall seek me, and find me, when ye shall search for me with all your heart."

You see, when we go to evil spirits to learn the future and what it holds for us, we are slaves to these demons, but when we seek God only, then we are not slaves. The full content of our divine nature lives in Christ Jesus. It is in Christ that we have been given our life in full union with Christ. Jesus is supreme over every spiritual ruler and authority.

"O Lord, I know that the way of man is not in himself: it is not in man that walketh to direct his steps" (Jeremiah 10:23). God is the master of our destiny. "Whatsoever the Lord pleased, that did He in heaven, and in earth, in the seas, and all deep places" (Psalm 135:6). God does whatever He wishes in heaven and on earth. No one can escape from God's power. "Yea, before the day was I am He; and there is none that can deliver out of my hand: I will work, and who shall let it?" (Isaiah 43:13).

No one can stop God from fulfilling his will (Job 23:13–14). God's plans will always be carried out (Proverbs 19:21). God brings both blessings and disasters (Isaiah 45:7). Good and bad come to everyone, and we never know what will happen next (Ecclesiastes 7:14). Everything that happens in this world happens at the time when God chooses (Ecclesiastes 3:1). No man will have anything unless God gives it to him (John 3:27). When God closes a door, no person or demon is going to open it, and when God opens a door, neither will any person or demon close it (Revelation 3:7).

"Trust in the Lord with all thine heart; and lean not unto thine own understanding. In all thy ways acknowledge him, and he shall direct thy paths" (Proverbs 3:5–6). We don't need mediums and fortune-tellers to direct our paths or to tell us what our future holds. God's eyes are on the sparrow (Matthew 10:29). God clothes the grass of the field (Matthew 6:30). God has every hair on our heads counted (Luke 12:7). How much more God cares for us. We don't need to seek the future from evil spirits; God holds our lives in His hands. His spoken word to us is this: "Behold, I have graven thee upon the palms of my hands" (Isaiah 49:16).

Did you know that both tattoo parlours and fortune-telling parlours are loaded with demons? Entering a tattoo parlour or fortune parlour is reason enough for an evil spirit to enter you. As believers in Christ, we should all stay out of these places. Through my own experience, I know that if you get your fortune read or get a tattoo, in doing so, you break down your protective hedge enough for evil spirits to enter. The people who do so give these spirits the legal right to enter them and stay.

The Taboo behind the Tattoo

The Bible tells us not to mark our bodies: "Ye shall not make any cuttings in your flesh for the dead, nor print any marks upon you: I am the Lord" (Leviticus 19:28). God always gives us commands for our own good because He knows the consequences that will follow our actions. God does not forbid to be mean. I often call it tough love when I refuse to give my dogs chocolate. With God, when He says no, He does so out of love. He only wants to protect us. If God says no, He has a good reason for it. I happen to know that a lot of Christians are now getting tattoos. If you have had your body marked with a tattoo, then you need to repent.

In America, people get tattoos out of ignorance. However, in some countries, people get tattoos to serve goddesses, which supports the demonic realm. Whether it is out of ignorance or to support a goddess, either way, getting a tattoo is making a covenant with a demon.

The puncture of many small holes into the skin during the tattooing process creates a portal into the human body. Demons can manifest through these portals, and they can come and go at will. If you have gotten a tattoo, then you need to close the portal so the demons cannot manifest. The breach must be closed. Ask the Holy Spirit to help you close the portal. You need to plead the blood of Jesus over the area of the tattoo. It is costly and painful to have a tattoo removed, but it is well worth it, and I suggest if you can financially afford it, you should get it removed. If, however, for any reason, the tattoo cannot be removed, don't panic. Ask the Lord's forgiveness, confess, denounce and renounce, and then ask the Holy Spirit to help you in closing the portal.

The portal of the tattoo is similar to the all-seeing eye. Witches communicate with evil spirits through the all-seeing eye, and demons manifest themselves through the portal of the tattoo. It makes no difference whether the tattoo is a picture of Satan's face, the number 666 or something sweet and seemingly harmless, such as a butterfly or a flower. The tattoo is a portal that demons can manifest through and look through. There is only one way to safely close that portal: to have the tattoo removed. I say this because when you do a spiritual house cleaning, there are some things you cannot just simply cast the evil spirit out of. You've got to destroy or remove all pagan objects; otherwise, if these types of objects are not removed, the evil spirits will continue to have their legal right to remain. Tattoos are pagan objects that give evil spirits of their sort their legal right to remain.

Body Piercing

The Church of Body Modification represents the collection of members who practice ancient and modern body-modification rites. Through the piercing of their bodies, they are engaging in rituals that strengthen the bond between their mind, body and soul. By doing this, they ensure they live spiritually complete and healthy lives. They have faced such allegations as physical violence, sexual assault, mental abuse, animal abuse, death threats, theft, identity theft and lies. They are an occult who takes their body piercing from ancient occult practices.

History tells us that the American Indians pierced their tongues as part of their religious rituals. They believed this brought them closer to their gods as a type of blood ritual. They practised septum piercing to appear fiercer to their enemies. Similarly, tribes in New Guinea and the Solomon Islands would pierce their tongues with bone, tusks and feathers.

Nose piercing has been practised by Bedouin tribes of the Middle East, the Beja people of Africa and the Australian Aborigines for many centuries.

Today body piercing is done for many different reasons: religious or spiritual reasons, beauty and cosmetic appearance, self-expression, sexual pleasure and conformity to culture. In some regions of East India, the woman, on her wedding night, wears a nose stud that, like a wedding ring on the left ring finger in America, identifies her as married. Furthermore, many youth today pierce their bodies out of rebellion.

My ears are pierced. I had them pierced for cosmetic purposes only, and I still wear my pierced earrings. I have nothing against piercing as long as it is only for the purpose of cosmetics; however, it is my opinion that in some cases, it is an abomination before God to pierce your skin. If you have done body piercing for a spiritual or religious purpose or to rebel, then I personally believe you should take out the jewellery or whatever else you are wearing in your piercing and let the skin grow in.

THIRTEEN

Lies, Deceit and Flattery

Many Christians believe they can tell a little white lie, and it won't hurt anyone. They don't believe it can cause damage to themselves, their blood relatives and other Christian believers. Since we, the church, are the body of Christ, our sins, whether they seem unimportant or big, affect the whole body of Christ. Every lie you tell gives the devil the opportunity to use it against you, the person you lied to and the complete body of Christ. So the answer is this: tell the truth in love. If you truly love a person, you will tell him or her the truth. If the relationship is for selfish gain, then you will not be truthful with that person. God is truth. Satan is deception. Just tell the truth, and you will sleep better at night.

When Christians tell a deliberate lie, they are opening themselves up to a demonic attack. They fully know it is a lie, but just the same, they deliberately tell it.

I don't know how Christians can deliberately lie and feel okay afterward. Following my three months in the hospital with my broken hip, I had a friend calling in on me every day, which I appreciated. One midmorning, I received a phone call from her that greatly disturbed me. She called at ten o'clock and asked me, "Are you still in your pyjamas?" I immediately picked up a spirit of sarcasm in her voice. Although I am a sincere God-fearing Christian, just the same, I was embarrassed. I was having a great deal of trouble dressing myself and manoeuvring around the house; therefore, yes, I was still in my pyjamas. My pride got the better of me, and before I could think of what I was doing or what to say, I blurted out, "No, I am dressed!" She then asked, "What are you wearing?" Again, I lied: "I'm wearing slacks and a sweater." Suddenly, guilt flooded my soul. I asked God to forgive me, but for days, the guilt would not lift. The guilt from telling her that lie lay heavy on my conscience. To top it off, the next day, she called again at ten o'clock and asked the same question with the same sarcastic tone, but this time, I answered, "It's none of your business whether I'm dressed or still in my nightclothes!" She never made that rude call again; however, it was some time before I got over the guilt I carried on my shoulders for telling that lie.

Here are some things the Bible says about telling lies: liars are failures; liars use bad tactics; liars will have a sword upon them; liars are deceivers, have naughty tongues and commit perjury in the spiritual world; the truth is not in them; liars set a trap for themselves; liars do not respect themselves; liars delight in lies, are false witnesses and make lies their refuge; liars lie to God's people, cause themselves to make mistakes and will eat the fruit of their lies; liars think up lies, teach and prophesy lies, trust in lies, are weary with lies and are an abomination to God; liars are recognized as liars; and liars do not walk in the Spirit, are false, lie to God, walk in darkness and speak in hypocrisy.

All things that are false are contrary to God and will cause trouble to the believer. Falseness can be found in individuals, families, religions, ministries and churches. This occurs when one is trying to be something that he or she is not. Falseness is the opposite of truth.

Lying leads to cheating, and cheating leads to lying; one works with the other. Cheating can happen in the areas of marriage and family; ministry and church finances; lording tithes and offerings (that is, not giving to God what is His); business and income tax, or cheating the government and, in general, taking ungodly advantage of others. Read (Ezekiel 16). God sees us as being in a marriage covenant with Him. Cheating on God is called spiritual adultery and whoring after other gods.

The dishonest person must lie in order to cover up his or her tracks. One lie leads to another lie, and then the Christian, who was once in his or her heart sensitive, over time becomes a compulsive liar. The dishonest Christian will try to lie to God or reason with God about his or her actions or will try to rationalize the actions in his or her mind. The Christian must first be honest with God and then with him or herself. It is better that we face the truth head-on. At the time, sure, it will hurt, but when it comes to where we spend eternity, telling the truth will be the better choice.

A pastor has a dreadful responsibility before God to tell the truth. God holds the pastor to a higher standard than the ones who do not teach. The pastor will be held responsible for every word he has spoken to teach God's children. The pastor needs to stand up to God's standard.

Read (Revelation 21:8; Revelation 21:27 and Revelation 22:15). Liars don't go to heaven. Lying is a gravely immoral act done with full commitment and knowledge. The Bible tells us that all liars go to hell. Furthermore, when you lie, you place a curse on yourself.

Prayer

In Jesus Christ's Name and through the power of the Holy Ghost dwelling in me, I come before you, Father. I want to be like you. You do not lie. I want to tell the truth. I repent for being a liar, a deceitful person and a cheat and for being dishonest; flattering others; giving a false appearance; having pride, ego and vanity; being false and faithless and pretending I am something I am not. I repent for falseness of dress, thoughts and actions. Help me to be what you made me to be. I want to be natural and not false. I ask these things in Jesus Christ's name. Thank you, Father, Holy Spirit and Jesus. Amen!

FOURTEEN

Evil That Lurks in the Darkness

Try mentioning angels, demons, evil spirits or the devil, and you will be quickly accused of having signs of pathological violence and shunned. Eighty percent of what I have placed in these next two chapters is information I have learned through personal experience. Through my deliverance with the Holy Spirit assisting me in casting spirits out of myself, I have come to this knowledge I have placed in these next two chapters. As the spirits came out, they gave their names and their ranks.

I have also been given the gift of discernment of spirits, and the Holy Spirit often opens my spiritual eyes to see the evil spirits and demons in the room. I have been through some horrific experiences that I would never wish on any person, but through them, I have gained much knowledge, which I share in these two chapters. Most of the next two chapters cannot be backed up with Bible reference. As shocking as you might find what you are about to read, what I share in the next two chapters truly occurred in my life. I have chosen to share my experiences because there are people who have been through what I have suffered through and worse, and they deserve to receive their freedom as well. Not only that, but also, by honestly telling my story, I am saying, "I've been there, I understand and I care." Don't shun this information, and don't panic or close the book; just hear me out. What I share with you about Satan's massive army in these next two chapters will later be helpful to you with your physical deliverance in Chapter 27 ("Warfare Deliverance Prayers").

Kingdoms in the Heavenlies and at Large

I have come to understand that most Christian believers are not aware of the massive demonic kingdom located in the second heaven. I have learned that Satan has a complete supernatural government under him. This is where the core of our spiritual battle lies. We need to wage war against Satan and his massive army. We need to go right onto his battleground. We need to march into the heat of the battle. We need to take up our two-edged swords and march into the second heaven. The authorities that Satan has are set over cultures, nations and regions of this earth. They are located behind natural and supernatural governments.

There can be little doubt that Satan has a highly organized empire of evil. Satan is described as the one who deceives the whole world. Behind the facade of our Christian life, a spiritual battle is raging. It is a fierce conflict. I have become aware that there are born-again believers who do not wish to take up their swords and battle this evil empire. The fact is, the Christian church of Jesus Christ will reach its high point when all born-again Christians know how to and start to:

- Bind the strongman by prayer.
- Command the evil spirits in the name of Jesus Christ and through the power of Jesus's blood.
- And deliver men and women from Satan's power.

We are to battle in spiritual warfare: "Know ye not that we shall judge angels?" (1 Corinthians 6:3). We are to judge the fallen angels; we are to bind the kingdom of evil. We are to bind principalities, powers, rulers of darkness of this world, spiritual wickedness in high places (that is, the second heaven) and the kingdom of Satan. We are to command evil spirits and demons. We are to cut and burn ungodly silver cords and ley lines. We are God's war clubs and weapons of war (Jeremiah 51:20). We are to break down, undam and blow up Satan's walls of protection. We are to besiege Satan's strong city just as God's chosen people marched in faith and brought the walls of Jericho tumbling down (Joshua 6:1–16 and Joshua 6:20–21). We will see the devil's strong fortress walls come down, for we have been given the authority to trample on serpents and scorpions and over all of Satan's powers: "And He Jesus said unto them, I beheld Satan as lightning fall from heaven. Behold, I give unto you power to tread on

serpents (that is demons) and scorpions (that is evil spirits), and over all
the power of the enemy: and nothing shall by any means hurt you" (Luke
10:18–19). We are to battle with courage; no harm will come to us. When
the wizard was coming into my home, he tried more than once to harm
me. Every time he tried, God sent massive angels who stood guard around
me, and the wizard was forced to leave. More than once, he had his hands
on my neck, squeezing—he was trying to strangle me. This wizard was a
human who had soul-travelled into my home, and he had his free will, yet
God sent angels to protect me. Believe me when I say that nothing is going
to harm you. I say this from personal experience.

Satan is the commander-in-chief. He has, in his levels of satanic
authority, thrones; dominions (that is, lordships); principalities (that is,
rulerships and princes); rulers of darkness of this world and spiritual
wickedness (that is, wicked spirits in high places, meaning heavenly places,
or the second heaven) (Ephesians 6:12).

We have different levels of spiritual warfare that we are to use if we
want to be achievers in this battle. The definition of our spiritual warfare is
this: conflict with demonic strongholds and moral deception. This requires
our spiritual weapons and our armour, as described in (Ephesians 6:10–18).
We should wear it as I described in Chapter 10, "Putting On the Whole
Armour of God."

Our warfare prayers hinder the prevailing spiritual strongholds that
hinder the gospel of Christ. It is as well our ground level that ministers our
activity over individual bondage and demonization. Our warfare prayers
bind the strongman; by engaging in spiritual warfare, we neutralize the
deceptive holds and enchantment the demonic powers have achieved over
human subjects. We break through the occult level; we judge the battles
of demonic forces that operate through Satanism, witchcraft, shamanism,
esoteric philosophy and other similar occult activities. On the strategic
level, we battle against demonic powers that are concentrated over cities,
cultures, churches and people. We battle against principalities and powers
of darkness; we battle against the demonic agents and the structures
that exert their deceptive control over co-conspiratorial human political
kingdoms and systems. We battle against the rulers of darkness that is of
this world—the demonic forces involved in the deception and destruction
manipulating the natural elements and systems. This is what we battle
against: strongmen, territorial spirits, principalities and powers of darkness
and the rulers of the darkness of this world.

The territorial spirits have been given demonic powers of controlling influence over cities, peoples, churches, governments and nations. Belief in such hierarchical arrangements is culturally widespread. Protective deities are often linked to homes, temples, clans, cities, valleys and nations.

Principalities are the forces and dominions who deal with nations and governments. They are the high-level satanic princes set over the nations and regions of this earth. They are the commanding generals in Satan's army.

Powers of darkness have authority and the capacity for action in the spheres that are open to them, including the supernatural and the natural government. They are high-ranking powers of evil.

The rulers of darkness of this world govern the darkness and blindness of this world at large. They operate within countries and cultures to influence certain aspects of life. They are the governing spirits of darkness.

Spiritual wickedness in high places refers to the forces being directed in and upon the church of Jesus Christ. Those in this category battle the church with wiles, fiery darts, onslaughts and every conceivable deception about doctrine they are capable of planning. These are made up of the many types of evil spirits and demons that commonly afflict people. They are the collective body of demon soldiers comprising Satan's hordes.

There are four levels of strongmen. There are the strongmen who rule over principalities or wide geographic areas on earth. There are the strongmen who rule over people, churches, families, communities and other specific groups or individuals. There are the strongmen who dwell within people; these rule over the evil spirits that dwell within people. These evil spirits are the lowest; they are at the bottom of the barrel. The principalities are ruled by princes, also called strongmen. These are the gods and goddesses of the evil underworld.

Because of our lack of understanding and knowledge and the lack of teaching we have received about Satan's vast kingdom, most born-again Christians believe that demons are the fallen angels. However, for the sake of argument, there are no scriptures in the Bible that indicate that the demons are indeed the fallen angels. This is simply no more than an assumption that lacks biblical proof.

Satan is not omniscient, omnipresent or omnipotent. He cannot be in more than one place at a time. He is nothing more than a fallen angel who, because of his own selfish pride, was cast out of heaven to the earth. However, he does have a vast amount of fallen angels, demons and evil spirits. (Hebrews 12:22) says that the number of angels is innumerable. This means there is an enormous multitude of them. There are more angels than could ever be counted. (Revelation 5:11) calculates at least 101,000,000 total angels. (Revelation 12:4) calculates at least 33,700,000 fallen angels that were thrown to the earth with Satan. There are millions of fallen angels.

Based on how many evil spirits that I cast out of myself and what the commanding officer spirit said as he was coming out of me, one person can house billions of evil spirits. The world has billions of people in it, and Christians alone can have billions of evil spirits in them, so there must be centillions of evil spirits. The number of digits in a centillion is the number 1 followed by 600 zeros, as shown here:

```
1000000000000000000000000000000000000000000000
0000000000000000000000000000000000000000000000
0000000000000000000000000000000000000000000000
0000000000000000000000000000000000000000000000
0000000000000000000000000000000000000000000000
0000000000000000000000000000000000000000000000
0000000000000000000000000000000000000000000000
0000000000000000000000000000000000000000000000
0000000000000000000000000000000000000000000000
0000000000000000000000000000000000000000000000
0000000000000000000000000000000000000000000000
0000000000000000000000000000000000000000000000
0000000000000000000000000000000000000000000000
0000000000000000000000000000000000000000000000
0000000000000000000000000000000000000000000000
```

Satan is the chief of staff of his army. The fallen angels are his officers. The demons are his soldiers. The evil spirits that are the most insignificant of all dwell in people and animals. When the Holy Spirit works with me to cast out evil spirits, these spirits are under total submission to the Spirit of God. When I command with the authority of the Holy Spirit that they speak, they speak; they give their rank, the name of their family, the time when they entered, the reason they entered and the number in their family. If only one spirit comes out, then he gives his name, his reason for entering and the time when he entered. Many of the families of spirits that came out of me, when asked their names, called themselves legions (Luke 8:30).

The general is in charge of a legion, which is 3,000 to 6,000 spirits. The prince will control a number of legions. A ruler or captain commands a cohort, which is 600 spirits. There can be chief captains and chief rulers with still more authority than this. A centurion controls 100 spirits. The spirit that controls fewer than 100 spirits is called a strongman. I cast out of myself generals, rulers, chief captains, strongmen and chief rulers, which all ruled over the evil spirits within me.

The top division of the demonic hierarchy supervises and closely monitors activities in the lower ranks without violating any of the ground rules in scripture. Through born-again Christians' own stupidity and ignorance, they divide and sow suspicion among believers. This is an astoundingly effective tool Satan uses; this tool is rated in Satan's spiritual domain as 90 percent successful.

There are spirits from the second heaven deliberately intervening to strengthen and reinforce the embattled evil spirits in humans. The most powerful of these spirits are those in the heavenlies charged with the overall direction of Satan's program.

The demons refer to the evil spirits that dwell within people as the bottom division. It is the middle division that encompasses the evil spirits whose job is to gain entrance into mortal bodies. The evil spirits who are at work to gain their entrance into the human body are always on the watch for people messing up. With my first deliverance back in 1999, the Holy Spirit cast out of me two spirits who confessed to watching me from around the corner of a tombstone, and as quickly as I spoke to my dead brother, the first one of the two entered me. Less than a year later, I again went down on my knees at a tombstone and spoke to my dear deceased friend, and the second of the two spirits, who was also hiding behind a tombstone, took the liberty to enter me. By the way, you should never talk to the dead. Talking to the dead gives evil spirits the legal right to enter you. Talking to the dead is called necromancy, and it is a dreadful, abominable sin.

Any spirit that is in authority will direct how many, when and where pain spirits are to attack and how sustained the attack is to be. Those who are in charge refer to the pain spirits as imps.

Because of this rigid authority structure, a person who is dealing with evil spirits needs to bind all spirits, especially the ruling spirits and the spirits of violence, fighting and murder.

Control of a geographic area seems to rest on the success of the prince in controlling the majority of the persons within that place. This also has to do with the ferocity and power of that prince.

Evil spirits degrade the bodies they dwell in, whether they be humans or animals. This influence is exercised both to mislead the unsaved and to wage an increasing war against believers. Thus commences the fierce battle raging between God and Satan for control of the human race. By the way, animals need deliverance too.

God told Adam and Eve to subdue the earth. In telling them this, God gave them dominion over the earth. Satan deceived Eve and Adam voluntarily followed his wife into the trap. With their fall from grace, Adam relinquished his crown to Satan, and Satan gladly took his dominion over the earth. Thus, Satan invaded the affairs of men.

By the time of Noah, angels had started having sex with the daughters of men. In doing so, they were able to create hideous, monstrous hybrid offspring that were half human and half angel. These were known as the nephilim, it is my believe they were demons. The Bible tells us that God was grieved because of how wicked man had become (Genesis 6:6) and (Jude 6-7). My theological guess is most likely at that time demons started breeding among themselves, and that would have created the evil spirits. I believe the tiny evil spirits were as early as Noah, entering humans in massive amounts making the human race vile and a stench to God.

The evil spirits that the Holy Spirit cast out of me made it clear how much they feared and dreaded eternal damnation and its consequences.

Wizards, Witches and Sorcerers

The evil that is lurking in the dark, sinister world is not made up of evil spirits and demons alone. Satan does his work through an organization of spirits and people. He has lied to people and placed powerful spirits in them, and these people are helplessly under Satan's demonic control. He has wizards, sorcerers, witches and Satanists working under him in his dominion. He has lied to them, promising them power. A wizard once told me, "Satan has promised me an elegant office in hell with a dark mahogany desk, a leather office chair, and my name in big block letters on a plaque on my desk." The devil put this belief in this person. Because he had made a binding obligation with the devil by signing his name in his own blood, he had sold his soul to the devil. He believed that because he had signed his soul over through a binding agreement, he was doomed to hell and could never get out of this signed contract.

Our soul consists of our personality, our intellect, our thoughts and our being that lives on. Through my own experience, I have learned that when wizards or witches place a spell on a person, they fill that person with fragments of their own souls. When the fragments of a wizard are within the targeted person, the wizard's personality mingles with the personality of his target. The personality becomes a little of the wizard and some of the person whom he placed the spell on. Along with his fragments, the wizard fills his target with families of spirits who bear their family names according to the way in which the wizard wants to control the person he has targeted. Through the wizard's soul fragments and the families of the spirits he places in his target, he operates his own will and personality in his target. He is able to place his target under his complete control. This person becomes the wizard's puppet on a string, his own personal marionette. He can make this otherwise morally outstanding person do things contrary to his or her moral beliefs.

Angels

Pride comes before a fall. This truth has ruined many pastors. The risk in being a pastor is power giving into pride. A pastor stands up at the pulpit and looks down at his sheep as the congregation respectfully and attentively listen without interrupting or questioning his authority. Then, after the service every Sunday, week after week, month after month, year after year, he's told, "Great sermon, Pastor!" This can go to a man's head and puff it up like a big beach ball. With all the attention and praise, it's easy for him to start thinking, *Gee, I guess I really am something awesome!* (Proverbs 16:18) tells us that pride comes before the fall. God opposes the proud. The verb *oppose* means "to fight" or "to obstruct." (First Peter 5:5) tells us, "God opposes the proud, but gives grace to the humble." My church had one pastor whose personality was like an open book. He was the humblest man I have ever known. His humility was what made me admire him most. Was he perfect? No! But he was humble before God, and to Him, this would have been counted as righteousness. It was as if I could read right through him. As a matter of fact, I have been able to read into every pastor we have had in our church, whether he was humble or given to pride.

We will start with Satan, an angel that, because of his wicked pride, was hurled with great force out of heaven to the earth. Read (Ezekiel 28:12–18). There was a certain angel, Lucifer. He was not just any ordinary angel; he was a guardian cherub. He was adorned in precious stones, including sardius, topaz, diamond, beryl, onyx, jasper, sapphire, emerald and carbuncle, all mounted in gold. Music was prepared in him on the day he was created. It is believed by many he was the head cherub over the music in God's throne room. He stood on the holy mountain; he walked up and down in the midst of stones of fire. God created him and found him perfect in every way—until the day when pride got the best of him. That was his great fall. He has gone down in history as the greatest example of the destruction pride can do to a man. Lucifer became prideful and decided he was going to rise above God and take over the throne of God. A great battle took place in which two-thirds of the angels battled against Lucifer and his third of the angels, and he and his third were thrown out of heaven to the earth. This is a lesson in pride that all born-again believers should take notice of. Satan's pride came before his great fall from heaven to the earth, and it's the same with all of humanity: pride will come before our fall. The great deceiver, Satan, was one of God's angels in heaven. Technically, Satan is still an angel, but he is a fallen angel; he is a deceiver and a liar.

The reemergence of the Christian church's teaching on angels dangerously runs parallel to the rise of the New Age angels in the neo-pagan revival of the secular culture. Our knowledge that, in the Word of God, a few spoke with angels causes today's born-again believers to blindly seek to communicate with angels. However, we are now living in what is called the New Age, in which many are fascinated with angels. The witches, who practice Wicca, use angels and interact with them.

I have lost count of how many Christians have approached me and asked, "Have you ever seen angels?" or "When was the last time you saw an angel?" Born-again believers are fascinated by angels, and many long to experience an encounter with an angel, as Abraham, Mary and Joseph had. Some Christians will tell you not to look for angels; let them approach you. However, I am leery of this, and as many times as I have seen angels and had them speak to me, I have never since I received Christ spoken with an angel. By the way, I have been approached a number of times about privately getting to know my so-called guardian angel. Every time, it was a demon masquerading as Gabriel that approached and suggested I start speaking with my guardian angel and find out his name. Do not let yourself be deceived by such spirits.

Some of the Wicca books mention angels. The names mentioned are Uriel, Raphael, Michael and Gabriel, angels that are actually in the Bible. However, these are demons masquerading as God's elect angels. Michael and Gabriel are God's elect angels. These are not the angels mentioned in the Bible; they are demons who lie and say their names are Michael and Gabriel. Remember that Satan and his demons masquerade as God's ministering angels, and if possible, Satan will deceive even the elect. "But though we, or an angel from heaven, preach any other gospel unto you than that which we have preached unto you, let him be accursed" (Galatians 1:8).

People interacting with angels is the neo-pagan New Age. Stay away from that garbage. If you go searching for angels and start talking to them, you are going to get more than you have bargained for. You will be communicating with demons, and this will open the door for evil spirits to enter you. The only spirit that born-again saints should ever speak to is one of the deities: Christ, the Father and the Holy Spirit. You do not ever speak with an angel. You only answer an evil spirit or demon with the gospel or to command him. I know my Bible, and I know that people spoke with angels in both the Old and New Testaments, but in today's culture, with the New Age spirituality as it now is, I have found it is safer that Christians just don't speak at all with celestial beings.

Angels stand 12 to 14 feet tall. Upon waking one night, I left my bedroom, in which God had me safely secured in by an army of angels who encircled my room, and went out into the hallway, where I saw huge dark shadows towering over me. I counted six of these giants. I stand five foot three inches, and my head came to their thighs. As I looked upward, I saw their nakedness. Taking in the massive size of these spirits, I knew in my spirit that they were three times my height, massive in size and power. I could see they were fully loaded with male reproductive organs. These giants had no clothes on. Amazingly, I was not afraid of them. I was, however, amazed at what I was looking at, and I asked the Holy Spirit, "What is this?" He told me, "They are angels who have fallen from grace. These angels showed themselves to you to intimidate you."

You need to remember that angels who have fallen from grace seldom leave the second heaven or mingle with humans. They are the highest ranking of the satanic system. Demons take their orders from these angels.

The evil spirits are the lowest. In today's culture, we would say evil spirits are at the bottom of the ladder.

God has two-thirds of the angels. They make up His army of angels. Then there are the other third of the angels who fell with Satan, and then there are the number of angels fallen from grace who fornicated with the maidens, they are in chains in hell (Jude 6). I have come to believe that the one third of the angels who fell are Satan's highest-ranking officers. Satan's army is made up of demons. Demons stand eight to 10 feet tall. We have no way of knowing just how many there are of them.

Just as God has given us free will, He has also given the angels free will. Out of His goodness, He has never desired that the angels or Christians would be puppets on a string without their minds or emotions. God's holy angels are His elect. This means God chose them. The angels who chose to follow Lucifer are lost and condemned. The angels who choose to remain loyal to God are secure in their decision.

There are three views people have of (Genesis 6:1–6). The first is the merging of the ungodly Cainite with the godly Sethites. The people who hold to this view believe the godly Sethite men entered into marriage with the daughters of the ungodly Cainites, and the nephilim were violent men who were produced through this unholy union. The second is the despot interpretation. Some scholars have sought to define the expression "sons of God" by comparing it with the languages of the ancient Near East, in which some rulers were identified as sons of God.

My problem with both the first and second view is this: everywhere you read in the Bible, you will find *God* referring to God the Father spelled with a capital *G*, and all man-made gods are spelled with a lowercase *g*. In (Genesis 6:2), *God* is spelled with a capital *G*. Also, in (Job 1:6), *God* is spelled with a capital *G*. Therefore, both mentioned in (Genesis 6:2 and Job 1:6) are indeed heavenly angels.

Then there is the third view, the fallen-angel interpretation. Some believe the angels changed themselves into sexy and charming men to build Satan a nation of people of his own. The young virgins would have seen these men as stronger, taller and more appealing to look upon than the average, wimpy-looking men being born to women. These angels of God and daughters of men together conceived and gave birth to the nephilim race, who were giants. They would be a powerful military race for Satan's use.

This is my own personal view, which I have come to believe through my bizarre experiences. In (Genesis 6:1–6), I believe the sons of God to be angels and the daughters of men to be young women. I have often been raped by spirits who revealed their physical form to me so I could see, through my spirit, their spirits. I have been raped by large giants and by four-foot trolls with the ugliest faces one could ever imagine. Believe me when I say these creatures that raped me were not the bodies and faces of human soul travelers. Satan took me as his wife, and I suffered under his filthy, dirty, depraved sexual acts. He raped me over and over again for more than three years. Another spirit took me as his wife. He revealed himself to me as a four-foot troll. My mother used to keep me up late at night to watch horror movies with her, and this spirit was uglier than any monster I had ever seen on TV. Then there was the wizard who had been soul-travelling into my home. He asked me to marry him in what would have been a marriage ceremony acted out in the spiritual realm. Our witnesses would have been demons.

My False Pregnancy

Christian counsellors were failing to help me, and therefore, I took it upon myself in desperation to search for freedom from my adversities. In great desperation, I endeavoured to find deliverance from the spirits I was helplessly suffering from, as they would overpower me.

I was 19 when my daughter was born. Eight months later, in the privacy of my bedroom, at the age of 20, I performed an abortion on myself. As a result, my uterus was damaged, making it so I would not be able to carry a baby past two weeks of pregnancy. My son was a miracle baby, as I should have never been able to carry another baby to full term. I had many difficulties with my second pregnancy. After the birth of my son, I would continue to miscarry at early stages of my pregnancies; therefore, my family doctor suggested I have my tubes tied, and when I was 24, my tubular surgery was completed. Therefore, the chance I would get pregnant and carry a child to full term would be one in a million. This is my personal experience with a false pregnancy.

There are two scriptures in the Bible that can back this up, (Genesis 6:1–6) and (Jude 6-7). However, these scriptures does not go into much detail. In my mid twenties, I started experiencing a large number of spiritual rapes. I was in my late thirties when Satan took me as his wife. After a number of months of him raping me, he told me he wanted me to carry his baby, but it was obvious to him that I would not get pregnant except by artificial insemination, so his conclusion was to artificially take my egg from my ovary and place it into my uterus. I felt his hand massaging my uterus as he talked me through the whole procedure of what he was doing. After that, I began feeling all the symptoms of a natural pregnancy: I had morning sickness, my menstrual cycle ended, my breasts got tender, my nipples started seeping fluid, my tummy started to enlarge and I started to feel the undeniable first stages of the infant fluttering in my uterus. At that stage, the Holy Spirit told me, "The baby you are expecting is a hybrid half angel and half human. It is an evil spirit, and this pregnancy must be terminated. You will feel me reach into your womb and remove the unborn baby. Because it is an evil spirit, it will be placed in hell." After this, I felt the Spirit of God reach into my womb and remove the spirit I was pregnant with. There was no baby, but a spirit came out of my womb. After this, just as after the birth of both my son and daughter, I went through the natural blood flow, which lasted six weeks, and then my menstrual cycle went back to normal.

My view of (Genesis 6:1–12) is that it is likely these sons of God performed in the spirit world a marriage ceremony in which they took these fair young maidens for their wives.

There is no doubt in my mind that these young maidens, being sexually active with these fallen angels, gave birth to demons that were offspring of the angels. Yes, they would have given birth to spirits. These creatures would have been half human and half angel.

I learned as the Holy Spirit assisted me in casting out my evil spirits that these spirits are not forced to give an account of how and when they were created. Wizards and witches are astral-travelling and performing astral sex every day, and I believe it is possible that through this spiritual sex, spiritual beings can be created. It is my belief that they are being created today as you read this book. Satan is hard at work at building his kingdom. Ninety-nine percent of the evil spirits the Holy Spirit assisted me in casting out of myself were cast into the abyss. Satan is hard at work at keeping his evil spirits numerous.

Angels are towering spirits anywhere from 12 to 14 feet tall. There is one place in the Bible that tells of the procreation of demons, (Genesis 6:1–6), although it does not go into much detail. Therefore, we have little knowledge of this factual event of how demons came into existence, and we have no biblical proof whatsoever of how the evil spirits came into existence. The offspring of both the sons of God and young women are in fact demons. These are the giants of renown whom we know in the Bible as nephilim, and since these demons stand anywhere from 8 to 10 feet tall it makes sense that these demons would be the giants conceived by the sons of God and daughters of men.

As I looked at these angels who had entered my home to intimidate me it was clear they were fully loaded with everything they needed to reproduce. It is evident that it was through these angels reproducing with human women that Satan was building his military army as we know it today.

Think about it: Where did demons and evil spirits come from? Today Satan has both demons and evil spirits. Actually, he has a complete military army in the second heaven. Somehow, this military army of Satan's was produced. (Genesis 6:1–6) tells of sons that are angels of God taking young women as their wives and producing offspring. I believe Satan found himself not omnipotent, omnipresent or omniscient. The people were quickly multiplying on the earth, and he knew he could never with his one third of his angels defeat God and His two thirds; it would take an army to carry out Satan's plans.

You might argue with me that angels do not have reproductive organs, according to (Matthew 22:29–30); however, the two best-known chosen angels of God have masculine names, Gabriel and Michael. Notice that their names are those of men, not women. It is clear that angels are men. Notice too that God and Jesus are identified as men: God the Father and Jesus, the Son of God. The men in Sodom recognized the angels who came to destroy the city to be men. The homosexual men of Sodom were capable of judging one's sexuality. They were sexually attracted to these angels' male bodies (Genesis 19:1–11 and Jude 6-7). I had a Christian tell me that according to (Matthew 22:29–30), we will be like the angels in heaven, not having reproductive organs. This is not at all what (Matthew 22:29–30) is telling us. Instead, the Word of God tells us that in heaven, we will be expected to live lives of celibacy. Jesus did not say we would all be eunuchs. Jesus said we were going to be as the angels by not having sex and not giving and taking in marriage.

At some point, evil spirits started dwelling in people. Paul recognized these evil spirits within himself: "Now if I do that I would not, it is no more I that do it, but sin that dwelleth in me. I find then a law, that, when I would do good, evil is present with me. For I delight in the law of God after the inward man: But I see another law in my members, warring against the law of my mind, and bringing me into captivity to the law of sin which is in my members" (Romans 7:20–23). Jesus cast many evil spirits out of people.

This is my belief: at the time when the angels started taking young women for their wives in the spirit form and started reproducing, demons and evil spirits came into existence, and the evil spirits started dwelling in people. The Bible tells us that at that point, people became unruly, and nothing good was in their hearts. (Mark 7:21) says that evil thoughts are within a man's heart. God saw that the wickedness of man was great in the earth and that every imagination of the thoughts of his heart was only evil continually (Genesis 6:5). This dismayed God so much that He chose to destroy all mankind with a flood, with the exception of Noah and his family. The Lord regretted that He had made the human race (Genesis 6:6–8). The Bible further tells us that this sexuality between humans and angels continued after the flood as well: "There were giants in the earth in those days, and also after that, when the sons of God came in unto the daughters of men, and they bare children to them, the same became mighty men which were of old, men of renown" (Genesis 6:4).

I knew from my own experience of being raped that women were still being raped by spirits, but I could not wrap my mind around the fact that we don't have powerful, towering giants today, and Jesus said that His saving grace is for all humankind. Therefore, the fact that there could still be hybrid half-man, half-angel nephilim walking upon this earth did not line up in my mind. Only after I conceived and carried part-term Satan's offspring in my womb and was later raped by a wizard travelling in the spirit form was I convinced that in fact, angels can, in the spirit form, rape a human woman and, as a result, create hybrid half-angel, half-human spirits. What I have said might sound bizarre and unbelievable, but personally, I believe that demons and evil spirits must in fact be the results of sexual acts performed between and with demonic spirits, sex with angels who fell from God's grace and astral sex with and between soul-travellers.

I later came to learn of the book of Enoch. Reading the book of Enoch gave confirmation to me that in Genesis 6, indeed, the sons of God, who are angels, and the daughters of men did create the demons as we know them today. That was the beginning of Satan's vast army. Plus, it confirms my spiritual rapes and my conceiving of that spirit. You can read the book of Enoch at http:book-ofenoch.com/.

Evil Spirits

Through my two deliverances, I learned that most evil spirits are no bigger than a half centimetre in size. These spirits can come out through a person's nostrils. When the Holy Spirit was assisting me in casting my spirits out, some came out when I would sneeze. Because they are so tiny, people can have billions of these spirits in them. They dwell in people in large families. I had families as large as 1,200,000 come out under one name. When one is casting out evil spirits, they can come out through the nose as well as through the mouth. A spirit can also come out through one's breath.

The last evil spirit to come out of me with my second deliverance was the highest-ranking captain in charge. There was only one of this spirit. All other evil spirits dwelling inside of a person are submissive under his charge and command. This includes all commanders, lieutenants and other officers. This spirit, the highest-ranking captain in charge, enters at the person's conception. All humans have this spirit in them. This spirit told the Holy Spirit and me that one human body can house more than 1,000,000,000 evil spirits at one time, but he said that makes living quarters quite cramped.

Everywhere Jesus went, He would cast out evil spirits. Jesus is the example we are to follow. Jesus cast out evil spirits in synagogues, in Galilee, outside, in the multitudes, in people's homes, at the seashore and on a ship. In every city and village He went into, He cast out evil spirits. Everywhere Jesus went, He cast out evil spirits from people. This is what Jesus wants us to do today.

Since the born-again Christian's body is the temple of the Holy Spirit, we can hold church anywhere where two or more Christians are gathered together. This can be you and a person you are ministering to. I have been called to private homes where I cast spirits out of believers. At my home, I have a prayer room in which I do this. (Mark 16:17) tells us, "And these signs shall follow them that believe, in My Name shall they cast out devils."

To cast out is to eject, cast forth, bring forth, drive out, expel, pluck, pull out, take out, thrust out, put forth, send away and send forth. When you cast out evil spirits, you are commanding them to leave. It is not a prayer; it is a strict command. An example would be to say, "Spirit of perversion, I command you to come out of [person's name] in Jesus Christ's name."

Here is a scripture that strongly applies to the people who fight against deliverance: "Give not that which is holy unto the dogs, neither cast ye your pearls before swine, lest they trample them under their feet, and turn again and rend you" (Matthew 7:6). These people will not appreciate your help but, rather, will use it to turn on you.

The Bible commands us to cast out demons, as in the following verses:

1. "And as ye go, preach, saying, The kingdom of heaven is at hand. Heal the sick, cleanse the lepers, raise the dead, cast out devils: freely ye have received, freely give" (Matthew 10:7–8).
2. "Verily I say unto you, whatsoever ye shall bind on earth shall be bound in heaven: and whatsoever ye shall loose on earth shall be loosed in heaven. Again I say unto you, That if two of you shall agree on earth as touching anything that they shall ask, it shall be done for them of my Father which is in heaven. For where two or three are gathered together in my Name, there am I in the midst of them" (Matthew 18:18–20).
3. "And Jesus came and spake unto them, saying, 'All power is given unto me in heaven and in earth. Go ye therefore, and teach all nations, baptizing them in the Name of the Father and of the Son, and of the Holy Ghost, Teaching them to observe all things whatsoever I have commanded you: and lo, I am with you always, even unto the end of the world'" (Matthew 28:18–20). Teaching to obey everything includes doing deliverance.
4. "The Spirit of the Lord is upon me, because He hath anointed me to preach the gospel to the poor. He hath sent me to heal the brokenhearted, to preach deliverance to the captives, and recovery of sight to the blind, to set at liberty them that are bruised, To preach the acceptable year of the Lord" (Luke 4:18–19). This was a general charge from Christ to the Christians not only to heal the sick but also to preach deliverance and set free those who are oppressed under demonic attack.
5. "Then Philip went down to the city of Samaria, and preached Christ unto them. And the people with one accord gave heed unto those things which Philip spake, hearing and seeing the miracles

which he did. For unclean spirits, crying with loud voice, came out of many that were possessed with them: and many taken with palsies, and that were lame, were healed" (Acts 8:5–7). The Word was being preached, unclean spirits were coming out of people and these people were being healed through their deliverance.

In some cases, the families of evil spirits that represent a disease need to come out first before the person can receive his or her healing. In a case where the person is bound, such as being paralyzed, there will be spirits within him or her that are strongmen. These families keep the person bound to his or her infirmity (Luke 13:10–17). I had a large evil spirit wrapped tightly around my spine preventing my spine from straightening. His name was Boa Constrictor; he was a snake spirit. I had six families named Door and six families named Key to Door. These families, as they came out, handed the keys over to the Holy Spirit. I also had six families named Doorkeeper. These families, as they come out, leave the doors open. There was a fortified wall around my spine that needed to come down; the fortified wall is the stronghold. Then the debris from the wall had to come out. Plus, the family that bore the name of the disease also needed to come out before I could receive the healing of my crooked spine. Only after the debris from the wall and these families of spirits came out of me did the Holy Spirit straighten my spine. You'll notice that the Key to Door has six families, Door has six families and Doorkeeper has six families. In total, all three had six families that needed to come out. The number six is Satan's number (666). Seven is God's number.

It is clear to see in scripture that Jesus was casting out evil spirits, and after Jesus had gone to the Father, through the power of the Holy Spirit, the disciples and Christians of that day were still casting out spirits, performing healings and raising the dead back to life. Today Jesus wants us doing the same. He wants today's Christians to follow in His ministry. Unless believers practise deliverance throughout every nation globally, this world will never be conquered for God and taken out of the grip that Satan has on it.

Any place can be church. I have laid hands on strangers and prayed for them in crowded shopping malls. If you feel the Holy Spirit is calling you to pray for someone, then do it.

The greatest enemy against God is the Christian who says, "A Christian can't have demons!" In saying this, Christians are keeping a world of

Christians in spiritual bondage, and some could be suffering as badly as I was or even worse. These are Christians who are in bondage and can't see any clear way out. These people cannot overcome just through simple salvation, full immersion baptism, Holy Spirit baptism with evidence of speaking in tongues and divine healings. I was full immersion baptized and baptized in the Holy Spirit with evidence of speaking in tongues, and I had received many healings. I was, in every sense of the word, a born-again-saint. I was washed in the blood of Christ and redeemed. I was also in trouble that I desperately needed help to get out of. Christians need a lot of deliverance. That is why everywhere Jesus went, He would cast evil spirits out of people. That is why we should be casting evil spirits out of people.

We need full-force spiritual warfare against Satan and his forces of evil. You can see clearly that Satan is winning the battle. You only need to look at world statistics to see this. Only a small percentage of the world's population will make it into heaven. I had read that it is estimated that only 2 percent of the world's population and 25 percent of the Christian population will make it into heaven. "Because strait is the gate, and narrow is the way, which leadeth unto life, and few there be that find it" (Matthew 7:14). Christians will go to heaven with or without their deliverance. I am just saying, "our daily walk with our Lord would be so much more easy if we were to have our evil spirits cast out."

With my second deliverance, the Holy Spirit cast out of me more than 6,000,000 evil spirits. Come on, my sisters and brothers in Christ; let us put on our armour, take up our war weapons and go to battle. There's a world of Christians out there who need our help!

This is my opinion: UFOs are demonic manifestations. Since the beginning of mankind, people have reported seeing aliens. These are demons and evil spirits. There are also water spirits and fire spirits. We also have nymphs, druids, undines, fairies, gnomes and mermaids. These are types of demons, both male and female. They can breed with their own kind as well as with humans. Many of these creatures stand close to a dwarf's height. As you can see, the toys today's children are playing with and the programs they are watching are all associated with demons and are causing our children to accept and feel comfortable with evil spirits.

FIFTEEN

What Is This We Battle Against?

God and Satan are involved in a cosmic struggle for the souls of mankind. The fact is, every Christian is involved, whether he or she wants to be or not. The battle is being waged worldwide in our courts, media, schools, military, churches and governments. It is up to the Christian believers to respond.

Satan has wiles, cunning schemes and temptations. He is dangerous and wicked and causes moral and spiritual corruption. His methods are premeditated, systematic and methodical. He encourages lust for control and power, illusions and lies, secrecy and darkness, brutality, mind control and dog-eat-dog competition. The attacks can vary from mild influence (temptation) to full demonic possession. Evil spirits can cause physical, mental and emotional oppression, affliction, sickness and illnesses; control the person's mind and body; exhibit extremely immoral behaviour and speech; have supernatural strength and affect sub- or superconscious minds (Mark 5:2-4). The devil is so clever that he can make himself and his demons appear as angels of light. He creates superstition and idolatry. People call on the devil so they can benefit from his powers. Some people choose to be wizards and witches because of their love of power.

Powers of darkness include the occult, fortune-telling, spiritism, magic and false cults. Satan has a false gift for every true gift of God, such as mockery, emotional or demonic tongues, falsely being slain in the spirit, babbling with empty and fruitless conversations and vain, foolish talk.

The highest satanic power has their councils, occult network and 13 bloodlines of German, Scottish, Italian and English families who use every demonic method to create a one-world government and dictator. Intelligence agencies act as occult cults in practising mind control.

In the fall of 2014, I was out with the Red Hat ladies for a fun afternoon of being entertained with 1930s music. Our entertainer was a talented one-man band. After an hour of our singing along with the oldies, he brought out a puppet and entertained us with his ventriloquism. From the beginning, I could see spirits in him that made me uneasy, and when he brought out his puppet, I could see some powerful spirits in the puppet as well.

The next day, he soul-travelled into my home. He was in my home in spirit form. I could see his soul. He said to me, "I am a wizard. You don't need to be afraid of me; I'm only here for the sex." While he held me down and raped me, in my spirit, I saw a demon enter the room. He saw the demon as well. The wizard looked up from where he had me pinned on the floor, and with a demanding tone in his voice, he shouted at the demon, "Get the $@&% out of here!" Now, as I said, these demons stand eight to 10 feet tall. At the wizard's command, the demon fled from the room faster than it had entered the room. This was my first encounter with a wizard. You can guess how shocked I was to find out that demons shudder and flee at the command of a wizard. This left me thinking, *What in the world is this man who has me pinned on the floor?*

We do not deal only with fallen angels, demons and evil spirits. We also contend with witches, wizards, sorceresses and Satanists, who astral-project out of their bodies and soul-travel often into our homes. They tamper with our computers and TVs, and they can rape us. Through casting spells, wizards, witches and sorceresses can place hexes, spells and enchantments on people.

Most Christians sit comfortably in church. The pastors, board members, music leaders and teachers are hard at work in the church, but they have no idea what is actually taking place in the spiritual world. This dullness in our spiritual understanding is ideal for Satan. Six years of writing this book caused me more spiritual excitement than I have had in my whole lifetime. The devil hates this book. I have heard demons refer to my book as the Book. They say this book is the talk of the spirit world. I have for some time now had a death sentence placed on me. A wizard, in order to try to kill me, filled me with spirits of suicide, cancer and a brain tumour. How do I know this? The Holy Spirit, as He assisted me in casting out the wizard's soul fragments, which bear his full first and last name, cast out the three families of suicide, cancer and brain tumours, and as they came out, they told us that the wizard had, through casting his spell, chanted them into me.

If born-again believers knew half of what is going on in the dark spiritual world, they would not be sitting on their backsides. Christians would be instead giving the devil one powerful run for his money. Satan does not want us to be aware of what is going on in his empire. To the greatest part of mankind, the devil's ruling kingdom is top secret, and that is the way Satan plans to keep it.

The fact is, Satan has a hierarchy of demons, with Beelzebub as his right-hand spirit. The externalization of the hierarchy suggests the hierarchy is getting more and more public. Satanism is creeping into all facets of life.

The Satanic Church

The Church Of Satan is an international organization with temples located worldwide. Although they proclaim themselves to be atheists, their beliefs are based on Satan's characteristics. They declare that they believe Satan to be no more than a mere symbol of human traits, and he does not exist. They claim that anyone who believes in supernatural entities demonstrates a level of insanity. They say, "There is no God, and there is no Satan." My question is this: Why do they call themselves the Church of Satan if they don't believe Satan exists? The Christian church believes in God, the Creator. Hindus believe in their gods (Shiva, Vishnu, etc.). The Church of Satan is not telling the true facts. The truth is, they believe in Satan. They are concealing their sinister truths.

Satanic Rituals

Satanic worship is open, blatant worship of the devil. This is black witchcraft of the worst kind. The worst form of occult ritual abuse is that done by Satanists who program people to follow Satan all their lives. This is trauma-based monarch-like mind control of programmed slaves—total and undetectable mind control. Their terrorized, fragmented, divided dark side creates multiple personality disorders (MPD), which are brutal, secret, immoral and controlled to function in illusions and lies. There are blood covenants and sacrifices, sexual sealing, invocations of demons, demonization of fetuses with moonchild rituals, voodoo, witchcraft, psychics, drugs, hypnotism, electronics, electroshock, hunger, fatigue, tenseness, threats, violence and other control methodologies.

Fear, terror and torture are used to split the mind and develop animalistic, demonic drives to survive. Controlled LSD-like trips include sensory deprivation tanks, chronology of layering in mind-control programming, cranial manipulation, movie mind control, implants, nanobots, thought transfer, soul entrapment, dissociative programmed multiplicity, mind control by means of electronics, energy beamed at minds and other secret techniques.

It is possible there could be 364 levels of demons, 169 principles after personalities, three ceremonial altars, beta and delta altars, MPD, dissociative identity disorders (DID) and the switching of altered personalities or fragments. Satanic ritual abuse creates total mind control consisting of altars, programming, implants, internal computers and dissociative states of the ego-physiological state of the mind. Some paranoid schizophrenics might be programmed multiples. Obscured concepts include programmed MPD, DID for trained multiples, recovered memories, hypnosis, demonic possession, aliens, mind control, the subconscious, sadistic and criminal altars and conspiracy to bring in a new world order.

You'll notice that many of today's children's shows and adults' shows on TV are being used for the devil's programming purposes. Most worldly people would be shocked to know that by going along with Satan's world system, they are contributing to his cause.

Let us take a short look at the satanic calendar. There are various days of the year set aside for sacrifices of humans and animals; sexual rituals; the kidnapping, holding and ceremonial preparation of people for human sacrifice; orgies; dismembering of corpses; cannibalism and sex with demons.

The Satanic church has a full calendar; they have activities planned for every month of the year. They have a celebration for Easter, which is their Black Mass, or Black Sabbath, during which they mock the death of Christ, who was sacrificed on Good Friday. They sacrifice a man or woman on that day and then undergo three days of fasting and chanting.

They celebrate Christmas as well. On December 24, they sacrifice both a man and a woman. December 25 is their Yuletide, during which they celebrate the birth of the sun as a young babe to the great goddess. They believe that every man is a god if he chooses to recognize himself as one, as quoted in their Satanic Bible.

I don't like to see a face hidden behind a mask. Halloween is satanic. Let's look at what the Satanic church is doing in preparation for Halloween while the Christians who are ignorant to Satan's schemes are helping their children carve jack-o'-lanterns and shopping for the most popular costumes and plenty of candy for the ghosts and goblins who will be trick-or-treating at their doors on Halloween night. October 22 to October 29 is sacrifice preparation: kidnapping, holding and doing ceremonial preparation of persons for human sacrifice. October 28 to October 30 are Satanists' high unholy days related to Halloween, which involve human sacrifices. October 31 is All Hallows Eve (Halloween), one of Satan's two most important nights of the year. Attempts are made to break the bond keeping the doors to the underworld closed. Blood and sexual rituals ensue. There is sexual association with demons, as well as animal and human sacrifice, male and female. November 1 to November 3 are high unholy days related to Halloween, which means more human sacrifices. When your children are dressed up as their favourite goblins and ghosts and you are handing out candy to otherwise innocent children, Satanists are killing human beings as sacrifices. They sacrifice a baby while it is alive. Starting at the throat of a living one-month-old baby, they slice one clean cut down to its lower abdomen, slicing the child's stomach wide open. The baby is screaming and making gurgling sounds as its life is coming to an end. The infant dies as the knife is slicing its stomach open. It takes its last breath, and the child's torment has ended. That's why I hate Halloween! And that's why you should hate Halloween as well.

There are Christian believers who find nothing harmful in children dressing up as their favourite characters and going from house to house collecting candies. Halloween is as big a celebration for the satanic church as Christmas is to the world. We start getting excited about Christmas as early as November 1. Across Canada, visions of sugar plums are dancing in children's heads as fast as Sears can distribute their Christmas wish books. Christmas celebrations can last from November into January. Well, I tell you that the satanic church has just as big a hoedown with their celebrations of Halloween.

As I said, on All Hallows Eve, Satanists attempt to break the bond keeping the doors to the underworld (hell) closed. Jesus died, and in three days, He rose again. During the three days before He rose, He was in the belly of the earth—that is, hell—where He took the keys of Hades and of death. By attempting to break the bond that keeps the doors of hell closed, the satanic church is trying to mimic what Jesus did when He took the keys of hell. Their attempt is to free spirits from hell. This is what Satan is orchestrating while gullible worldly people and Christians alike are handing candy out to children dressed as witches, wizards and ghosts.

Participating in Halloween is abominable, wretched and vile. Christians should not be giving out candies and should not be letting their children participate in going from house to house collecting candies.

There is far more I could tell you about Halloween, including the history of the jack-o'-lantern; the history of dressing in costumes, such as ghosts and zombies; and the history behind going from house to house receiving treats. I suggest if you need more proof of the sinister reality of Halloween, go on the Internet and read about the history behind this depraved and sinister night of dark evil.

Possibly the darkest satanic ritual involves the grail drinking of blood, which is a sex ritual related to the goddess Cerridwen.

They have altogether eight Sabbaths:

February 2	Candlemas
April	Good Friday
(the date follows along with our Easter)	
April 30	May Night (the maypole dance, when they dance in the nude in a group setting)
May 1	Beltane (May Day)
June 21	St. John's Eve
August 1	Lammas
October 31	Halloween
December 1	St. Thomas Day

One of their main colours is black, which represents darkness, night, evil, the devil and sorrow.

Many well-meaning Christians will say, "If these human sacrifices are taking place, then why don't we hear about them?" It is possible the remains of the bodies are buried in graves, eaten or cremated. A baby's body parts and bones could be easily disposed of in a kitchen sink garbage disposal.

Children and adults often go missing, and many of them are never found. The satanic church will put a dreadful fear in the governing authorities; therefore, kidnappings done close to Halloween are possibly never reported and are quietly slid under the table. The satanic church also, within their communes, breeds babies for the purpose of sacrificing them. Also, child sacrifices and ritual murders linked to witch doctors are common even to this day. Witch doctors believe the brutal dismembering of body parts and sacrifice of a boy child will bring wealth and prosperity. Furthermore, according to the judicial system, a person cannot be charged with the crime of sacrificing humans; they can only be charged with murder. Therefore, chances are, you will never hear of a human sacrifice; however, that does not mean these sacrifices are not happening. Witch doctors are not being charged for their crimes. I believe it is out of fear that these crimes are overlooked. This fear is global. It is much easier to brush this crime under the carpet than to deal with it and the possible consequences that would follow.

Witchcraft Attacks

The practice of witchcraft includes sorcery; white, grey and black magic; charms; enchantments and irresistible influence; whispered spells; enchantments; the practice of magic, sorcery or witchcraft; influence through trickery; the practice of dealing with evil spirits and soothsaying.

Enchantment is when witches and wizards use their human voices to bring another person under their psychic control. They use incantations and pronounced spells of evil spirits. Hypnosis and casting spells fall under enchantments. To cast a spell is to hiss, whisper a spell, prognosticate, divine, enchant, to practice magic, to cover, to cloud over, observe times, enchantments-practices of magical arts, and soothsaying, which is all the art of a sorcerer.

Depending on the legal rights Satan has been given, witchcraft has the power to control and affect individual people, families, churches, cities and nations. How many Christians, ministries and churches have been destroyed by witchcraft when the people were not even aware of the attack they were under?

Wizards and witches can besiege church congregations and have the pastors and board members under their wicked spells. I have been aware of this occurring in a healthy evangelistic church, and for this reason, this question remains in my heart: What percentage of Christian churches are under the control of witchcraft? I believe it is possible that 99 percent of all Christian churches have unidentified wizards and witches comfortably nestled in their church bodies. I want you to take note that priests and priestess of the Church of Satan can make their way into Christian churches as pastors and secretaries.

I have come to understand that few Christians grasp the overall nature of Satan's conspiracy. This deals with the occult science, which is a complicated system of witchcraft that is interconnected. There is a revival of the occult worldwide. The world's religions and political entities are being fragmented, divided and conquered. Witchcraft is experiencing one of the greatest revivals in history around the world. The scope and power of modern occultism are vast. The world apparently is in the midst of what scripture calls the last days. It is obvious to me that Satan is mobilizing all his forces into a worldwide conspiracy for a final all-out attack on the world and especially on God's church. Trauma-based occult mind control might be the greatest danger to our human race. You only need to take a look at Satan's attack against our children. By introducing our children into the occult through cartoons, movies, games and toys, Satan is building up a whole new generation of sorcerers and wizards.

Demonic influences include spiritualism, parapsychology, martial arts, occultism, oppression, psychic phenomena, deception, satanic rituals, abuse, ancestral demonism and seizures. For the Christian, the occult can cause a departure from the faith, open apostasy, doctrinal corruption, perversion of the truth, babel of the cults, Christian disunity, corrupt conduct and practice, indulgence in defiling lust, ritualistic formalism, unbelief in God, suicide and insanity. Ungodly lifestyles can cause sexual promiscuity, racism, addiction to drugs, eating disorders, theological heresy and demonic meditation.

Many Christians are falling into the devil's occult snare by consulting witches, mediums, clairvoyants and astrologers. Demonization of Christians includes violence, uncleanness, blasphemy and failure in their Christian walk. Christians can compromise their beliefs; tamper with the occult; participate in idolatry and sin; be influenced, oppressed, vexed, depressed and bound by demons; and have spiritual blindness, hardness of heart toward the Word of God and antagonism toward God.

Beware of witches, Satanists and wizards in Christian churches. They come in as fellow believers. They will be pleasant and well liked, and they blend in quickly. You could be sitting next to one of these every Sunday morning. Writing this book has gotten me a lot of negative attention. Since I have started this book, I have dealt with attacks from wizards, Satanists and witches, some from within the Christian church.

Our dream world is an arena of spiritual warfare that we know little about. Just as God works through our dreams, Satan also uses this method. Sleep is a war front of demonic manipulation and attacks. As we slumber with our beautyrest, our mental awareness is shut down. This makes us fully unprotected from the demonic spirit world. This is another good reason why Christians should always have their protective hedge in good shape with no tiny pinholes. It is our healthy Christian lifestyle that surrounds us through the night. Knowing that I am right with God helps me to rest in peace. I have noticed that since I have given my life to Christ, I am never raped as I sleep, and other attacks, such as spinning my soul at a massive speed, have never again occurred. The two wizards who did rape me only did so when I was awake, with my full faculties to be able to fight them off. You will learn later in Chapter 18 how to do a spiritual house cleaning and then later on in this book you will find spiritual warfare prayers that you can use to ensure your safety as you sleep at night.

Charismatic witchcraft is witchcraft practised by Christians against other believers. This includes Jezebel-type practices, prophesy used to control and pastors who are dictators. It is basically anyone who attempts to control others. When a Christian prays out of God's will—for instance, he prays that his wife will die so he can marry Miss Sussy, who teaches Sunday school—his prayers are psychic prayers. Psychic prayers are directed to Satan, and the answer to a psychic prayer comes from Satan rather than from God. Be careful what you pray for. It might just get answered. "For rebellion is as the sin of witchcraft" (1 Samuel 15:23).

A consulter with familiar spirits is a medium. Mediums use demons or evil spirits to tell them about the present or future of individuals or the location of a lost person or object. Mediumistic powers come by heredity and occult-practised transference. *Fortune-telling* is a general term used in any supernatural process of gaining hidden knowledge that cannot be discerned through the natural mind or senses—for example, water-witching, mediums and horoscopes. Witchcraft means to distribute or determine by lot of magic scroll or to divine. A soothsayer or diviner is one who uses false means to discover the divine will of God. The six forms of fortune-telling are astrology (the interpretation of human destiny), palmistry (the practice of reading palms), reading cards (both playing cards and tarot cards), psychometry (getting information from an object belonging to a person), crystal balls and the Ouija board.

Charmers use amulets, potions and symbols to hypnotize; cast spells; bring good luck; charm away warts, disease and sickness; and give protection from evil. To charm is to fascinate, cast a spell, join in spells or enchant. This includes hypnosis. To charm is to put a spell upon. This is an example of charming: I was told of a woman who would take a raw piece of meat, rub it on a wart, bury it in the ground, and forget about it. She did this to get rid of the wart. What she did was witchcraft.

A *pharmakeia* sorceress is a medical poisoner, druggist and magician. This magic is done through oriental science, drugs and chemicals to produce stupor, spells and mind-altering influences. To mention three would be yoga meditation, acupuncture and meditation music. This is sorcery and witchcraft.

Necromancy is communication with the dead. Séances are necromancy. When people do this, they call upon familiar spirits—that is, they call upon demons. Necromancy is calling forth the spirits of the dead. A necromancer is a medium who consults demons that mimic a dead person. The necromancer will often go into a trance in which he or she lets an evil spirit take over his or her body to speak through.

The observer of times is a soothsayer. This is one who pretends to tell future events. This practice includes the following of horoscopes, omens in the sky and nature, astrology and monthly prognostication. This includes star gazing, prognostication and observing times.

Occult television shows, to name a few, include *Night Gallery*, *Sixth Sense*, *Ghost Story*, *The Amazing World of Kreskin* and *Bewitched*. Occult programs are anything featuring the supernatural. When you watch such programs, the evil spirits will leap off the TV screen into the room. Watching these programs breaks down the Christian believer's protective hedge, and these evil spirits then have the legal right to enter that Christian—and they will enter. Use caution when watching TV. When a commercial or TV program is not appropriate for Christian viewing, then either change the channel or shut the TV off. I have seen evil spirits leap out of the TV screen at me and other people, and the Holy Spirit has assisted me in casting spirits out of myself that entered me from the computer screen as well as from the TV screen.

New Age in the Church

New Age concepts include exploration of human sexuality, environmentalism, Christian apostasy, modern-day occultism, worship of Mother Earth and embracing a different god. In these last days is a time of the worst religious deception this world has ever seen from the beginning of humankind. Satan had this agenda fully planned long ago, and he is now pushing ahead in full stride. Jesus warned in (Matthew 24:24) that psychic powers would produce counterfeit great signs and wonders in the last days, which we are now living through. People are attracted to these psychic powers in a fundamental way. These powers draw them in like powerful magnets. Jesus warned that in the last days, there would be a religion of the demonic sort. We are in a time when the Christian church is denying the teachings of Jesus Christ yet still saying they are faithful to the gospel of God.

This deceit is so pervasive that many believers are manipulated into not recognizing this prophesied demonic invasion. Jesus warned that this would happen just prior to His return. Christians are facing the greatest challenge in all of history. This demonic power is subtly seducing and changing biblical interpretations and undermining the faith of Christian believers.

I have come to believe that many Christians believe the Enemy is safely outside of the Christian church, even though the truth is, he is tucked right inside our midst. Many Christian believers cannot tell enemy from friend. Many are attracted to Christianity today because of the false teachings that are attributes of the Antichrist. These new Christians are being fooled into believing they are following the true gospel, but the truth is, they are being led astray by wolves in sheep's clothing. The prophetic scholars know that humankind must be both religiously and politically made ready so as to embrace the coming Antichrist when he comes into power. The Antichrist will claim he is Christ.

A part of Satan's aim is to cause as many as possible in the Christian church to fall from grace. I believe when Christ comes for His church, any who have fallen from grace will not be taken up, and when the Antichrist comes into rule, those who have fallen from grace will be so badly twisted in the New Age teaching that they will not know the Antichrist, even though he is standing right in front of their faces.

What people find so appealing about this New Age doctrine is that it offers a new way of perceiving reality and religion. This New Age is not a passing fad. This New Age offers spiritual reality, fulfillment and world harmony, although in reality, it is a spiritual counterfeit. Scripture warns numerous times of spiritual counterfeits, counterfeit Christians, counterfeit prophets, counterfeit miracles, counterfeit angels, counterfeit gods, counterfeit good works, counterfeit converts, counterfeit spirits, counterfeit doctrines and counterfeit gospels.

Satan knows that Christians will not accept the frontal assault of the New Age occult doctrines and themes, so he has the New Agers change their occult-related words into Christian terms, such as *faith*, *God*, *Christ* and *born again*. Many churches today are being pulled in hook, line and sinker. The devil knows how to mix just enough truth with falsehood to make it appealing to even God's elect.

With all this said, remember this: we Christians do not fight against people. We fight against principalities of the air, seas and earth (evil spirits, Satan, demons and rulers of darkness) of this world; spiritual wickedness in high places; and the kingdom of Satan. (Matthew 5:44) tells us to love and pray for our enemies. This includes wizards, witches, sorcerers and Satanists. We are to pray daily for their salvation. Jesus gave up His life for these people as well. "But I say unto you, love your enemies, bless them that curse you, do good to them that hate you, and pray for them which despitefully use you, and persecute you" (Matthew 5:44). If you know a Christian who is struggling or you yourself are struggling because you came out of such an entrapment as this, I have included in book 2 some deliverance prayers that wizards, witches, sorcerers and Satanists can pray to find their freedom in Christ Jesus.

SIXTEEN

Demons Connected to and Dwelling in Man-Made Objects

It may not be your Rice Krispies joyfully greeting their sidekick homogenized milk when, in the night, you suddenly hear in the silence of your home the creepy sounds of *snap*, *crackle*, and *pop*.

The Haunted House

On May 17, 2013, I took a trip to visit a haunted house. In order to get a feel of the atmosphere both surrounding and within this so-called spooked house, I walked through the old house and then through the forest surrounding the house. I was surprise to see that this house was not any more frightful than the house I grew up in. My mother's practice of witchcraft, card reading and other magic arts she operated in, plus my dad's perverted extramarital affairs, caused our home to be heavily inhabited with demons. It was not uncommon to witness cast-iron frying pans and coffee mugs floating to the ceiling, floating across the room and then dropping down. These objects would just miss dropping onto the head of whomever they were aimed at to hit.

As I explored the rooms, I found myself comparing the haunted house to the houses I spent my younger years growing up in, and this house was mild and peaceful in comparison. I could, in my spirit, see the demons who were attached to wall hangings, ornaments, fixtures, antique furniture and even the window coverings. If one would have dared to remove the handsomely made antique hutch and taken it home, he or she would have brought along an unwelcome part of that old house, because the demons were dwelling in and attached to the hutch. The spirits in the hutch would then cause the same havoc in the next home. This demon will not leave your home. Only through a spiritual house cleaning will you get rid of him.

Every home I grew up in would have been classified as a haunted house, although the truth was that these houses were inhabited by the demons my mother's and dad's ludicrous actions had given the legal right to enter and remain. Evil spirits, oddly enough, seem to need a place to live, and once they have taken up their lodging in an object—whether in an animal, house or person—they will not be willing to leave and, as long as they have their legal right to stay, will not leave.

I commonly hear evil spirits cursing at me. It only takes my finding some written material pertaining to doctrine about evil spirits to set them off, and they call me some pretty rank names. I immediately found this house to be quiet. As soon as I entered the house, the demons took off into the basement and surrounding forest in order to hide from me. None of them cursed at me or desired to be anywhere close to me. I found it surprising to see how quiet the house was. When these demons saw me, they recognized the spirit in me, and they knew I would be able to see them. That caused them to take off into hiding. When evil spirits see a Christian, they see the blood of the Lamb. They did not like the light I represented, so some took to hiding in the basement, while others took to hiding in the surrounding forest.

In the forest were two unmarked graves the homeowners were aware of. The co-owner told me that back in the 1800s, their great-great-aunt had been given in an arranged marriage to a vile and deranged man. She hated him. He would come into her bed every night and rape her. When she found herself pregnant, she would throw herself down the staircase in order to miscarry the child.

I took my time as I made my way from one room to the next. I followed my spiritual instincts as I carefully searched for the room where the rapes had taken place. When I discovered this room, the Holy Spirit gave me a clear picture of just how these spirits had gained their legal right to remain in the forest and house. The rapes had taken place in the last room I entered: the front bedroom on the second story of the old farmhouse. Entering this room, I could, in my spirit, feel the pain and suffering she had felt. I could also see the woman in her bed, frantically fighting off her husband as he raped her. The room was dark with gloom, which I could feel. At that moment, it became clear to me that the tiny unwanted embryos had been buried in shallow graves in the forest surrounding the haunted house. Thus, the continual rapes over the many years in the upstairs bedroom, as well as the murders of the unborn babies, had given the demons the legal right to remain in the house. The babies buried in the forest surrounding the house had given the demons the legal right to remain in the forest.

After discovering this in the final room I entered, I went out behind the house, where I saw the demons in the forest. They knew I could see them; therefore, they were trying to hide from me behind the trees. I chose to follow one of the demons to see how he would act. As I would walk up to him and start to close in on him, he would move from one tree to hiding behind another. I would then follow him to that tree, and he would move and hide behind another. I did this for some time, and then I just walked away, letting him go.

As the co-owner of the house and I were departing down the dirt road, we stopped the car and turned to watch what would next take place. Looking back at the old haunted house, I saw coming up from the foundation of the farmhouse something that looked like a filmy cloud. As it rose, the cloud formed a dome that enveloped the entire house. I believe the cloud was made up of the spirits that had hidden in the basement from me, and now that I had left, they were coming back up and entering back into the old farmhouse.

Although many would possibly rather simply burn down the house, it is possible to spiritually clean a haunted house. This is because you are dealing not with ghosts but, rather, with demons. As long as an object is not an image of man-made gods (demons), artifacts, witches and satanic symbols, you can cast demons out of it. If you have images of man-made gods, artifacts, witches and satanic symbols, then you will need to burn them.

A haunted house occurs when a person does some sort of sin that gives demons the legal right to move into the home and stay there. It does not have to be something as violent as murder. It can be a sexual sin, such as rape or pornography. It can be playing with a Ouija board or fortune-telling with a deck of cards. The demons given the legal right to come into the house and remain will not move out of the house even if the person who gave them rights through his or her sin moves out or passes away, and this is what makes a house or any building haunted. When the person who gave the demons the legal right to stay no longer lives there, still, the demons will remain, and it is up to the next people who lives there to annul the demons' rights and boot them out.

A lady was renting rooms out, and she had a boarder living in her home who was deeply into pornography; in this case, he was watching it on the computer. When he moved out, he left such a spiritual mess that she had to ask me to come into her home to do a spiritual cleaning. I first went onto her computer and logged in to his site. I then went into his saved pictures and deleted all of the offensive pictures he had saved. This computer was kept in the hallway, so it was accessible for all of the other boarders. I then went into the bedroom he had lodged in. This room was darkened with a large amount of demons that had remained after he had moved out. The demons cursed at me, demanding that I leave. I took their legal right away and made them leave.

A Christian lady called me in to do a spiritual house cleaning of a house she had recently purchased. The house was only 15 years old, yet she was convinced it was haunted. Walking into the second-story bedroom, I saw in my spirit that with the previous owners, a seven-year-old boy had been raped many times by a man. The Holy Spirit opened my spiritual eyes to the fact that this man had been in the habit of, in the night when the parents were not home, leaving his room, going over into the boy's room and raping the boy. Although this house was only 15 years old, because of the sexual sin that had occurred in that bedroom, it was a classic case of a haunted house. Before I could cast the demons out of the house, I had to break the curse and remove the demons' legal right to remain in the house. A month later, I followed up by calling and asking if there had been any more occurrences, and the new homeowner told me she had had no more trouble with the spirits. In that case, as with all other haunted houses, the curse that gave the spirits the legal right to remain had to be broken. Once the curse had been broken and the spirits cast out, the house was no longer haunted.

It is easy to break these spirits' legal right to remain and then cast them out. Place in the space provided below the name of the sin that was performed. Once you know what sin gave the evil spirits their legal right to remain in the house, then you can break their right by saying with firm authority, "I break, renounce and denounce the spirit of [name of sin committed]'s legal right to remain." You no longer have any legal right to remain in this house. I command you in the name of Jesus Christ to leave and not come back. I do this through the power of the Holy Spirit, who dwells in me."

A word of advice: if you are like me in the habit of shopping in antique shops, make sure to always ask the Holy Spirit to refresh your gift of discernment of spirits before you purchase your rare treasures.

Satan's Picture Book

I learned much from my mother about the astrology connected to the common deck of playing cards. I have also done a great deal of research about the sinister, dark history of playing cards as well as further reading on the astrology interwoven into the deck of cards. Through this, it is my conclusion that Christians should not have decks of playing cards in their possession. It is also my personal belief that having these cards in one's home could negatively interfere with a person receiving his or her deliverance. On the personal note, I myself did not receive my first spiritual physical deliverance until after I had trashed my deck of playing cards, and I do not think this could have been only by coincidence.

In the many years since my conversion to Christ, I have never heard preached from the pulpit the evil, sinister darkness that hides behind the deck of playing cards. Even when I went to Christian counsellors for deliverance, none of those professionals gave me any warning about playing cards and their links to astrology.

My mother did her fortune-telling through the use of a deck of playing cards. She turned over the death card, and within two weeks of doing that, she murdered my baby brother. To this day, I know my brother's life was taken because the evil spirits within her went after his life to prove the accuracy of my mother's fortune-telling. I believe playing cards are the devil's tool. Because of the strong link to astrology, I strongly believe that today's modern deck of playing cards must have been developed and designed by a Satan worshipper or an occultist.

Many Christians today are fascinated with playing card games and gambling. The reason for this is because our pastors fail to warn us of the evil that lies within the common deck of cards. There is an evil, sinister force behind the history of card playing, and because of the neglect of our spiritual leaders, few Christians are even aware of this. Most card addicts have no clue that each one of the 52 cards has a secret meaning. There's no doubt in my mind why, over the centuries, many good people have looked upon cards with great uneasiness and suspicion. The two most common nicknames given to the deck of playing cards are the *Devil's Bible* and the *Devil's Picture Book*. I recall my parents often calling the deck of cards my mother used the Devil's Picture Book and the Devil's Bible.

The cards are darkly tainted with indecency and dishonesty. At one time, the Christian church did take a strong stand against card games, and pastors and churches would warn about the sinister danger of these cards. However, although these playing cards have not lost their evil influence or their meaning, our churches today have kept strangely silent on the issue. This greatly saddens me when I think of the heavy load of misery I had to suffer because of the hold my demons had on me.

I came to believe through my personal experience that if you have decks of playing cards in your home, then you have given demons a legal hold on your life, and they have the legal right to stay in your home. When I removed the cards from my home, I removed the demons' legal right to stay. I feel the whole idea of my doing a spiritual house cleaning is to remove from my home the spirits causing me havoc, and the only way I can do this is by removing that which they believe gives them their legal right to stay.

It is important to note that the person who first created the playing cards had no decent regard for our glorious and marvellous Lord Jesus in designing a message in the cards that was the direct opposite of the true scripture as given in the Bible. You will note that decks of cards are commonly found in the possession of prostitutes, gamblers, prison inmates, hotel patrons, thieves and murderers, and they are used by fortune-tellers, but you will not see them in a prayer meeting.

When I asked my mother how she could look at the cards and get such an accurate reading, she explained to me, "The king represents a prince of darkness." In card reading, the king is Satan, who is the Prince of Darkness (Ephesians 2:2). He is the enemy of our Lord, Jesus Christ. She said, "The ten card is the spirit of lawlessness." This is in opposition to our moral law (the Ten Commandments) in the Bible, the Word of God. She continued, "The club is similar to the ten card." Back in the 1300s, clubs were the main weapons that murderers would use. As you can see, this suit of cards represents a spirit of death by violence—murder. Then she said, "The queen card represents Mary, the virgin mother of Christ Jesus. But in the language of the deck of cards, she is called the Mother of Harlots. The jack card represents a pimp, lustful adulterer and whoremonger whose only goal is to please his sex-driven fleshly lust." Now, what do you think of this? The joker represents our Lord, Jesus Christ. Yes, the Son of God. The meaning of a joker is a fool; this sets up our Lord, Jesus Christ, to be ridiculed. To add to this, my mother said, "The joker represents Jesus Christ; he is the birth son of the lustful jack and the Mother of Harlots." There are hidden blasphemous meanings to all of the remaining cards to the deck. This is true of all seemingly innocent decks of cards found in homes of Christians who are blind to the truth.

The decks of playing cards that many Christians have in their homes and play with have a Satanic origin. Few Christians know that today's modern deck of playing cards has many evil symbols and hidden meanings. According to what a witch openly told me, tarot cards, which fortune-tellers commonly use to reveal the futures of the ones searching, are the ancestor of our modern deck of playing cards. It is believed that ancient Egyptian occultists brought tarot cards from Egypt to Rome, where they were kept in the possession of the pope. Later on, the tarot cards were circulated throughout all Europe and were embellished by such Satan worshippers as Aleister Crowley. As I said, they are a tool of the devil. Satanists, witches, psychics and occultists all use playing cards to cast spells and curses and perform magic, divination and fortune-telling.

I believe it could be possible that the deck of playing cards might have been, in the beginning, intended for reading one's future. Then, later, people started developing games they could play with them. These playing cards are fully equipped for the use of fortune-telling.

There is an occult symbol put into every card of our modern deck of cards. This was how my mother identified men and boys from women and girls when she would read one's future. The heart and diamond are female symbols, while the club and spade are male symbols. The male colour is red, and the female is black. Both sexes are symbolized on each card that has a symbol of one sex and the colour of the opposite sex. The trinity, or the complete family, is viewed in the three highest cards: the jack, or knave (in the German language, it is pronounced *knabe*, meaning "boy"), king and queen. Therefore, you see, in the deck of cards, we have the father, mother and child. This is the perfect family, or the natural trinity. We have four suits, which symbolizes the male triad and female unit. This is forming the four gods of Arabel.

There is a powerful link between the astrology of ancient witchcraft science and playing cards. I believe a witch, wizard or occultist designed the deck of cards and patterned the numeric arrangement of the cards to coincide with both the occult science of astrology and the zodiac. The deck's 52 cards represent the 52 weeks of the year. The 12 cards with faces in the four different suits represent the four weeks in a month as well as the four different seasons of the year: winter, spring, summer and fall. The 13 cards in each of the suits represent the lunar months. When you count the jack as 11, the queen as 12, and the king as 13, not forgetting to add the joker, then the number in the card deck equals 365 to represent the total number of days in a year. Some decks have a second joker. When the second joker is added to the deck, it then represents the extra day in a leap year. My mother used the second joker in that way. Red and black in card reading represent day and night. As you can see, the one who designed the deck incorporated astrology into the cards.

Now you can see how easy it was for my mother to read one's future through the handling of a deck of cards. Should it be of any shock that many years later, after my mother had become a Christian, when she used a deck of playing cards to read a person's future one day, she suddenly got a horrible migraine that took her to her knees in pain?

God has made us stewards of the money He has loaned to us. We are to first of all tithe to Him a tenth of all income we receive. We are then expected to give to the needy and to the missionaries located around the world (Matthew 25:34–46). In heaven, Christians will be held accountable for how they manage their finances and how willing they were to give to the poor and needy (Matthew 25:14–30). Whether one is buying a lotto ticket or betting in a card game, in my opinion, he or she is gambling away God's money. Christians should shun all gambling like the plague. This includes card games and bingo. A good child of God's would never waste money on buying a lotto ticket when it could be used to feed the homeless.

There was a time when nearly nine-tenths of all gambling was done with decks of cards, and many Christians were participating in it. Some Christians even learned how to gamble with cards in their own homes. The main choice of gambling games was poker; it was a common game for many to pass the time. People played poker in saloons, dance halls and whorehouses, in which it was often accompanied by smoking, drinking, stealing, violence, murder and prostitution. In the long-past years, many Christians were forbidden from even having a deck of cards in their home. The Presbyterian preachers, like my grandfather Campbell, believed it was a sin for a Christian to have such an abomination in the home. Gambling is an expensive and addictive habit that will lead you into spiritual bondage and financial ruin.

Having a deck of cards in your home is no different from having a Ouija board in your home. Your playing cards, however harmless they might seem, have a hidden secret that makes them designed for fortune-telling. The Ouija board is designed to call on and talk back and forth with demons. Therefore, I believe one is as serious an evil as the other.

According to the Word of God, our heavenly Father forbids us from joining the world in playing games and passing our time in things that are of the world—that is, of Satan (1 John 2:15–17). I personally believe the deck of playing cards is of Satan, and I also believe we as Christians will never glorify God by having playing cards in our homes or playing with them. Remember, you were bought at a price. Therefore, honour God with your bodies (1 Corinthians 6:20). Everything we do should be for the glory of God (1 Corinthians 10:31). I found that I became addicted to playing solitaire with a deck of cards—the game was all I was doing. Playing with cards for numerous hours at a time stagnated my spiritual growth, and the cards became a god to me. I was replacing my time of worship, prayer and Bible reading with solitaire. "See then that ye walk circumspectly, not as fools, but as wise, Redeeming the time, because the days are evil. Wherefore be ye not unwise, but understand what the will of the Lord is" (Ephesians 5:15–17).

I personally believe it is a huge abomination to have a deck of cards in a Christian home, and all believers of Christ Jesus should remove their decks of cards and burn them. I discovered through my own personal experience that having playing cards in my home and playing with them gave the evil spirits their legal right to remain in my home, and this put curses upon me and my household. "Neither shalt thou bring an abomination into thine house, lest thou be a cursed thing like it: but thou shalt utterly detest it, and thou shalt utterly abhor it; for it is a cursed thing" (Deuteronomy 7:26). Perhaps you have experienced an uneasiness or a dark evilness with decks of playing cards. I have included in a later chapter of this book helpful prayers that will break these spirits' legal right to remain.

We should take a lesson from our early brothers and sisters in Christ and do the same as they did in (Acts 19:19): burn the abominable things. If you have a card game saved on your computer, then it is in your house. If you play a card game on your computer, then you are playing with a deck of cards.

Demons in the Toy Box

I would like to start by saying that not all children's dolls and toys are bad to have in the toy box. Don't panic and throw out all your kid's toys. Children need to play, and toys can be, if well chosen, an essential part of a child's physical and mental growth. Ask the Holy Spirit to give you discernment of spirits, and ask Him to work with you in following your mission.

Demons are hidden in toy stores. They are on the shelves, attached to the toys your children are begging you to purchase for them. I always ask the Holy Spirit to guide me as I Christmas shop for my grandchildren, and I have seen these spirits. Today many toys have evil spirits connected to and dwelling in them as they leave the factory. When you are shopping for toys, you should always ask the Holy Spirit to help you discern the spirits. You are going to be surprised just how many new toys are possessed with demons. I would like to add that I do buy toys for my grandchildren; however, I am careful to shop for toys that will not bring unwanted spirits into their bedrooms and homes.

Your child could possibly have a toy box full of demons. One night, while I was babysitting my grandchildren, my grandson asked me to come into his bedroom and take a look in his closet. He said, "You can see the monsters in my closet. I know you can. Mom and Dad don't believe me, but I know you do." He then told me, "I can see the monsters in my closet!" I answered, "Yes, I do believe you." As I looked in his closet, I could see the demons—the closet was loaded with them. A massive amount of demons will appear as a dark cloud in a room, and I saw with my spiritual eyes that his bedroom closet was clouded in a dark grey. He then said to me, "Grandma, you know how to get rid of them. I know you do." The fact was, yes, I knew how to get rid of the demons, but the truth was, I needed my son and his wife's consent to remove the things that were giving the spirits the legal right to stay. Without their permission, I could not start taking toys out of the house and start burning them. I told him, "Your mom and dad would need to give me permission to remove the things that make the monsters hide in your bedroom closet. I can't just take them out and destroy them without your parents' approval." He never spoke to me again about his monsters.

Voodoo is real. In many countries, even to this day, witch doctors perform dark magic by poking pins into voodoo dolls to cause pain and, in many cases, even the death of the person they are targeting.

My granddaughter was only into collecting Monster High dolls for one year before she started experiencing demons manifesting themselves in her bedroom. She was so freaked out about the spirits in her room that she could no longer sleep comfortably in her bedroom. She showed me a video on YouTube of one character in Monster High sticking straight pins into another character, who was a voodoo doll. Another of the Monster High characters started crying out, "Ouch! Don't do that!" This is witchcraft. Satan has legal grounds to our children through many of the toys they play with and the programs they watch. Children who have these dolls and toys in their possession will have demons in their bedrooms. Not only that, but also, I believe children who watch *Monster High* and have these toys already have had evil spirits enter them. Perhaps you have felt an uneasiness toward these dolls or these programs. That is the tender, sweet Spirit of God warning you.

I have known for many years that watching immoral programs can cause evil spirits to leap off of the TV screen and enter the observer. Therefore, as with any other program that is unwholesome for Christian viewing, while viewers watch *Monster High*, these spirits will leap off of the screen and enter them. I Googled *Monster High* and went into the *Monster High* site for a couple of minutes. Within that short time, 40,000 evil spirits with the name Monster High entered me, and 200,000 entered me with the name Evil Doll. I cast these spirits out of myself after I lost a night's sleep. I would like to add that I went onto this site as a Christian, and investigating the dolls was enough to damage my protective hedge and let the spirits in. Through my own experience, I have been left with no doubt in my mind that the children who watch these programs and have these dolls in their possession have the evil spirits with the names Monster High and Evil Doll dwelling in them, and it is possible that large families of these two spirits are dwelling in them. The fact is, evil spirits like to travel in families.

These spirits entered me as families. It has been my experience that most often, evil spirits enter as families, and when their legal rights are properly dealt with, they will come out as families. Furthermore, all programs with sorcery and witchcraft in them will also give evil spirits the legal right to enter a child who is viewing the program. For instance, if your child has been reading and watching Harry Potter stories, then your child has families of spirits with the names Harry Potter, Wizardry and Sorcery dwelling within him or her. By the way, in the movies of Harry Potter, the boy Harry is a practising wizard. Perhaps Harry Potter books and movies give you an uneasiness. If so, it is likely the Holy Spirit is warning you that your child should not be viewing them.

I am not against little girls having dolls. Every small child needs a baby doll. Little boys should have a baby doll as well. Loving and caring for a baby doll plays a role in helping the child learn how to be a warm and loving mommy or daddy later on when one has his or her own family. However, you need to discern the spirits in the toys you are bringing into your child's nursery, playroom and bedroom. I babysit my youngest grandson five days a week, and I have a toy box that is loaded to bursting at the sides. It is good for kids to have toys. We just need to be careful that the toys they have are spiritually healthy for them.

I have not yet seen a marionette puppet or a ventriloquist's doll that had no evil spirits connected to it. Therefore, it is my opinion that children should not watch these puppet shows.

I personally believe that you can look through people's eyes into their souls. I have often said the eyes are the window to the soul, and I have often looked into people's eyes to see if they had a gentle spirit in them. The all-seeing eye is an object or picture that has one or more eyes in it. In the spirit form, it has a hidden camera and microphone within it that is actually an evil spirit called The Watcher dwelling inside of it. Witches later soul-travel to where the all-seeing eye is and ask the spirit within what they have seen or heard. You could unknowingly have one of these objects or pictures in your office or your home. I had an all-seeing eye on a post in my backyard that was there for three years before I knew what it was.

The Minions movies are demonic. When I look at these creatures, I can see the all-seeing eye. This means that if your child has in his or her bedroom the Minions, then the child has an evil spirit watching him or her through the eyes of the Minions. The all-seeing eye origin comes from ancient mystery religions. Furthermore, I believe that through our children watching these Minion movies, they are being prepared to accept the Antichrist. I also believe that through a child fondly watching these creatures, the devil is enticing the child to be comfortable with evil spirits. The reason I believe this is because these Minions are characterized in these movies as being small, strange-looking creatures with little self-control. They are pesky when they are doing weird interactions with people and animals. They have criminal masterminds. In every way, they remind me of the evil spirits who dwell in people. Your children should not watch these movies or have these toys and posters in their possession. I have no doubt in my mind whatsoever that having these creatures in your child's room has the child under the watchful eye of an evil spirit whose name is The Watcher.

The German word for "demon" is pronounced as *Smurfs*. Papa Smurf is a wizard; he casts spells and mixes potions, and he is often referred to as Beelzebub in the cartoons. See who is referred to as Beelzebub in the Bible: "And the scribes which came down from Jerusalem said, He hath Beelzebub, and by the prince of devils casteth he out devils. And he called them unto him, and said unto them in parables, How can Satan cast out Satan?" (Mark 3:22–23). Jesus, in (Mark 3:23), says Beelzebub is Satan. In this cartoon, Papa Smurf is often referred to as Beelzebub—that is, Satan. Papa Smurf practises sorcery and witchcraft. God ordered in the Old Testament that witches and wizards be put to death (Exodus 22:18). Watching the Smurfs on TV, regardless of how cute, amusing and innocent they might seem, gives respectability to that which God forbids. I have come to the knowledge that it opens up the viewer to satanic bondage.

The Star Wars theme is based on a cosmic force taken from Buddhism and Eastern religions. In *The Empire Strikes Back*, Yoda is referred to as a Zen master. *Dungeons and Dragons* is a fantasy game fought in the minds of the players. It teaches demonology, witchcraft, voodoo, murder, rape, blasphemy, suicide, assassination, insanity, sexual perversion, homosexuality, Satan worship, barbarism, cannibalism, sadism, demon summoning, necromancy, human sacrifice and divination. Elves are inferior spirit beings with great powers. Gremlins are violent and sadistic.

Children can be easily influenced to accept demons. They have healthy and widespread imaginations, which are a playground for evil spirits. Demonic movies are aimed to frighten children, deceive children and familiarize children with their hideous characters. This entices the children to accept evil as good. I believe children's movies are teaching our children sorcery and witchcraft. Harry Potter is a good example. Some movies to avoid are *Christine*, in which a 1958 Plymouth violently murders its enemies while playing vintage rock songs; *Star Wars*; *Dark Cauldrons*; *Rosemary's Baby*; *The Exorcist*; *The Lion, the Witch, and the Wardrobe*; *The Lord of the Rings* and all Harry Potter movies. Through watching movies of this sort and reading books of the same kind, children learn to accept evil, menacing demons as their friends. These spirits become their imaginary friends. My grandchildren have mentioned demons manifesting themselves to them. While my grandchildren were fearful of them, some children are quite comfortable with them and eagerly accept these evil demons as their friends. They play with them. I know from my own as well as my grandchildren's experiences that these imaginary friends are demons who are there to rob, kill and destroy the children.

Walt Disney movies are part of the devil's plan. Most of them, with the exception of a few spiritually harmless movies, are full of occult workings. It was Satan's plan to make children feel comfortable with and even love the evil presented in these movies. I will never forget my grandfather Campbell's words repeated by my dad. My dad told me, "Back in the 1940s, your grandfather told me, 'The TV is the devil's tool!' Oh, if he could see it now, what would his words be?"

Children and adults alike live in their fantasy worlds. It is a major problem. Even adults have a hard time living in the real world. For many, their fantasy worlds have become real. Their fantasies cost them their satisfaction in life and work. When I was not yet a Christian, I was out with my sister for dinner, and she started to tell me about a soap opera she watched daily. As I listened, I thought she was telling me about some juicy gossip, perhaps involving someone she knew. After 20 minutes of her talking and my listening, I realized she was telling me about *The Young and the Restless*. She was so involved in this daytime drama that it had become a fantasy world to her that was, in her mind, real. These movies and programs our children watch become real in their fantasy worlds. If they are watching sorcery and witchcraft, then that is what their fantasy worlds are all about. The fact is, there is nothing that is fantasy about demons, witches, wizards and sorcerers. They're real. "And they shall turn away their ears from the truth; and shall be turned unto fables" (2 Timothy 4:4). We are in the last days!

I firmly believe children's cartoons and movies are aimed at stealing the souls of little children. The average child spends six hours in front of the TV each day. I further believe sorcery and witchcraft are formed into their minds as they sit in front of the TV. Because of my involvement with writing this book on spiritual warfare, I have battled a great deal of hard-core demonic attacks, one of them being in the form of sleepless nights. I learned to play "O the Blood of Jesus" through the night as I slept, and I found this helped me a great deal in receiving a good night's sleep. When I wake in the morning, and throughout most of the day, I hear "O the Blood of Jesus" playing over and over again in my head. When your children are watching sorcery and witchcraft being performed for six hours every day, they are going to have witchcraft and sorcery revolving in their heads for the rest of that day. I can clearly see this with my own grandchildren. My grandson was watching *Paw Patrol* every day while I babysat him, and then at home, again he watched *Paw Patrol* on demand on TV. As a result, while he was awake, all he could talk about was *Paw Patrol*. When it came to his third birthday, he wanted all toys to do with *Paw Patrol*. Any gift he opened that was not on the theme of *Paw Patrol*, he just threw it carelessly to the side, but everything to do with *Paw Patrol* he clung to with great pleasure, even clothes. As you can see, this child was in a fantasy world of *Paw Patrol*. I keep hearing "O the Blood of Jesus" all day, my grandson thinks about *Paw Patrol* all day and a child watching Harry Potter movies spends the rest of the day thinking how to perform sorcery.

Many fairy tales and Walt Disney movies are full of occult practices. A couple would be *Mary Poppins* and *Cauldron*. Most video games encourage destruction and death. Here are the names of some games that open children to the influence of occult power, wizardry, violence, mind control and witchcraft. Take notice that these are only a few of the many games that are on the market (ask the Holy Spirit to help you discern what is bad and needs to go): all Harry Potter games, all *Monster High* games, *Thundarr-Barbarian*, *Pandemonium*, Magic 8-Balls, *Monster Mansion*, *Krull*, *Herself the Elf*, *Gremlins*, *Dragon Master*, *Mythical Cards*, *Dungeons and Dragons*, Ouija boards, *Dark Towers*, magical crystals, *Dragon Lords*, *Towers of Night*, *Forest of Doom*, *Fires of Shadar*, *Star Wars*, *Zombie and Yoda*, fantasy card games, *Hell Pits of NightFang*, *RuneQuest*, *Chivalry*, *Sorcery* and *Arduin-Grimoire*, just to mention a few.

Subliminal music can put you into a semiconscious state much like the one soul-travellers put themselves into so they can astral-project their souls out of their bodies. Soul-travellers put themselves into a hypnotic state to leave their physical bodies just as subliminal music puts the listener into a hypnotic state in order to heal the inner body. Both are playing with the occult and should not be done.

Both rock-and-roll music and subliminal music are meant to operate on the stimuli that exist below the threshold of your conscious mind. The goal is to awaken the energy centre in your brain and expand your mental awareness. Music is more powerful than drugs! New Age kids' music is made to incite rebellion and self-elevation. Rock music leads our young people into sexual perversion and violence. The danger is not only in the lyrics our children are listening to but also in the instrumental music. I have felt a sexual arousal while listening to Christian rock music. I then quickly shut off the music, and the arousal was gone just like that. In her preteen years, my daughter became involved in rock-and-roll music. She would start to play her music, and like switching a light on, her sweet, tender personality would become violent and hard core. As fast as I would shut off her music, she would once again settle back down to a calm and peaceful state. Read (Isaiah 14:11) and see how it describes Satan: "Thy pomp (ceremony and splendid display) is brought down to the grave, and the noise of thy viols (a musical instrument six-stringed and bow"). (Isaiah 14:4–21) is speaking of Lucifer's fall from heaven. (Isaiah 14:11) tells us that Lucifer was created with musical instruments embedded in his body. He thinks he's a god; therefore, he must have music because gods must have music. Since he is all about music, it only makes sense that Satan would come against the youth by using his music.

Christian rock-and-roll and secular rock-and-roll music leads young people into sexual perversion and violence because besides the words, Satan has managed to work his perversion into the actual instrumentals. Most worldly rock groups are members of the Witchcraft Church. When they play their music, they ask the witch coven of the temple to cast a spell over the song so it will become a hit and sell. The witches then cast a spell as they order the demons to do their work. This is done by witches casting spells on the music, so the music is written in witch's language by the witches themselves. If a Christian performer writes rock-and-roll music using Christian lyrics and using in the instrumentals even a tiny amount of a worldly rock tune, the song will have in it witch's language, and it will draw demons and affect Christian youth in a negative way. "The thing that hath been, it is that which shall be; and that which is done is that which shall be done: and there is no new thing under the sun" (Ecclesiastes 1:9). All things done on this earth have been done before; everything is history repeating itself. Every tune added to a new lyric has, in past history, been played before, and Satan is into music; it is a part of his being. Believe me when I say he is involved with creating the Christian rock music that our youth take great joy in listening to.

A vest came in for me to do repairs on. On this vest was the skull-and-crossbones symbol as well as a few other occult symbols. Knowing that this vest would bring evil spirits into my home, I put it out of the house and brought it in only to do its repairs. Then I took it back out until my customer came to pick it up. In the morning, as I walked into the room where this vest was waiting for its delivery, I saw, through my gift of discernment of spirits, evil spirits that resembled hundreds of maggots crawling over this garment as if they were on a dead carcass. I also saw four eight-foot demons standing around the vest, guarding it. This customer has brought me plenty of sewing over the years; therefore, I knew it was not he who'd called these spirits to guard his vest. I knew that what looked like maggots were indeed evil spirits connected to the vest. The eight-foot-tall demons were there to protect the garment so that I would not be able to destroy it by fire. I have learned through my many years of spiritual house cleaning that in a case in which an object has evil spirits connected to it, where there is a Christian, there will always be three to four large demons standing guard around the object. I watched and tested the spirits to see what action they would take. I slowly walked closer to the garment, watching the eight-foot demons' facial expressions and body language. I also watched the tiny evil spirits connected to the garment. When I took my first step, the demons moved quickly, leaping into position to protect the vest from me. Their facial expressions, however, remained calm. When I took my next two steps, the demons' facial appearances changed. I saw fierce anger in their faces, and they started to bare their teeth and growl like fearsome dogs. They resembled my first Chihuahua, Lisa, when she was at her worst. When she was angry, her chin would turn beet red, and the sight of her snarling jaws would be enough to give the bravest of hearts horrid nightmares. With my last few steps, the four demons became submissive; they no longer snarled at me or bared their teeth. They submitted themselves to me and started to back away from the vest, giving me, the Christian, the freedom to take hold of the spirit-infested vest and destroy it (Luke 10:19). On the other hand, the tiny evil spirits the vest was infested with did nothing more than continue to crawl all over the vest like maggots on a dead carcass. Of course, this vest belonged to my client, so I did not destroy it; instead, I walked away and put the results of my experiment into my book. The demons acted as bodyguards and protected the vest.

The Holy Spirit told me, "When a Christian takes charge and goes into spiritual warfare, there will always be three to four eight-foot or taller demons standing guard over the object the Christian is going to destroy. With the first step the Christian takes to close in on the object, the demons leap into position. As the Christian walks closer to the object, the demons start to bare their teeth and growl. However, when the Christian closes in and takes hold of the object, the demons grow submissive and back away, allowing the Christian to take the object and destroy it. When the Christian walks right into the war ground and takes hold of the spirit-infested object, he or she is showing no fear, and this renders the demons defeated. The Christian who shows fear has already lost the battle. The devil has defeated that Christian." As much as the spirits who infested the vest were tiny and appeared to be the less aggressive they can attack and cause bodily harm. If this person who is performing spiritual warfare is not a Christian covered in Christ blood then both the evil spirits attached to the vest and the demons who stand guard will attack this person who is performing the spiritual warfare. Note however, that these spirits will not attack a Christian.

(Acts 19:13–16) says,

> Then certain of the vagabond Jews, exorcists, took upon them to call over them which had evil spirits the name of the Lord Jesus, saying, We adjure you by Jesus whom Paul preacheth. And there were seven sons of one Sceva, a Jew, and chief of the priests, which did so. And the evil spirit answered and said, Jesus I know, and Paul I know; but who are ye? And the man in whom the evil spirits was leaped on them, and overcame them, and prevailed against them, so that they fled out of the house naked and wounded.

The seven sons of Sceva were not followers of Christ. That is why the evil spirits answered them, "Jesus I know, and Paul I know, but who are you?" And that is why the evil spirits could manifest themselves in the possessed man and attack them.

In the case of objects dedicated to demons (idols, artifacts, etc.), the only action to take is to destroy them. As I said before, if you want your freedom badly enough, then no matter the attachment you might have to a cursed object, you will destroy it.

SEVENTEEN

House Curses

Any idol brings into your home a curse. My mother-in-law had, for a long time, a little white sitting Buddha in her kitchen, on the fireplace mantel. It stayed there until my sister-in-law took it and trashed it. You might think they are cute, but the truth is, these little white Buddhas bring curses and bad spirits into your home, your body and those living in your home. If you have a Buddha in your house or car, you need to destroy it.

I have seen altars of candles and pictures set up in people's homes to honour their dead loved ones. I believe this may be spiritual idolatry, and it could bring curses to your family. You do not talk to the dead, not to your family or to your friends. You do not worship your dead loved ones. You do not build altars in memory of your dead loved ones. In the Old Testament, God told the Jewish people not to build an altar to anyone but Him. If they built an altar on the high places, they would be cursed.

All books and objects identified with anything related to Satan's kingdom will attract demons. All sinful activities on the part of the former residents will account for the house needing to be spiritually cleansed. Many people hear in their homes sounds and voices; these are poltergeists. *Poltergeist* is a German name meaning "knocking ghost" or "noisy ghost."

(Deuteronomy 7:25–26) says,

> The graven images of their gods shall ye burn with fire: thou shalt not desire the silver or gold that is on them, nor take it unto thee, lest thou be snared therin: for it is an abomination to the Lord thy God. Neither shalt thou bring an abomination into thine house, lest thou be a cursed

thing like it: but thou shalt utterly detest it, and thou shalt
utterly abhor it; for it is a cursed thing.

Demons are attracted to houses by objects and literature that pertain
to false religions, cults, the occult and spiritism. All such materials should
be burned or destroyed. Houses or buildings suspected of having demon
infestations should be cleansed by the authority of Jesus Christ's name.
Those who live in such places should stand on the provision of Jesus
Christ's blood. It is a great abomination to God to worship other gods in
any form, and this includes having them in your home.

Good luck charms, ankhs, astrological symbols and other jewellery
with hex signs will interfere with you receiving your deliverance later in
this book. Some rings, bracelets, necklaces and other jewellery given to a
person by someone in witchcraft will cause curses and bring bondage with
them. A wizard, witch or sorcerer places a spell on the object and then gives
it or sells it to his or her intended victim. I witnessed this with a friend who
bought a stuffed toy from a fortune-teller and then later had to burn the toy.

There is a reemergence of hex signs and ancient geometric and mystical
motifs, which are being incorporated into designs for clothing, handbags,
jewellery, decorative objects and china. In antique shops, you will often
find selections of rings, pendants, pins and various kinds of jewellery
that were originally designed to bring good luck and act as talismans
to chase away evil. Some of the most popular are the Egyptian ankh (a
cross with a loop at the top), which was an ancient fertility symbol. I have
seen the Egyptian ankh hung around Christian ladies' necks. This is not
some kind of a funky cross; it will place a curse on you, your family and
your home. To mention some would be the ancient witchcraft sign of the
broken cross, most popularly known as the peace symbol; the chai, which
consists of Hebrew characters spelling the word *life*; Polynesian tiki figures;
a wiggly tail called the Italian horn; protectors from the evil eye; a hand
with the index and little finger pointing up, which is a satanic witchcraft
sign meaning "I worship Satan"; and a large variety of crosses, clovers,
stars, wishbones, lucky coins, mystic medallions, horseshoes and other
items. Always ask the Holy Spirit to help you recognize and see the spirits
connected to things. A demon-infested object could be something like a
child's lock of hair that has been kept as a good luck charm. When I was a
teen, I carried in my pocket a smooth stone that I claimed gave me good

luck. There is a demonic power in religious fetishes and statues. This is also true of artifacts and artwork from Far Eastern countries.

I have seen dream catchers hanging in many Christians' homes. They're often on the dash of the car and in the kitchen and living room. Dream catchers are intended to be hung in the bedroom, near where you sleep. The circle in the centre of the dream catcher has webbing similar to a spider's web; it is intended to catch bad dreams while allowing the pleasant dreams to filter through as you sleep, so you only have pleasant dreams and not nightmares. Burn your dream catchers, for they will put a curse on you, your house and everyone living in your home. I have noticed that anyone who likes wolves will have pictures of white wolves hanging in his or her home. The white wolf was, and possibly still is, worshipped as a spirit. These are objects that must be destroyed. Don't cast the spirits out; destroy them. They are images of demonic spirit guides.

All people who have broken from Freemasonry need to denounce and renounce their vows. They need to write the lodge and ask that their names be deleted from the membership roll. It is important that all personal regalia and anything handed down in the family be destroyed. All associated clothing should be burnt, and all metal objects, including swords, should be defaced or smashed and disposed of. Some relatives are sometimes superstitious about disposing of family relics, but these things are cursed, and if they are kept, they will bring the judgment of God upon the household.

I have run into situations where demonic books, paper and cloth would not burn, or I had a dilly of a time trying to burn them. Demons might try to prevent these occult objects from being destroyed by hiding the means of destruction or preventing objects, such as paper or fabric, from catching on fire. If you cannot destroy it, then throw it into the trash.

When I first became a Christian, I often thought my newfound sisters and brothers in Christ to be a little on the eccentric side. They were so full of rules that it seemed they were taking all the fun out of it. One of the first rules I received was "Throw out all of your incense sticks." Now, I had never burnt incense, as I had associated it with smoking weed, but I thought, *What are these fanatics going to come up with next?* However, I have long since grown up measurably in the Lord. I recently attended a small Christmas bazaar at which I saw a lady selling silk scarves that were strongly scented. In my spirit, I could see a dark grey cloud over and covering her table of scarves, and the scarves were saturated in tiny evil spirits. Christians must be careful about bringing incense into their homes. Most people are oblivious to the fact that most incense sold in curio and novelty shops has been manufactured by devotees of the Hare Krishna cult. Their wares are dedicated to this demon goddess of the Hindus and can cause much trouble.

I recommend that if possible, two Christians work together in agreement, led by the Holy Spirit, to go through a dwelling place to discern demonic objects that will need to be destroyed. I have done this with just the Holy Spirit and myself as a team, but having someone agreeing in worship and prayer moving from room to room with me is welcome. "For where two or three are gathered together in my name, there am I in the midst of them" (Matthew 18:20). A three-strand rope is stronger.

If you are spiritually cleaning another person's home, then it is up to the homeowner if he or she does not want something destroyed. I often say, "You can lead a horse to water, but you can't make it drink." I have spiritually house-cleaned for people who, although they were desperate to remove the demons, did not want to part with the things giving the demons their legal right to stay. Most people, by the time they ask for help, are hair-yanking desperate enough to let go of anything as long as their problem leaves with it.

Crosses, pictures and objects can be godly or ungodly. You need discernment of spirit to spiritually clean a house. There are ungodly crosses. Always ask the Holy Spirit to give you a fresh discernment of spirits. I ask the Holy Spirit every time I do a spiritual house cleaning to open my spiritual eyes so I can see. All these things place curses on your home, on you and on everyone living in your home. Cast demons out of houses; command demons to go by these names or their association with these objects:

1. Books and objects identified with anything related to Satan's kingdom. Any books written by psychic mediums, spiritual counselors and energy healers. It's alright to have books written by Christians about these subjects, but not books written about how to practice these abominations.
2. Sinful activities of former residents who have left curses.
3. Knocking or noisy ghosts, such as poltergeists and apparitions.
4. Owl and frog images.
5. Witch masks and fetishes used by witch doctors.

6. Objects and literature pertaining to false religions, cults, the occult and spiritism.
7. Graven images of gods (demons).
8. Objects dedicated to demons (idols and artifacts).
9. Ouija boards, decks of playing cards and other occult paraphernalia.
10. Prayer to and worship of demons, which bring curses into your home.
11. Mexican sun gods; idols; incense; buddhas; hand-carved objects from Africa, Jamaica and the Orient; anything connected with astrology, horoscopes or fortune-telling; books or objects associated with witchcraft, good luck charms, cult religions, metaphysics or Christian Science; rock-and-roll records, CDs, DVDs, tapes, posters and T-shirts; and New Age music.
12. Jewellery given to a person by someone in witchcraft, hex signs, ancient geometric motifs and jewellery designed to bring good luck and act as a talisman to chase evil.
13. Egyptian ankhs, broken-cross (peace symbols), chais, Polynesian tiki (statues of gods), African jujus, Italian horns, protectors from the evil eye, hand with index and little finger pointing up, clovers, stars, wishbones, lucky coins, mystic medallions, horseshoes and religious fetishes and statues.
14. Products with cryptic curses (hidden, secret occult curses).
15. Dolls used for witchcraft and magic, puppets and cult objects or representations.
16. (Use discernment of spirits, many kids' toys, movies and games are loaded with evil spirits) objects used in the practice of occult arts; toys, movies, DVDs logos on clothing and prints on clothing; occult-related role-playing fantasy games; artifacts of Eastern religions and all other occult religions, such as statues of gods; literature and tapes on the occult and pagan religions; New Age and rock-and-roll subliminal tapes, CDs and similar items.
17. Clothing and jewellery devoted to the Hindu goddess Krishna.
18. Every time you do a spiritual house cleaning to cover all possible items ask the Holy Spirit to give you a refresh infilling of the gift of discernment of spirits.

If you have a cursed object, you become cursed by God. Remove all cursed objects from yourself and your home. Destroy them by breaking them, burning them or at least throwing them in the trash can. Do not keep the cursed silver or gold of that object. If the object belongs to someone else and you can't throw it out, then anoint it with olive oil, and cast the evil spirits out of it. Do not give the things you are throwing out to someone else. If you give a cursed object to another person, then you are placing a curse on him or her. Anoint your home with olive oil, and cast the demons out from your house and possessions. Being a seamstress and working my business in my home, I often have sewing come in that will bring evil spirits into my home. When these items come into my house, since these items are not my own but belong to someone else, once I have mended them, I store them in a safe place outside of the main house until my clients are ready to pick them up. In doing this, I keep the evil spirits connected to the garments out of my home.

You must clean your body and your house of all cursed objects. Through my own experience, I have learned that all people, including Christians, who have cursed objects in their homes are cursed and could possibly have evil spirits from these objects living in them. These spirits don't just come to live in your house or in your person; they come to torment you and your family (Deuteronomy 7:25–26).

I mentioned in my autobiography that a dear friend with good intentions gave me a child's storybook for my first born grandson. She said she'd purchased it from a Christian bookstore, so I thought no more of it. I thought the book would be perfectly safe. However, every time I walked by the bookcase the Holy Spirit would urge me to take the book out and look through it. However I just kept walking by and not touching it. Therefore, the book remained there on the shelf. At that time I had been a Christian for 10 years, and since I had accepted Christ as my Lord, my spiritual life had been much more peaceful than before my conversion to Christianity.

As a result this book sat on the bookcase for three months. Then, suddenly, all hell broke loose. It started with me not sleeping, and the spiritual rapes that had been dormant for the past 10 years started back up. Three months into not sleeping and suffering these continual rapes, somewhere between October 13 and 31, through a spiritual ritual, Satan took me as his wife. For three years, I did not sleep while I underwent cruel and filthy rapes. The spirits would throw me across the room. They would also yank objects out of my hands and throw them across the room.

I spent bundles of money on Christian counsellors, but none could help me. Only when I read *Good Morning, Holy Spirit* by Benny Hinn and started talking to the Holy Spirit did I finally get my freedom through the Holy Spirit delivering me.

In that short time of three months when the child's storybook was sitting on my bookshelf, powerful spirits left the book and entered me. It is important that you clean your home of these things that carry curses. If possible, burn them. I can't express enough how important it is that you do spiritual house cleaning. These evil spirits can leave the unclean objects they are dwelling in and enter the unsuspecting Christian. I repeat: the spirits can leap out of cursed objects and enter upright born-again saints. These spirits left that book and entered me, which resulted in my 1999 deliverance.

If you have cursed objects on your body or in your possession that you carry around or in your home, then you are cursed by God. You have invited demons and evil spirits to enter you and attack you and to attack the other people who live in your home. If you have a cursed object in your home, you are cursed. A cursed object does not just sit idly in your house. It will cause you trouble. There are demons living around and evil spirits living in every cursed object. You might feel an unusual attraction or repulsion to some object in your home, office or car. If so, it is possible you have a demonic tie to it.

Signs and Symbols

The five-pointed star has been used by witches and wizards for centuries and is called the pentacle or pentagram. With the two points up, as in the Eastern Star, it is called the sign of the goat or Satan. One point up symbolizes witchcraft. When witches and wizards want to talk with demons, they will stand within a pentagram, and the demon will appear within the six-pointed star by two triangles. The hexagram—commonly called the Star of David or the Magen David—was a magic cabalistic symbol for white magic, and the word *hex* comes from *hexagram*.

The wiggly horn called the Italian horn is also a witchcraft device. The leprechaun's staff or unicorn's horn means you trust the devil for your finances. Destroy all those pretty unicorns you have in your house. Having a unicorn might be why you, as a Christian, can't get financially ahead. Having a unicorn in your house is a way of saying, "I trust the devil for my finances instead of God." Don't wear the Italian horn on a chain around your neck. It will bring a curse unto you.

The Egyptian ankh, which is a cross with a loop on top, is a sex-goddess symbol meaning you despise virginity, believe in fertility rites and worship and serve the Egyptian sun god, Ra, which is the Egyptian name for Lucifer.

This is what the peace sign (the broken cross) symbolizes. If people who were raised in a Christian church, whether they were Christians or not, want to join witchcraft, in order to be initiated in, they will have to take a ceramic cross, turn it upside down and break the cross bars down, symbolizing their rejection of Christ crucified at Calvary and the Christian church.

The signs of the zodiac are occult symbols, as are the Mexican sun gods and Buddhas. The crescent moon and the star are the signs of an initiation into witchcraft. The use of these signs and symbols and others that are the property of Satan will for sure bring demons into your home and possibly evil spirits into yourself and others.

There is a symbol for each of these hex signs listed. Some symbols of hex signs you should remove from your person and your possession are the following:

1. Six-petal rosettes and lucky stars (these are your lucky stars).
2. The Irish shamrock hex (this represents good luck, a fast life, good fortune and fidelity).
3. Unicorns (these symbolize virtue and piet.
4. Fertility symbols.
5. Twelve-petal rosettes (these ensure that each month of the year is a joyous one).
6. The distelfink (the bird of happiness that's always near you and brings good fortune).
7. Your lucky stars (lucky stars that guide your heart).
8. Rosettes and hearts of love and romance.
9. Eight-pointed stars (star and rosette to bring abundance and goodwill).
10. Friendship symbols.
11. Tulips (these symbolize faith, hope and charity).

There are many Masonic trinkets, tokens, jewels and regalia that cause trouble for Christians. Their symbols are disguised. Baphomet is the Satanic Goat of Mendes and the best known representation of Lucifer in occultism. Caduceus is an emblem of the Supreme Deity of the Masons and represents the active power of generation and passive power of production conjoined. The inverted pentagram is used to call up the power of Satan and is one of the main symbols of witchcraft and occultism. The square and compass symbolize the human reproductive organs locked in coitus. The crescent moon and star are used by witches. The lambskin apron is an emblem of innocence and the badge of a Mason. The hexagram is a power symbol to witches, sorcerers and magicians. Christians and Jews wear it as the Star of David. If you have worn the Star of David around your neck, throw it out, repent and ask for forgiveness!

Let's look at more demonic symbols:

1. Many symbols are of demonic origin, such as the fleur-de-lis. In India and Egypt, it was a common decorative device used as a symbol of life and resurrection, the attribute of the god Horus.
2. The mobile winged horse, or Pegasus, was a symbol of Mercury or Hermes, the messenger of the gods, the god of commerce and the god of fraud and cunning.
3. Caduceus, the winged wand of Mercury, is used by doctors and the American medical profession.
4. Nike is the goddess of victory in Athens.
5. The cornucopia represents the goat mother Amalthea, who suckled the infant god in a cave. Zenus is said to have given it to her to ensure a plenteous supply of food.

God never overlooked the Hebrews' worship of Satan and his demons, and I give my word to you that God promises not to overlook ours either. To truly follow God's demands as Christians, as soon as we learn of something we have that is an abomination to God, we must remove it from our lives immediately. Then, after we have done our research and submitted it to God, we follow His directions. There is a good chance that our Christian friends might not agree with us and might criticize us. But that is their problem; don't let it be yours.

EIGHTEEN

How to Do a Spiritual House Cleaning

If possible, it is best for two believers to go on a spiritual house cleaning with Bibles in hand. This results in two or more working in agreement.

Some Things to Burn

Look for Mexican sun gods, idols, incense, Buddhas and hand-carved objects from Africa. Jamaica has held on to their black tribal occult spirituality. Look for carved objects from the Orient and Far East; Ouija boards; and anything connected with astrology, horoscopes or fortune-telling. Also search for books or objects associated with witchcraft, good luck charms or the cult religions (e.g., metaphysics and Christian Science). Look for decks of playing cards and rock-and-roll records. New Age music, tapes, DVDs and CDs are also often loaded with evil spiritual power. Ask the Holy Spirit to guide your steps and give you discernment. Search closets, cabinets, shelves and drawers; leave nothing untouched. If you were at some time involved in an occult religion, as harmless as it might have seemed, you will need to break, renounce and denounce your involvement in that religion as well as destroy all objects that pertain to that false religion.

There is power in our spoken words. Verbally renounce Satan and his power. Here are some excellent scriptures to use. Read them out loud in the house you are spiritually cleaning: (Revelation 12:11; Revelation 22:3; Colossians. 2:14–15; Galatians 3:13; Deuteronomy 21:23 and 2 Samuel 7:29).

Witches have been using the five-pointed star for centuries. As I've said, it is called the pentacle or pentagram. This is a satanic symbol used by witches and Satanists. Also, Jewish ladies wear the Star of David on chains around their necks. If you have this star in your home, then you should destroy it. The Star of David has nothing to do with Christianity. It is not King David of the Old Testament that this star is named after. This star gets its name from Magen David.

Long before Freemasonry began, all the Masonic symbols they use were ancient witchcraft signs. The rituals for witchcraft and for Masons are the same. The Masonic roots come from witchcraft. The only difference between the two is that the witch disrobes completely at the close and signs with his own blood.

The wiggly horn called the Italian horn is also a witchcraft device. The leprechaun's staff, unicorn's horn and Italian horn symbolize that you trust Satan for your finances.

As I have said, the Egyptian ankh is a sex-goddess symbol. I have seen Christian ladies and men wear the Egyptian ankh on chains around their necks. I can understand a Christian with little knowledge of the demonic symbols mistaking the Egyptian ankh for a funky cross symbol, but it is a powerful tool of the devil, and if you own one, then you must destroy it. Your problem won't go away until after you destroy this ankh and get it out of your home.

All the signs of the zodiac, Mexican sun gods and Buddhas are all occult symbols. The crescent moon and star are the signs for initiation into witchcraft. These signs and symbols are the property of Satan. Having these signs and symbols in your home and wearing them around your neck as jewellery will give the demons the legal right to remain in your home and will open the doors for evil spirits to enter you.

Cleaning House

"The graven images of their gods shall ye burn with fire: thou shalt not desire the silver or gold that is on them, nor take it unto thee, lest thou be snared therein: for it is an abomination to the Lord thy God. Neither shalt thou bring an abomination into thine house, lest thou be a cursed thing like it; but thou shalt utterly detest it, and thou shalt utterly abhor it; for it is a cursed thing" (Deuteronomy 7:25–26). It is a dreadful abomination to God to have graven images of gods in your house. As a matter of fact, one of the most detestable abominations Christians can do is worshipping other gods in the form of having idols in their homes. These graven images of gods can cause sickness in anyone living in the house. Should you have in your home these idols and artifacts, which are objects dedicated to demons, the only possible action you can take is to destroy them—if possible, by fire. Nevertheless, you must destroy them.

Here is a list of some cursed and demon-infested objects you might find in your home that will give demons the legal right to remain:

1. Books related to Satan's kingdom, including the Satanic Bible and all other false religion Bibles.
2. Some owl and frog images.
3. Witch masks and fetishes used by witch doctors.
4. All objects and literature relating to false religions, cults, the occult and spiritism.
5. Graven images of gods (demons), including Lord Vishnu and all Hindu gods; Egyptian gods; and all Buddhas.
6. Objects dedicated to demons (idols and artifacts).
7. Ouija boards and other occult paraphernalia (anything used to call upon demons or the dead).
8. Idols and images, prayer cards, amulets and scapulars.
9. Mexican sun gods; idols; incense and scented candles; Buddhas; hand-carved objects from Africa or the Orient; everything connected with astrology, horoscopes and fortune-telling (tarot cards, decks of playing cards, etc.); all cards, books and objects associated with witchcraft; good luck charms; objects of cult religions; rock-and-roll records; and New Age music, CDs and tapes.
10. Jewellery, clothing or any other objects sold or given by someone in witchcraft; hex signs; ancient geometric and mystical motifs; jewellery designed to bring good luck and act as a talisman to chase evil away.
11. The all-seeing eye, Egyptian ankh, broken cross (peace symbol) and chai; Polynesian tiki statues of gods; African jujus; Italian horns; protectors from the evil eye; hands with the index and little finger pointing up; some crosses, as the Holy Spirit guides you with discernment of spirits; four-leaf clovers; stars; wishbones; a lucky rabbit's foot; lucky coins and anything you have claimed gives you good luck; anything you have claimed gives you bad luck;

mystic medallions; horseshoes; religious fetishes and statues; and unicorns.

12. Anything with cryptic curses (hidden, secret occult curses).

13. Dolls used for witchcraft and magic (voodoo dolls, puppets, marionettes, etc.) and cult objects or representations.

14. Children's toys, dolls, books, movies and music, as the Holy Spirit gives you discernment. Remember, not all children's toys, movies, games and music is bad, ask the Holy Spirit to give you a fresh discernment of the spirits connected to these items. (Don't throw out all your kids toys.)

15. Dream catchers, mystic wolves, owls and sun gods (I was recently in an antique shop where I came across a three-foot totem pole, and looking at it from five feet away, I could see some powerful evil spirits connected to it; they would carve into the totem pole the image of the boy's personal spirit guide, which is a demon).

Here is a list of some activities that can give demons the legal right to remain in your home.

1. Sinful activities of former residents will leave curses.

2. Prayer to and worship of demons (Buddha, sun gods, tiki gods, etc.) and worship of any god outside of the Lord will put a curse on you, your family and your house. Worshipping other gods is spiritual adultery. This includes speaking to your dead loved ones and friends.

3. Fortune-telling, reading horoscopes, playing with Ouija boards and performing séances (calling on the dead) will bring evil spirits.

4. Watching any movies, TV shows or commercials and listening to music that are abominations to the Lord will brings curses. This includes New Age music and rock-and-roll records, CDs, DVDs and tapes.

Any specific areas of demonic activities or influence of which you are aware should be broken, renounced and denounced by name (Proverbs 3:33). You should also do this for any objects you don't own and cannot destroy.

The following is the five-way prayer of forgiveness:

1. Forgive your ancestors, descendants and all others. Then ask God to forgive them and bless them. Then ask God to forgive you, and you must forgive yourself for sins against your own body. You should also ask forgiveness for spiritual idolatry.
2. Break all curses and soul ties from others and to others. Break curses of psychic and occult prayers.
3. Clean out the house of cursed objects and exorcist objects.
4. Anoint the house with olive oil, and drive the demons out of the house.

Prayer

Holy Spirit, You are welcomed in this place; fill this place with Your glory and grace. In Jesus Christ's Name, Lord God, I come to you about cursed objects and demon infestation in my possessions and my home. I forgive my ancestors, descendants and all others who have had a spiritual influence over me. I forgive everyone who in past years put curses in this house. I ask you, Lord God, to forgive and bless them, especially with salvation. Please forgive me, and I forgive myself for spiritual idolatry. I forgive those who have cursed me; Lord, forgive me for cursing others and myself. I break the curses and demonic soul ties, including psychic and occult prayers. I will clean out my house of all cursed and exorcist objects. I will anoint my house with olive oil, Jesus's blood and your protective hedge of thorns, and I will, with your guidance, Holy Spirit, drive all evil spirits and demons out of my house. Dear Holy Spirit, show me the cursed objects, demon infestation and evil spirits that need to be cast out of this house. I will do this through the power of the Holy Ghost within me. And in the wonderful Name of Jesus Christ, amen!

The five steps to spiritually clean a house are as follows:

1. Say the five-way prayer of forgiveness. You forgive your ancestors, descendants and others. You ask God to forgive them and bless them. You ask God to forgive you, and you forgive yourself for your sins against your own body.
2. Break all curses and soul ties from others and to others; break curses of psychic and occult prayers.
3. Clean out the house of all cursed and exorcist objects.
4. Anoint the house with olive oil, Christ's blood and God's hedge of protection, and then drive out of the house all evil spirits and demons.
5. Never speak directly to a soul-traveller. Speak to evil spirits and demons only to command them, such as to cast them out. You don't need to say any more than "In Jesus Christ's name, I tell you, evil spirit, to leave this house." Speak loud and firmly, and show them you mean business.

How to Do a Spiritual House Cleaning

First of all, start by asking the Holy Spirit to guide you in the discernment of the spirits. When the Holy Spirit opens your eyes to bad spirits or closets and cabinets pertaining to things that are drawing bad spirits into your home, through the gift of discernment given to you through the Holy Spirit, you will see and know there is something unclean in the closet or cabinet. I will see with my spiritual eyes a dark cloud blanketed over that spot, and then I know in my spirit that there is something unclean in there.

1. You must first, before anything else, looking through your spiritual eyes, search for any items that would be drawing evil spirits into the house you are spiritually cleaning. The Holy Spirit will cause you to see everything in the room that is giving the evil spirits the legal right to enter and stay. You will be able to look at closed closet doors and know in your spirit that there is something giving legal rights to demons in that closet that needs to be removed and destroyed. When you know there is something in the closet or cabinet that needs to be destroyed, then do not hesitate; immediately look for

it and remove it from the house. Pile the items you find outside the house to destroy them. Your items could be dolls, movies, rock-and-roll music, etc. (see the previous lists). If it looks questionable yet you feel positive the Holy Spirit is guiding you to remove it, then out it goes. All satanic and witchcraft symbols, foreign gods and other occult items I previously mentioned must be burned; you cannot cast demons out of such things.

2. You then again carefully look around the room while using your spiritual discernment. If the room now in the spirit looks clean, then you can move on to the next step. If not, then again do the spiritual cleaning of items. Continue to do this until the room looks clean through your spiritual discernment.

3. After you have cleaned the room of all items giving the demons their legal right to remain, open all the closets in the room, and if you should see spirits hiding in them, then through the Holy Spirit dwelling in you, with authority and using Jesus Christ's name, command these spirits to come out. After the spirits have left the closet, then place your hands on both side frames of the closet and say, "In the name of Jesus Christ and through the power of the Spirit of God dwelling in me, I cover this lintel and these frames with the blood of my Lord, Jesus Christ, and I put a hedge of protection around this closet so that no evil spirits will be able to again enter this closet." Repeat this with all remaining closets in the room or anything else the Holy Spirit guides you to cast spirits out of. If you sense a spirit is hiding in a cabinet or some other odd place, then open it and command the spirit to come out. I have cast evil spirits out of toilet bowls, the backs of clocks and refrigerators. They will hide in the most ridiculous places to avoid being found and cast out of a house.

4. Anoint all door lintels, window lintels and window sills with olive oil. After you have done the oil, place your hands on both sides of the window frames and say, "In the name of my Lord, Jesus Christ, and through the power of the Spirit of God dwelling in me, I cover this lintel and these frames with the blood of Jesus Christ, and I put a hedge of protection around this window so that no evil spirit will be able to enter or leave through it." Repeat this with every window and door in the room, but leave one door untouched. Then place the blood of Jesus Christ over all walls, and place the

hedge of protection around all of the walls in the room. This traps the demons so that they have nowhere to go except out the door that you left untouched. You will command these spirits to leave through the door you have not covered with the blood and hedge of protection. (Note that it is important that the Holy Spirit give you clear sight of these spirits so that you can see them to command them to leave.) The blood of Jesus and the hedge of protection are in the spiritual form. You cannot see them, but they are real and do protect.

5. Follow through every room, doing the same procedure, until you come to the last room. (Note that this last room needs to have a door that leads outside the house.) As you have done in all other rooms, first search through the room for all items that could be giving demons the legal right to enter and stay. Again, anoint all windows, doors, closets and walls with olive oil, Jesus's blood and the hedge of protection. Then open the door leading outside, and command the spirits to leave the house through this door. Then anoint this door with oil, Jesus's blood and the hedge of protection. Remember that upon entering each room, before you anoint with the oil, blood and hedge of protection, you always must make sure that the room is spiritually clean and that there is nothing in the room giving the evil spirits the legal right to stay.

6. When you enter a room and see that it is spiritually clean that there is nothing giving the spirits legal rights to stay, then pronounce that the room is clean. Although the room is clean, you still need to anoint the room and drive the evil spirits out of the room.

If you have done the spiritual cleaning and the casting out of the demons but they continue to reenter the house, it could be that you have missed something that is still giving the spirits the legal right to come back in. If this is the case, you should do another spiritual search through the house, and if everything comes up clean, then it could be that the previous owner or someone in your household has done something to give demons the legal right to remain. In that case, you shall treat it as a haunted house and ask the Holy Spirit to give you the discernment to know what sin has been done that has given the demons their legal right to remain. Then walk through the house, entering every room. You are now searching for the sin that has given the spirits their legal right to remain in the house. Again, the Holy Spirit will show you in your spirit the sinful activity that gave these spirits their legal right. Once the Holy Spirit has shown you what the sin was, then you shall break the curse by renouncing and denouncing by name the demonic activity or influence the Holy Spirit has made you aware of. Say, "In the Name of my Lord, Jesus Christ, and through the power of the Holy Spirit that dwells in me, I break, renounce and denounce all legal rights you have to remain in this house. I command you, spirit of [name of the sin committed] to leave this house now." By doing this, you break the demons right to stay.

Then start over again to spiritually clean your home and casting the demons out. Note that you can follow this same method when staying in a motel. I always do a spiritual house cleaning when I stay overnight out of town. My imagination of what sinful activities might have gone on in the motel room with previous overnight guests is enough of a warning signal for me to seek out all previous sins committed and break, renounce and denounce these committed sins. By doing this, I am cancelling all evil spirits' and demons' legal rights to remain in the motel room. I plan to get a good night's sleep without any spiritual disturbance.

When you are finished casting the demons out of the house, then, if it is possible, burn all the unclean items you have removed from your home. Some items will not burn. They need to be destroyed in another way. It is important that you do not give any of these items to someone else. They must be destroyed! We discovered that we had a cast-iron all-seeing eye in our flower garden. Of course, we could not burn it, so we used a reciprocating saw to demolish it and then threw it into the garbage.

The Box

Sometimes you will come across a stubborn evil spirit that simply does not want to leave. If this happens, then place him in the box until he decides to willingly leave.

The box is the most effective tool of spiritual warfare. The demons hate it. The box is invisible but real. You might get a really stubborn demon that will not budge, and it might not talk. With this kind, you can use the box. The Holy Spirit taught me how to use this tool. You can also use the box when casting stubborn evil spirits out of people.

With a stubborn spirit, say, "*Do you want to go in the box?*" In most cases, the demon will say no.

If the spirit says no, then say, "*If you don't want to go in the box, then I command you to leave now in the name of Jesus Christ.*" Most of the time, they do leave.

If, however, the spirit won't leave, then say, "*I am going to count to ten, and then I am going to put you in the box.*" Start counting. Most of the time, they wait until you get to 10 and then go; however, if the spirit still won't leave, then say:

> "Father, in the name of Jesus Christ, I put this demon in the box. I tie that box up with iron chains and fetters. I fill that box with the blood of Jesus Christ. I ask for two angels to go into the box to read to this demon the Word of God both day and night. Demon, you will get no peace and no rest. I fill the box with the glory of God to blind you. I put a gag in your mouth so you cannot communicate with any other demons or the devil himself."

Then ask him, "*Do you like it in there?*" Most of the time, the spirits say no. Ask, "*Are you ready to leave now?*" Most of the time, they say yes, and then you command them to leave in the name of Jesus Christ.

However, sometimes you get a really tough one who in defiant says he is still not going to leave. With this kind, say, "*In the name of Jesus Christ, I shrink the box to fit like a body glove. I ask you, Lord, to boil the blood in the box.*" Then give the demon one more chance to leave the house. Ask the spirit, "*Are you now willing to go?*" If he refuses, then say, "*I am going to leave you in the box until you beg to come out.*"

If you keep your home spiritually clean, then you will know if something pertaining to demons is brought into the house. In my home, a sure sign is a sudden spiritual tension that develops (a spirit of bickering). It could be a spirit of any type of sin that enters with the unclean item. As soon as you know what has been brought into the house, you must immediately destroy the item. If you have school-aged children living at home, then you should do spiritual house cleaning more often, then do the spiritual cleaning of your house every three to six months.

This is a sample of how to spiritually clean a house:

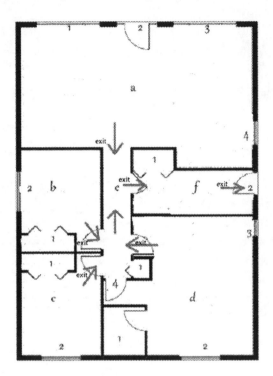

1. Enter the room (a). With spiritual discernment, look around the room for anything that makes the room unclean. Remove all unclean items by placing them outside of the house. Anoint and hedge the windows (1, 3 and 4), and anoint and hedge the door (2). Anoint and hedge all of the walls. Command spirits to enter into the hallway (e). Anoint and hedge the door that the demons left through.

2. Enter the next room (b), and with your spiritual discernment, look around the room for anything that makes the room unclean. Place all unclean items outside of the house. Then command any evil spirits to leave the closet (1). Anoint and hedge around the door of the closet (1) and anoint and hedge around the window (2). Anoint and hedge all of the walls. Command spirits to enter into the hallway (e). Anoint and hedge around the door that the demons went through.

3. In the next room (c), perform the same routine you did in the previous room (b).

4. Enter the next room (d), and with your spiritual discernment, look around the room for anything that makes the room unclean. Place all unclean items outside of the house. Then command the spirits to leave the closet (1). Anoint and hedge around the closet (1), and anoint and hedge around the windows (2 and 3). Anoint and hedge around the door (4). Then anoint and hedge around the walls. Command any demons to enter the hallway (e). Anoint and hedge around the door the demons went through.

5. Enter the hallway (e), and with your spiritual discernment, look around for anything that makes the hallway unclean. Place all unclean items outside of the house. Command spirits to leave the closet (1), anoint and hedge around the closet (1), anoint and hedge around the walls of the hallway (e) and command spirits to enter the next hallway (f). Anoint and hedge around the doorway the demons went through.

6. Enter the last hallway (f), and with your spiritual discernment, look around for anything that makes the hallway unclean. Place all unclean items outside of the house. Command demons to leave the closet (1), anoint and hedge around the closet (1), anoint and hedge all of the walls in hallway (f). Open the door leading outside and command the spirits to leave the hallway (f) through this open door leading outside of the house. Anoint and hedge around the door you have commanded the demons to leave through.

7. Be sure to destroy all unclean items; burn them with fire if possible. Do not give these unclean things to another person.

It would be good for you to check any second-hand vehicles you have, because if the former owners had occult paraphernalia or were involved in any serious bondage to sin, then evil spirits will have the legal right to linger behind, and these spirits will cause trouble to the new owners. I have often gone to car shows with my husband. Some decals I have seen are dragons, naked women, Satan and the Rolling Stones' lips-and-tongue logo. These will give demons their legal right to stay. Any vehicle that sexual sin or drug deals have been performed in will have demons attached to it. Although your car might not be as scary as the one in the movie *Christine*, still, when I think of some of the close calls I have had while driving and realize that my husband has always bought second-hand cars, I know it is a good idea to do a spiritual vehicle cleaning.

BOOK 2

Receiving Freedom

INTRODUCTION

Now that you have spiritually cleaned your house, you are ready to receive your deliverance. In order for you to receive your deliverance, your curses must be broken. Read (Deuteronomy chapters 27 to 33).

A curse is a supernatural power that inflicts harm upon a person or animal. Simply put, a curse is the opposite of a blessing. Do you have a curse on you? The answer to this is yes; all of creation is under a curse that came on all humankind through the original sin of Adam and Eve. Sin entered the earth through one man, and in this way, death came to all men because of the original sin: "Wherefore, as by one man sin entered into the world, and death by sin; and so death passed upon all men, for that all have sinned" (Romans 5:12). Spiritual and physical death is a curse.

A curse, from a biblical perspective, is anything that is undesirable and emerges from spoken or written words that wish sickness or misfortune on a person, animal or object. Whether spoken or written, a curse needs to be uttered. You cannot put a curse on someone or something by simply feeling angry or feeling hatred toward a person. A curse is a telepathic or physical play of words.

A curse cannot be placed through a dream, vision, apparition or spiritual phenomenon. The curse cannot be placed through the spiritual realm; it can only be placed through the physical and earthly realm. Wizards and witches can place a curse on you by the play of their words, by physically uttering or thinking them. God speaks curses into existence. For example, "Because thou hast hearkened unto the voice of thy wife ... Cursed is the ground for thy sake" (Genesis 3:17) and "Cursed shall be the fruit of thy body [your children], and the fruit of thy land, the increase of thy kine [cattle], and the flocks of thy sheep" (Deuteronomy 28:18).

A curse is:

1. the expression of a wish that misfortune, evil, or doom will fall on a person or group;
2. a formula or charm intended to cause misfortune;

3. the act of reciting such a formula of words mentally or verbally;
4. an evil that has been invoked upon someone;
5. a cause of evil, misfortune or trouble or
6. something that is accursed.

To utter a curse is to excommunicate; afflict with great evil; or wish calamity, injury or destruction upon. The curse is the appeal to a supernatural power for harm to come to a specific person or group of people. It is a play of words that causes harm and evil to fall upon the victim.

We receive a biblical curse when we oppose God's plans. A curse is placed on a whole nation or individual persons because they oppose God's will. Curses are on those who violate the community standards and traditions defined by God. Thus, a curse is a play of words to invoke evil against the person who violates God's written contract or will. In this book, we will take a look at the various types of curses and how to break them.

NINETEEN

God Is Boss; He Says How His Kingdom Is Run

We are made by God. We are the works of His hands (Isaiah 66:2). God is our potter, and we are his clay (Isaiah 64:8). God gives us breath and spirit (Isaiah 42:5), and in our mother's womb, He calls us by name (Isaiah 49:1). He forms us in the womb (Jeremiah 1:5). He created man upon the earth, and He mentioned our names in our mothers' wombs. We are God's workmanship, and He formed us (Ephesians 2:10). God knew, sanctified and ordained us before conception. Jesus was conceived by the Holy Spirit. John was filled with the Holy Spirit while he was in his mother's womb.

Ancestral curses are started by our ancestors committing some sin against God that is mentioned in the Bible. Our Father in heaven is a loving God; He would not curse us without warning us beforehand. One good example of this would be the curse of worshipping other gods in (Deuteronomy 5:7–9). If our ancestors worshipped other gods in this manner, as described in this passage, then they have cursed the next three to four generations of their descendants. Fact being that we have not done the same thing—we are innocent and have not committed this sin—but we still are cursed because of our ancestors having authority over us. However, it is not hopeless; God gave us a way to break these curses on ourselves and our descendants: Christ became a curse for us. "Christ hath redeemed us from the curse of the law, being made a curse for us: for it is written, cursed is everyone that hangeth on a tree" (Galatians 3:13). By Christ becoming a curse for us, He made it possible for us to break our curses.

You can be cursed by others aside from your ancestors, including those in the grip of the devil: Satan worshippers, witches, wizards, covens, fortune-tellers, tattoo artists and anyone who practices witchcraft or sorcery. This also includes those in Christianity who would speak against you, those who practice charismatic witchcraft and Christians who pray psychic prayers. A curse can also come from a family member or anyone in general who speaks a negative word into your life.

You might ask, "How can I be cursed by these people?" Adam was the first man; he is our beginning and our human father formed from dust. God, in the beginning, gave Adam dominion over the earth and everything created upon the earth. Through sin, Satan took Adam's dominion for himself. Through this act, all curses were formed against the earth and all living creatures. It is because Adam and Eve were our forefathers that these curses were handed down to all humankind: "Cursed shall be the fruit of thy body." Adam's sin produced death (Romans 5:12, 14, 15), judgment (Romans 5:16, 18) and condemnation (Romans 5:16, 18). All of these cause curses. His sin brought guilt upon all humankind. In Adam, we have therefore all sinned. However, the good news is that in (1 Corinthians 15:45), we read that Jesus Christ is the last Adam. Christ became a curse for us by hanging on the cross, and for this reason, we can now break all curses formed against ourselves, even as far back as Adam. Read (Romans 5:12–21). The fact is, both Christ's righteous actions and Adam's sinful actions affected all of mankind.

Contrary to popular Christian belief, sorcerers, wizards and witches can put spells on the average born-again believer. Christians who practise spiritual warfare on a daily routine have 40-foot glass domes around them at all times, which prevents soul-travelling witches, wizards and sorcerers from getting nearer than 20 feet to them. The glass dome is spiritual and not visible to the naked eye. It is 10 times the width of the thickest bullet-proof glass made by man. The thickest bulletproof glass is 3.5 inches thick. This makes this spiritual glass dome 35 inches thick. The Holy Spirit told me I would see this glass dome come down and form around me. As I watched it come down, I saw that it was milky in colour, resembling a cloud. Average Christians do not have this luxury; therefore, witches, wizards, sorcerers and all other soul-travellers can enter their homes and watch them or sometimes even assault them. Unfortunately, this 40-foot glass dome cannot prevent a wizard, witch or sorcerer from casting a spell on a Christian. Our curses that have not been dealt with make it possible for a spell to be placed on born-again believers. Therefore, our curses need to be broken all the way back to Adam and Eve.

There have been a few times in my Christian walk when I came to a point where I knew there was no going back. It was as if the Holy Spirit were telling me, "Girl, there's no going back; you can only go forward. Don't look back; only look forward. The past is behind you, and your future lies ahead of you, so keep going forward." It made me think of Lot's wife. Lot and his wife were told not to look back but to run as fast as they could. Lot's wife did look back, and she turned into a pillar of salt.

A good example of a time when I knew there was no going back for me was in 1999, when the Holy Spirit gave me my first deliverance. After my deliverance, I went right back into the sin that one of the spirits' names had represented. A few of the evil spirits came back in with seven more powerful than themselves, and I was in a horrid mess. Read (Matthew 12:43-44). After the Holy Spirit cast those spirits out, I knew I would never go back to my past, even the last three days. I knew I had to go forward and never again look back. It was as if my existence from only three days before had been written out of my life forevermore.

You have got to be a serious Christian to walk away from what you were only three days before and from then on live a whole new lifestyle. It was as if I had gone into protective custody and received an all-new identity. A person who only wants to follow Jesus when it is fun and easy could never go through the life-altering change I went through. I had to endure it to the end, and with this life change, I did for a time suffer persecution.

As I prepared to write this book, I studied Satan and his tactics. Every Christian should study the Enemy to recognize him and know how to battle him. He is out to destroy every one of God's children, and to stand up against him, we must know his strategy. We must study our enemy and his tactics well enough to recognize him and know how to destroy his works in us and around us.

I believe 99 percent of all Christians are living in a fantasy world where they play church. I was no different. I believe if most people were perfectly honest with themselves as well as with God, they would admit to having problems in their lives that they cannot seem to conquer even after they become Christians. Oftentimes, these people become discouraged and give up. Some even, out of defeat, walk away from the faith. One of the problems is that we have an unrealistic expectation of the Christian life and how to live it. You need to study up on the 12 disciples. They did not have it easy, and most of them left this world as martyrs. Read and consider the Bible passage (Philippians 2:12).

As I said before, the Old Testament is just as important as the New Testament. We should read and study both. In the Old Testament, God gives us information about both curses and blessings. Like it or not, God is our boss, and He has the right to say how His kingdom is run. In (Deuteronomy), the blessings and curses are explained to the children of Israel.

Wizards, witches and Satanists sometimes come into our Christian churches as part of the flock. Think of it this way: a person can be too good to be true. Not one person is perfect; only Jesus is perfect. You've likely heard these words: "He's got me under his spell." I had a romantic love spell placed on me. A wizard can put a friendship spell on you. Through casting his friendship spell on enough people in the church, he can make everyone like him, even possibly to the point of worshipping him, making himself in the eyes of the church body the most outstanding man in the congregation. They mingle in, and through putting spells on pastors and board members they become highly respected and prominent people in the congregation, oftentimes becoming elders, church secretaries and board members. Because of the spells they place on their victims, they seem charming and are some of the most liked people in the church. You could have a wizard or witch sitting next to you in church every Sunday morning and never know it.

If these people have placed a spell on you, then they have placed a curse on you. I pray warfare prayers every day for my church, my family and myself. According to the Bible, there is no one who is blameless, sinless and perfect. If we were perfect, then there would not have been a need for a Savior to die for our sins. Even listening to gossip is a sin. Christians are saved by God's grace. There has to be a reason why curses land on worldly people and Christians alike.

I felt the Holy Spirit impress upon me to break the curses in my own life so as to undo the evil spirits' legal right to remain in me. Believe me when I say you won't lose anything by breaking a curse that never existed, but you have freedom to gain by breaking a curse that does exist.

The curse of Ahab and Jezebel is traced back to the fall of man. One of the families that came out of me was the family of the Curse of Jezebel. I was surprised when the Holy Spirit called this family of evil spirits out of me, since I had always believed the husband should be the head of the household, and to my best effort, I had always tried to respect both God and Maurice on this matter. The speaker of this family of evil spirits told me the Jezebel and Ahab families were some of the oldest, dating as far back as Adam and Eve. The family of Jezebel always enters a baby girl at conception. The Ahab family always enters a baby boy at conception. These spirits have been entering babies at their conception right back to the fall of man in the Garden of Eden.

The relationship of Ahab and Jezebel provides an excellent illustration of the curse brought through a husband and a wife being out of God's divine order for the family. This curse is found in the Bible being manifested in different families, a famous one being Ahab and Jezebel's evil union. God has placed the greatest burden of this responsibility on the men. If the men were not Ahabs but instead were the priests and heads of their homes, then the women would not be the Jezebels. Face it, men: you cannot escape your responsibility by blaming all of your problems on your wives, whom God has given to you. To my shame, I preach this to myself as well. For me, allowing my husband to be the head over me is an everyday struggle. However, knowing that I have God's approval in my life makes every part of this battle worth it. I want my husband to be my leader and the head over our home. When Maurice takes authority, it gives me comfort and a sense of safety. I feel safe under my husband's shelter of authority and his spiritual strength. My husband is the spiritual leader and priest in our home.

Do you have more than the usual problems in finance, housing or family? This could be a curse of an improper family structure. I have come to learn through experience that if believers in Christ do not step up to the plate and stop this pattern of living in this curse, it will continue to follow down their generations.

The Jezebel mother will raise Jezebel daughters and Ahab sons. Ahab fathers will raise Ahab sons and Jezebel daughters. If the sons do not see their fathers as respected in his office as a father and husband, they have no other example to the contrary and will follow their dads. Likewise, in most cases, a girl will choose a husband more like dear old Dad.

When you have a Jezebel-Ahab marriage, you will have men who are not committed to God, their home and their children. They prefer to play games, pretending they are men. My dad would put on a show and act masculine to the many women he slept with, but it was apparent in our home that my dad was weak. My father's actions deceived himself, as is the case with all other Ahab men. Likewise, a woman who has taken over the financial care and total responsibility for the children is equally deceived.

These are the results of the Jezebel-Ahab relationship:

1. They set a pattern for their children to follow.
2. The children spend the rest of their adult lives trying to live normal lives.
3. Husbands are wrongly influenced by their wives.
4. Husbands let their wives do their jobs.
5. Ahab men are weak spiritually and might be evil.
6. Ahab men turn away from their families and God to achieve satisfaction with other things, such as alcohol, women and money.
7. The husbands shift their blame to their wives.
8. The women are placed in the position of priest and head of the home, which they cannot handle.
9. They open our families, churches and nation to demonic attack.

The following result from the Ahab-Jezebel rebellious influence in the world:

1. Divorce and one-parent families.
2. A bungling father and clever mother.
3. Sex with no restrictions.
4. Young people who are confused and rebellious.
5. Drugs, sex and vile music.
6. A society with emotional problems.
7. Effeminate, emotional, weak men, spiritually and physically.
8. Women's false strength being put to the test and usually failing.

Children from Ahab-Jezebel families will experience confusion, frustration, disgust and hatred, which can lead to suicide. In trying to find their place, these children will often give in to spirits that drive them to the love of power, money, praise and fame. Read (1 Kings 21:20). These children have fear, insecurity, frustration and difficulties in learning. This will lead to potential corruption, discord, growth in the occult and cults, selfishness, doubt, the inability to achieve, fake sickness, hypochondria and church splits.

The Ahab father places curses on male children; the Jezebel mother places curses on female children. Male children tend to become homosexuals; female children tend to become lesbians. Read (Romans

1:24–27). God gave them over to lustful shame; men were having sexual relations with men and women were having sexual relations with women.

Children will have broken marriages and families like their parents'. Jezebel mothers cause their children to be manipulative. The children are full of rebellion and under pressure to prove their love to their parents. These children are open to satanic attacks big-time and will usually become like their parents.

These are the Ahab characteristics. Ahab brought grief and judgment on himself and the nation. He opened the doors for idol worship to enter the nation. He did not despise murder for greed or any other purpose. Once entered into the mind of an Ahab man, he will accept more and more the acts of a depraved nature. This man loses both manhood and fatherhood. Jezebel's aim was accurate in the perspective, but her actions were against God and His plans. By not opposing Jezebel, Ahab gave his consent, and he was guilty of being an accessory to crime. Ahab broke the Tenth Commandment; he coveted a man's field.

Satan's evil desires are seen in the evil acts of men (John 8:44). Influence is what an evil spirit does to you; from the outside, he controls the inside. We need to be careful with what we allow to influence us, because the evil spirits hope is to later gain control—that is, enter you—through that influence.

Ahab married a woman who was devoted to everything God hated and forbid. This opened a breach upon Israel through which Satan gained great power and flooded Israel with evil. Even so, a man opposed to God who submits to his wife or another woman opens the floodgate for evil to pour upon his family.

Ahab's major rebellion was against God with his Baal worship. He went after other gods and idols. Worshipping idols is one of the two worst rebellions we can do against God, the other being sin of a sexual nature.

Ahab displayed the characteristics of confusion, disobedience, resentfulness, sullenness and greed. He was an accomplice to Jezebel, believed a lying spirit, refused to believe God and begat rebellious children.

Jezebel had God's prophets killed, which was rebellion against God. She exhibited hatred, retaliation and threats. She turned from the role of a woman and wife to try to upstage the king, her husband. She belittled her husband. Some women and men today use what seems to be religious motive to control others, such as prophecy—telling others what to do. Soulish prophecy is charismatic witchcraft.

Another motive behind Jezebel's rebellion was that she wanted worship and admiration. Her actions were true sorcery. Rebellious Jezebel-like men and women will ask questions aimed at causing the other person to doubt his or her worth, ability and decisions. Jezebel ended up being thrown out of a window, run over by chariots and eaten by dogs. There is no doubt in my heart that she went to hell.

Prayer

In Jesus Christ's name, through the power of Christ's blood and through the power of the Holy Spirit dwelling in me, I ask you, Father, to forgive me and forgive my ancestors for being Jezebels and Ahabs. I renounce and denounce idol worship, passivity, irresponsibility, fear, weakness, sexual impurity, pride, selfishness, witchcraft, control, criticism, jealousy, rebellion, competition, retaliation, marriage breaking, child abuse and worship of gods in my life and the lives of my ancestors. Please forgive me for idol worship, passivity, irresponsibility, fear, weakness, sexual impurity, pride, selfishness, witchcraft, control, criticism, jealousy, rebellion, competition, retaliation, marriage breaking, child abuse and worship of other gods. I ask this in the precious name of Jesus Christ, my Lord, Master and Savior. Amen!

TWENTY

The Origin of Curses

The first curse to be issued out would have been to Lucifer and the one-third of angels who were cast out of heaven (Luke 10:18 and Revelation 12:4), as they were most likely cast to the earth when it was void and without form (Genesis 1:2), possibly much like a planet in outer space. Later, the fallen angels, Satan, and the demons and evil spirits will all be thrown into the lake of fire, which is the second death (Revelation 20:14). This is for eternity. I would consider this a curse placed upon the angels who chose to rebel against God.

However, the original curse upon the earth and man dates back to (Genesis 3:1–19). In (Genesis 2:17), God warned Adam not to eat from the tree of knowledge of good and evil, as in doing so, he would certainly die. God was warning Adam that a curse of a spiritual death would occur with his disobedience of God's command concerning this tree. The death God was speaking of was the spirit within the body. "Of every tree of the garden thou mayest freely eat: But of the tree of the knowledge of good and evil, thou shalt not eat of it: for in the day that thou eatest thereof thou shalt surely die" (Genesis 2:16–17).

(Genesis 3:1–19) tells of the first curses God issued out:

> Now the serpent was more subtil than any beast of the field which the Lord God had made. And he said unto the woman, Yea, hath God said, ye shall not eat of every tree of the garden? And the woman said unto the serpent, We may eat of the fruit of the trees of the garden: But of the fruit of the tree which is in the midst of the garden, God hath said, Ye shall not eat of it, neither shall ye touch it,

lest ye die. And the serpent said unto the woman, Ye shall not surely die: For God doth know that in the day ye eat thereof, then your eyes shall be opened, and ye shall be as gods, knowing good and evil. And when the woman saw that the tree was good for food, and that it was pleasant to the eyes, and a tree to be desired to make one wise, she took of the fruit thereof, and did eat, and gave also unto her husband with her; and he did eat. And the eyes of them both were opened, and they knew that they were naked; and they sewed fig leaves together, and made themselves aprons. And they heard the voice of the Lord God walking in the garden in the cool of the day: and Adam and his wife hid themselves from the presence of the Lord God amongst the trees of the garden. And the Lord God called unto Adam, and said unto him, Where art thou? And he said, I heard thy voice in the garden, and I was afraid, because I was naked; and I hid myself. And He said, Who told thee that thou wast naked? Hast thou eaten of the tree, whereof I commanded thee that thou shouldest not eat? And the man said, The woman whom thou gavest to be with me, she gave me of the tree, and I did eat. And the Lord God said unto the woman, What is this that thou hast done? And the woman said, The serpent beguiled me, and I did eat.

The first curse to be issued out was this:

And the Lord God said unto the serpent, Because thou hast done this, thou art cursed above all cattle, and above every beast of the field; upon thy belly shalt thou go, and dust shalt thou eat all the days of thy life: And I will put enmity between thee and the woman, and between thy seed and her seed; it shall bruise thy head, and thou shalt bruise his heel. (Genesis 3:14–15)

The Bible does not go into detail on this curse pertaining to the serpent; however, I have for many years assumed this reptile might have been more like a lizard walking on all four legs, and with this curse, God performed the first amputation, removing the snake's legs, forcing the snake to crawl on his belly and eat dust.

The next curse on the snake was between him and the woman. Most men and women alike are fearful of snakes. I am sort of okay with them. I have lived my whole life in Southern Ontario. The biggest snake I ever came across was a garter snake measuring one metre in length. The only boa constrictor and rattlesnake I ever saw were kept restricted behind glass walls in a zoo. I have held snakes, and I am fascinated by their beautifully decorated bodies. I like the feel of their slithery coats. It fascinates me how they can shed their skin and how they can open their mouths wide enough to swallow their meals whole and then later digest their prey as it sits in their bellies. But I also like speaking in public, although every time I stand in front of a microphone, I break out in a cold sweat, my knees start to buckle and my heart starts to race. I feel similar when I handle a snake: my heart starts to race, I break out in a cold sweat, my knees start to buckle out from under me and I put on my best show. "See? I'm not afraid." Honestly, however, I'm afraid of snakes! When I see a garter snake in the grass, the first thing I do is start chasing the poor little critter while he tries desperately to get away from me. It is clear to see that the little snake is more afraid of me than I am of him. This fear that humans and snakes have shared between each other has followed down the generations since the fall of mankind in (Genesis 3:15), when God placed the curse between the offspring of the woman and the offspring of the snake. This is never going to change. The snake strikes the heel with his sharp fangs, and man tramples the snake's head with his foot. Thus, the snake has received his curse.

"Unto the woman he said, I will greatly multiply thy sorrow and thy conception; in sorrow thou shalt bring forth children; and thy desire shall be to thy husband, and he shall rule over thee" (Genesis 3:16). I had my children by C-section; therefore, I have little clue how much pain there is in giving birth. I understand that today's painkillers help significantly with the pain to the point of feeling nothing more than a mild pressure from the contractions; however, before the invention of these painkillers, women gave birth without any drugs at all, and the pain would have been unbelievably horrendous to bare. To add to this, their sexual desire would still draw them to their husbands' masculinity, even though they knew the unthinkable pain that would again be in store for them nine months later. Now, when it comes to the husband ruling over the wife, I know few women who are not touchy about hearing that the man rules over the woman per

(Genesis 3:16). Face it, girls: if you want God's perfect plan for your life, then your husband needs to be your spiritual leader. I have learned through the spirits cast out of me that fighting against your husband's spiritual leadership will place a curse on you, your husband, your children and your generations to come.

"Thorns also and thistles shall it bring forth to thee; and thou shalt eat the herb of the field" (Genesis 3:18). As pretty as the purple flower is that grows on the stem of the thistle, the weed itself is one heartless brute to dare take hold of with your bare hands and pull out of the ground. You only dare to grasp that weed in your hands with thick leather gloves since the entire plant is covered in relentless prickles. Then, once you have a good grip on that weed, the root is impossible to pull out. Then there is the remorseless thorn bush. As a teenager, I found nothing more refreshing to the soul than hiking through the forest. The only downside to this was the dreadful thorn bush. I only hiked once in shorts and a sleeveless shirt, and I came home looking as if a sabre-toothed tiger had mauled me, although the truth was, I had tangled myself in a thorn bush. Do I need to explain any further why the Holy Spirit taught me spiritual warfare by placing hedges of thorns around rooms to keep the demons and evil spirits out? Also, a crown of prickly thorns was pressed onto Jesus's head. When you think about it, thorns and thistles are a curse to every person who has ever gardened or hiked in the bushes.

Regarding the curse to "eat the plants of the field," how many kids and even adults do you know that like their vegetables? My husband does not like his green vegetables. My son does not like vegetables at all, and my grandkids will only eat peas. Would some call Brussels sprouts a curse? "In the sweat of thy face shalt thou eat bread" (Genesis 3:19). Imagine you are a prehistoric bachelor of that time. After an hour bent over digging up your carrots and potatoes, you come into your dwelling; your back feels as if it has been snapped in two, and you are covered in dirt from head to toe. Blood is oozing out of your flesh from the thorn bush you had to battle through to get a cup of blackberries. The sweat has caused the dirt and blood on your flesh to turn to mud, and you are not finished yet. You still need to build the fire and cook dinner. Before you can take a bite, your nodding head falls into your dinner plate, and there in a lump of potatoes, you sleep for the night. Sounds like a curse to me. To top this all off, the Lord ends by saying, "Till thou return unto the ground; for out of it wast thou taken: for dust thou art, and unto dust shalt thou return" (Genesis

3:19). Putting this into today's modern language, it would be spoken like this: "You made your bed; sleep in it!"

Just as these curses are still to this day in effect, so are all the other curses that were later issued out. All curses should be dealt with. Biblical curses come from God. He has Satan carry out the curse, and Satan can only do this through permission from God. Curses can come to us through ancestors and through people who are not our relatives. You can also place a curse on yourself. There are the biblical curses, and our sins as well as our ancestors' sins place curses on us as well. Through procreation, curses follow down the bloodline from one to the next generation (Deuteronomy 28:18).

Christians can put curses on their brothers and sisters in Christ through charismatic witchcraft—that is, by exercising control over other born-again believers. No one has the right to control people. God has given everyone free will, and God will never try to control us. For this reason, should we try to control another person, we are entering into agreement with Satan, and this is called witchcraft. A psychic prayer is any prayer that does not line up with the Holy Bible. If we pray contrary to the Word of God, then we are not praying to God but, rather, to Satan. Then Satan has the legal right before God to attach his evil spirits to the person who was prayed for as well as the person who prayed the prayer. Through psychic prayers, we curse others, and we will be cursed in return. All people have the free will to accept or reject the things of God. God has given them their free will, and you and I do not have any right to violate their freedom.

Curses take effect when we or our ancestors commit certain acts that are contrary to the Word of God. This is the action of sin, which then will bring a curse on us and our descendants. The evil spirits will then perpetuate this curse through our descendants to 3, 4 and 10 generations. They do this by entering the child while it is in its mother's womb. The child then is born with this curse, which is actually an evil spirit within the child. In the case of cancer or heart disease, the heathen world says the child has inherited the disease from his or her ancestors. However, what was indeed inherited was an evil spirit passed down through the bloodline. First time with the partner at the point of the man's full orgasm, when the two become spiritually one, the evil spirits leave the one partner and enter the other. If there is a child conceived, then the evil spirits will enter the child, thus carrying the inherited curses to the next generation. This will be true for every child the couple conceives. It was when the bloodline curses were cast out of me that I learned this.

Even heathens can recognize a curse; they just don't know where it came from or what caused it. For example, perhaps in a family, five generations of adult children have been estranged from their parents, and like in my case, there is no reason for this separation. The heathen would say, "This is a family curse." Now, the next question would be this: What is the original sin that started this generational line? As Christians, if we cannot identify the sin by name, then we need to ask the Holy Spirit what the name of this curse is so that we can break, renounce, denounce and cancel the evil spirits' legal rights. Next, we need to forgive all of our ancestors who have sinned and caused this curse. Only after this can we cast out our evil spirits, and then we and our descendants will receive the ultimate freedom from this curse.

Every one of us lives with the results of our actions. Our blessings are the result of obeying God. Curses are the result of obeying the devil—that is, disobeying God. Man had the blessings in the Garden of Eden. The curses of God began in (Genesis 3:1–19). The woman does not suffer the pain of childbearing alone; her husband suffers emotionally at that time as well. In a sense, he feels her pain. The fact that Adam disobeyed God's command by heeding to his wife cursed the ground so that it would yield thistles and thorn bushes. The woman then suffers to watch the stressful, back-breaking work of her husband. This would have started the power struggle between men and women (Ahab and Jezebel).

Once our curse is identified, then we know there is a sin in the camp. We then should deal with our own sin. In order to deal with this, we need to break, renounce, denounce and confess our sins and the sins of our ancestors, especially our parents, for bringing curses and torment into our lives and our families. After we have asked God to forgive all parties involved in the sins that brought the curse and have repented, then we have the right to break the curse in Jesus Christ's name through the power of Christ's blood and through the power of the Holy Spirit dwelling in us. I had to do all of this before I could be delivered, and as a result, I received my freedom.

Once the curse is broken, the Holy Spirit can start assisting you in casting the evil spirits out of yourself. He will reveal the spirits' names to you and assist you in calling them out by their names and families. After the evil spirits are out, it is important that the Holy Spirit fill the rooms the evil spirits have left. You can then pray for physical healing of your body and mental healing of your mind. Then you go and sin no more, lest this spirit come back in, bringing with him seven worse than himself (John

5:14). Even though this curse was brought upon you by your ancestors, you need to change your own way of acting and thinking, just as I had to with my deliverance.

If the evil spirits have the legal right to stay because of a curse, then they cannot be cast out of a person. If, by chance, they are cast out, they will reenter the person. Follow these steps to freedom from curses:

1. Identify the name of the curse and the sin that caused the curse.
2. Forgive your ancestors (in the case of ancestral curses) for their sins against you in placing the curses on your family line.
3. In Jesus Christ Name break, renounce and denounce the curse, repent of it, and pray to God to take away the right for the curse to be in your life.
4. Cast out your evil spirits. The Holy Spirit will assist you in casting out your spirits.
5. Discipline your life, and sin no more.

Once you know you have cursed objects in your house, you need to get rid of them. The cursed things you have in your home will curse you.

1. God cursed the earth when Adam and Eve fell.
2. Biblical curses apply to people—and their descendants—who have committed these sins.
3. Hex signs and all associated with these symbols are demonic. "Thou shalt not bow down thyself to them, nor serve them: for I the Lord thy God am a jealous God, visiting the iniquity of the fathers upon the children unto the third and fourth generation of them that hate me" (Exodus 20:5). Curses of idol worship extend to the fourth generation of great-grandchildren. "A bastard shall not enter into the congregation of the Lord; even to his tenth generation shall he not enter into the congregation of the Lord" (Deuteronomy 23:2). The curse of the bastard extends to the 10th generation of descendants. Per (Deuteronomy 28), blessings are for those who obey the Holy Bible, and curses are for those who do not obey the Holy Bible. All curses are the wrath of God.

Notice how a family can be cursed to the 4th and 10th generations by ancestors. There are curses on us that go back to Adam and Eve. Blessings can go from generation to generation if not broken by sin. Curses can also go from generation to generation if not broken. It is this simple: we are blessed for obeying God's Word and cursed when we disobey God's Word. God promises both blessings and curses, which will either bring down the wrath of God or bring His favour on your family. God will supply all your needs: mental, physical, spiritual and material. He can become your Savior, Baptizer, Healer, Deliverer and Prosperer. These things will only come to pass if you follow the Bible for every promise!

Ask the Holy Spirit to bring to your mind the names of curses that need to be broken. Add in the blank the family curses that come to your mind. Here is a list of possible curses to break: mistreating God's chosen people; willingly deceiving; committing adultery, harlotry or prostitution; disobeying God's Word; worshipping idols and keeping cursed objects; refusing to fight for God's house; not giving to the poor; stealing; swearing falsely by God; failing to give God the glory; robbing God of tithes; dishonouring your parents; hearkening to your wife rather than to God; making graven images; murdering secretly or for hire; being prideful; putting trust in man; doing the work of God deceitfully; rewarding evil for good; performing abortion or causing the unborn to die; having bastards; murdering indirectly; striking parents; kidnapping; cursing parents; not preventing death; sacrificing to gods; performing witchcraft; turning someone away from God; following horoscopes; rebelling against pastors; losing virginity before marriage; listening to false prophets; committing rape; not disciplining children; teaching rebellion against God; cursing rulers; refusing to warn sinners; engaging in astral travel or astral projection; defiling the Sabbath; sacrificing humans; performing séances or fortune-telling; having intercourse during menstruation; being homosexual or lesbian; being a necromancer; blaspheming the Lord's name; being carnally minded; engaging in oral and anal sex; rebelling as a child; being unproductive; being a fugitive or vagabond; having an improper family structure; destroying the family priesthood; refusing to do the Word of God; creating family disorder; failing; committing any sin worthy of death; touching God's anointed; offending God's children who trust in Christ; loving cursing; choosing that which God hates; looking to the world for help; adding to or taking away from the Bible; being stubborn and rebellious; and perverting the gospel. When we fail to hearken unto God's voice and observe all of His commandments and statutes, then all these curses will come upon us and overtake us.

Prayer for Breaking Curses

In the name of Jesus Christ and through the power of Christ's blood and the power of the Holy Spirit dwelling in me, Father, I renounce, denounce and break all curses placed on me or my descendants from speaking a wish of evil against anyone that would cause them evil, call for mischief or injury to fall upon, execrate, bring evil upon, blast, vex, harass or torment with great calamities. I break these curses in Jesus Christ's name. I break the curses back to 10 generations or even back to Adam and Eve on both sides of my family, and I destroy every legal hold and every legal ground these demons and evil spirits have to work in my life. I break the following curses: [place in names of the curses]. In the name of Jesus Christ, my Lord, amen!

Prayer Continued

Through Christ, my Lord, and through the power of Christ's blood and the power of the Holy Spirit dwelling in me, Father, I come to you. I want to bless others and be blessed by you rather than curse others and be cursed. Please make me a blessing, and take away the curse. I will get rid of all cursed objects in my possession. Father, please forgive me for anything I have done by cursing others. I ask that my descendants and other people will forgive me for anything I have done by cursing my descendants and others. I forgive my ancestors and others who have placed curses on me. Father, please forgive these people for psychic prayers, spoken curses, ancestral curses, parental curses, cursing others, charismatic witchcraft and all other curses found in the Holy Bible. I break these curses back to 10 generations or even back to Adam and Eve on both sides of my family. I destroy all legal holds and legal grounds that evil spirits have to remain in me and to work in my life. I do this in Jesus Christ's name.

TWENTY-ONE

Old Testament Curses

God's iniquity is God's curse. God is visiting His curses upon children and great-grandchildren. Read (Exodus 20:1–5); the curse of idol worship extends to the fourth generation of great-grandchildren. Read (Deuteronomy 23:2); the curse of the bastard extends to the 10th generation of your descendants. Notice that a family can be cursed to the 4th or even the 10th generation by their ancestors.

With my second deliverance in 2016, I had families of curses cast out of me that went back to Adam and Eve in the garden, that is back to the fall of man. These curses follow down every person's family line. There are no exemptions to this rule. I had the curse of the reptile: "I will put enmity between thee and the woman, and between thy seed and her seed; it shall bruise thy head, and thou shalt bruise his heel" (Genesis 3:15). I had the curse of Jezebel: "And when the woman saw that the tree was good for food and that it was pleasant to the eyes, and a tree to be desired to make one wise, she took of the fruit thereof, and did eat, and gave also unto her husband with her; and he did eat" (Genesis 3:6). Because it was Eve who first took the fruit and then offered it to Adam, she was the strong, domineering wife. Because Adam was the one who took the fruit from his persuasive wife, he was the weak, passive, easily manipulated husband—he had no backbone. You'll notice that after Eve impelled Adam to eat of the forbidden fruit, God told her, "Your husband will rule over you" (v. 16). I also had the curse of menstruation and the curse of menopause, which went back to Adam and Eve. The speakers for the curse of menstruation and the curse of menopause told the Holy Spirit and me that in the addition to the pain of childbearing, the woman would suffer discomfort with her menstrual cycle and menopause. The speakers for these four families of curses that came out of me told the Holy Spirit and me that they followed the bloodline back to the fall of man in the Garden of Eden. "Cursed shall be the fruit of thy body" (Deuteronomy 28:18)—in other words, the fruit of your womb.

As the curse of the Jezebel family was coming out, their speaker told us that this family of curses follows down the bloodline by entering every girl baby at conception, and the Ahab family curse follows down the bloodline by entering every boy at his conception. The speaker for the curse of the reptile family told us that this family follows down the bloodline by entering every boy and girl at conception. The speaker of the curse of the menopause family and the curse of menstruation family said that they enter every girl at conception, following down the bloodline. You should believe that you have evil spirits in you, as these families of curses have entered every child at conception, starting from Adam and Eve's fall from grace in the Garden of Eden in (Genesis 3). These curses will follow down every generation to come. God said to Adam, "I will curse the ground because of you." God said to the serpent, "Because you have done this, cursed are you above all livestock and all wild animals."

God called them curses. Per (Deuteronomy 28), blessings are for obeying the Bible, and curses are for disobeying the Bible. (Deuteronomy 28:1–14) gives promises of blessings. (Deuteronomy 28:15–44) gives promises of curses. You'll notice that in this passage of scripture, God said, "You shall be cursed": "Cursed shall be the fruit of thy body" (18) and "Cursed shalt thou be when thou comest in, and cursed shalt thou be when thou goest out" (19). (Deuteronomy 28:45–68) gives promises of God's wrath. You'll notice that in (v. 46), God said, "And they shall be upon thee for a sign and for a wonder, and upon thy seed (descendants) forever." You can see that these curses are following down the generations as bloodline curses. In most countries of the world, abortion has been legalized. This is the curse mentioned in (Deuteronomy 28:53–57), which follows down the bloodline. Mothers and fathers kill their unborn infants. (Deuteronomy 28:30–34) describes how the husband is plundered of all his possessions when his wife files divorce. This is the curse of divorce. (Deuteronomy 28:58–63) mentions curses of sicknesses. Fornication, adultery, incest and many sexually transmitted diseases, some of which cannot be cured, are curses. Today, on account of sexual promiscuity, there are many sexually transmitted diseases.

Blessings can go from generation to generation if not broken by sin. Curses can also go from generation to generation if not broken by prayer, repentance and deliverance followed by a disciplined life. It is simple: we are blessed for obeying the Word of God and cursed for disobeying the Word of God. Blessings and curses are promises from God. They will either bring down God's wrath or bring God's favour on your family. God will supply all of our needs: mental, physical, spiritual and material. He can become our Savior, Baptizer, Healer, Deliverer and Prosperer, but this will only happen if we follow His Bible. For every promise, there is a condition. If we do not meet the condition, we will not receive the promise.

Many Christians believe that the Old Testament curses are no longer in effect, yet strangely enough, they believe that all the Old Testament blessings are in effect. How does this make any sense? In my early years of being a child of Christ, many of my Christian brothers and sisters in Christ told me, "We are in the time of grace." This might be why many born-again believers believe that the curses of the Old Testament are no longer in effect; however, the thousands of evil spirits of curses that came out of me prove without any doubt that to this day, these curses are still in effect in our lives, and they will continue to be as long as people continue to sin and Christians don't break their curses.

You can't choose to accept the candy-coated parts of the Bible and not accept the parts of the Bible that don't make you feel good. In (Matthew 5:17–18), Jesus said He did not come to do away with or undo the law. In (Revelation 22:18–19), furthermore, Jesus said if anyone removed text from the Bible, that person would not share in the tree of life and the Holy City. To say that anything written in God's Word is no longer in effect is to say it has no value. I ask you this: Would you say such an opinion is removing curses from the Word of God? I say it is removing curses from the Word of God. In the Old Testament, God was concerned with outward actions. In the New Testament, God was concerned with our inner thoughts and emotions. The requirements of the law were not changed; rather, they were enforced. I can tell you from my own painful experience that not dealing with curses and their results will only bring confusion, calamity and grief into your life. Read (Matthew 19:17–19; Matthew 15; Mark 7 and Romans 12:14).

I never got into hard-core street drugs; therefore, I have little knowledge about them. Neither have I smoked marijuana. But I can tell you that all sin has its penalty of curses. Because of my own experience with the spirits of curses being cast out of me, I know without a doubt that if you have been addicted to or even tried street drugs one time, then you will have within you evil spirits bearing the names of the drugs you have taken. Not only that, but also, you will have their families dwelling in you as well as the curses bearing the names of the street drugs. Evil spirits like to travel in groups of families, and that is how they like to enter. They bring their relatives in, and they all take up lodging together.

As a child, I was a loner. I could not pass grade 1. I could not read a first grader's book. I was simply moved on from one grade to the next. In grade 8, I was voted least likely to succeed. In that class, we had the perfect blond. She had blue eyes, a pretty face and a great body, and to boot, she was smart. She brought in an A+ grade in all of her classes. She was amazing in every way. Of course, at the end of the year, she was voted the most likely to succeed. However, I did not know about her deep, dark secret. When grade 8 graduation was over, the summer was quickly passing, when, at the end of July, I got the shocking news that she had overdosed on street drugs, which had left her no more than a vegetable. This meant her brain was still functioning; she could think. She knew what she had done to her body. Her body was frozen in position. She could not even blink an eye, and she would never again talk. That was the way she would stay until her physical death. This smart and beautiful girl had destroyed her life and her future.

My high school sweetheart was into the drug scene. One afternoon, he proceeded to tell me of a horrifying experience he had had while mixing drugs and alcohol. He had a look of horror on his face as he told me what he had seen. He said, "I saw the devil. He walked into the room and looked right into my face as he told me, 'I have your soul. You will burn in hell.'"

I was rejected by both of my parents at conception. Then I was rejected in school. I knew nothing but alienation my whole life. Why do some people do harmful drugs, become obese, become workaholics or live in terrible fear? These are things that often have their root in rejection. I suffered rejection my whole life. There were three things I would drown my pain in. Number 1, I was a workaholic. Number 2, I was an alcoholic. One drink was never enough. Number 3, I was a glutton. I was ashamed of my poor eating habits. I would hide my eating even from my husband. When I became a Christian and altogether stopped drinking, my eating habits took a dreadful turn for the worse. My gluttony was out of control. This was all due to my self-pity in being rejected. Working oneself to death, doing harmful drugs, drinking too much alcohol and being gluttonous all have roots in rejection.

I understand that a part of what drug users enjoy is the altered mind. I have mentioned only three of the illegal street drugs. Marijuana (cannabis) alters the mental and physical faculties. Magic mushrooms affect the mind by causing hallucinations. Angel dust makes the person confused and causes hallucinations. Doing drugs alters one's mind. It is our mind that Satan is after. When your mind is in a delusional state, the door is wide open for evil spirits to enter into your mind. If you have been doing drugs or your earlier ancestors did drugs, then you have evil spirits in your mind, and you need deliverance.

Prayer

> Through Christ, my Lord, and through the power of the blood of Christ Jesus and the power of the Holy Spirit dwelling in me, Father, I come before you. I take authority over all of curses and their existence back to the 10th, 9th, 8th, 7th, 6th, 5th, 4th, 3rd, 2nd and 1st generations. I command that they be obliterated, erased, eradicated and severed, never to return to me again. I command that every part of my body affected by curses go back into perfect order as God made it. Thank you, Jesus, Father and Holy Spirit. Amen!

TWENTY-TWO

Curses of the Bastard

I was conceived through my mother being raped by an Italian hooker my dad had paid to impregnate her. As a result of this, I am a bastard, and the 10-generation curse of the bastard was in me: "A bastard shall not enter into the congregation of the Lord; even to his tenth generation shall he not enter into the congregation of the Lord" (Deuteronomy 23:2). This is a curse that falls on all children conceived out of wedlock. I can tell you this much: I have, on account of my unfortunate beginnings, suffered great misery. The first curses we receive are those placed on us by our ancestors, including our parents. "Cursed shall be the fruit of thy body" (Deuteronomy 28:18). I was innocent, and I had not committed any sin, but still, I was cursed because of what my ancestors and parents, who were in spiritual authority over me, had done. If you were born out of wedlock, then you too are innocent. You are not guilty of your parents' sins.

When a bastard is conceived, it is not out of love. It is not true love; it is lust. True love protects and provides. Most of these children will grow up not having their fathers in their lives. Whereas the mother nurtures, it is the father who encourages. The dad is just as important in a growing child's life as the mother is.

Families of spirits of lust followed me and gained their entrance into me, which has caused me to believe these spirits will do this with the children conceived of this line. I also believe that besides these spirits, all types of evil spirits follow these children and try to gain entrance. Out of the millions of evil spirits that came out of me, two-thirds were spirits of the sexual nature. Today more and more children are born out of wedlock, which I believe contributes to family and personal rebellion, sickness, suicide, inability to feel welcome or at peace in church, murder, delinquency and mental illness. I have come to believe this is on account of the babies who are conceived outside of the marriage union.

I have found through my own abuse I endured that a common example of cursing a child after it is born is rejecting the child in some way, such as a parent wanting a boy when a girl is born and then not quickly changing his or her mind. Other examples would be cursing a child in one's thoughts or words or mistreating the child mentally, physically, spiritually or materially, such as committing physical, emotional or sexual abuse.

The point is, I was conceived through rape. Of course my mother did not want me. The man who raised me and whom I called Dad would often tell me that my mother never had wanted me and had tried to murder me while I was in her womb. I always felt, as far back as I can remember, a distance between myself and my mother. After my birth, my mother gave my dad three more girls and a boy who were of his flesh; therefore, my dad treated me with contempt, often telling me that I was not pretty or smart enough to be his biological child. He would tell me, "Someone born with the Campbell blood would never be that ugly."

It is obvious to me that I was cursed in my mother's womb through the unfortunate way I was conceived and through rejection on my parents' part. My painful childhood has made it clear to me that parents can curse their children in the womb and can curse the children after they are born. My dad died at 72, and even then, he was still rejecting me; therefore, I can see clearly that parents can curse a child until the child's death. I believe an example of cursing the child in the womb is not wanting the child when it is conceived. I also believe that after the birth, the way the child is talked about or thought about places a curse on him or her. When I was pregnant with my daughter, had I wanted a boy and had a girl instead, and had I continued to hold on to this disappointment, I would have been rejecting her, which would have placed a curse on her. I can place a curse on my child in my thoughts and in my words. If I mistreat my child mentally, spiritually or emotionally, my words I say will hold a curse on my child for the rest of his or her life. For instance, if I were to say to my son, "You will never amount to anything," or "You're useless like your old man," by saying this, I have placed a curse on my child.

My life has been living proof that the curse of the bastard does in fact affect the illegitimate person's spirituality. In fact, my life has been a perfect example of how the Christian church is dreadfully affected by people who are conceived outside of wedlock. I believe that like me, many people who are conceived outside of the marriage union have a greater difficulty in going to church and participating in church services. Those who have sexual evil spirits might act religious in church to cover up their guilt about their sins, as I did. But in reality, just as I needed deliverance, they too need deliverance.

Through my spiritual battles and my deliverance, I have come to know that Satan will never leave illegitimate people and their descendants alone until they have broken their curses and repented of their sins. Only after I had renounced, denounced and broken the curses on my family line did I find my freedom. Evil spirits need to be cast out. People who are under spiritual bondage need to cancel their evil spirits' legal right and boot them out, and then they need to live according to the Bible. However, should these people or their children later sin again in this nature, then the curse will return upon them and their generation to come.

In this day and age, sex outside of marriage is no longer looked at as taboo. I remember that in my first year of high school, a girl in my class was dating a man who was in the army. Halfway into the school year, she was in a dreadful mess. Her friends gathered around her as they did their best to comfort her. She had gotten pregnant with this man's baby, and he had bailed out on her. The problem with this was that back in the 1960s, a girl who got pregnant out of wedlock was scorned as a bad girl; furthermore, these girls were put into special hostels run by Catholic nuns and were treated scornfully for their actions. After the baby was born, it would be immediately taken from the girl and adopted out. Only after the baby's birth could the girl go back home.

Today people actually praise and encourage unwed mothers for their sexual promiscuity. Social workers will go as far as to tell girls, "If you don't want to work and you want to collect money for staying home, go out and get yourself pregnant. The system will pay you for having babies." I personally knew a young girl who was told this by a social worker. The convenience of the mother's allowance checks was the beginning of this new era. With this, I personally believe that everyone in America now in this new generation is conceived with the curse of the bastard. I believe this is just another way in which Satan is going after our children. I believe we are talking about a whole generation of people participating in sexual immorality and possibly not attending church at all. Since this is a 10-generation curse, it can only get worse.

Incest is having sex with one's blood relative, such as father with daughter, brother with sister or mother with son. A bastard is a child who was conceived before his or her parents were married. Because the sin of fornication was committed before marriage, even if the parents get married after conception, the child is still illegitimate. If the child was conceived in incest, that child is also illegitimate. Through the casting out of my many evil spirits of curses, I have come to know that this illegitimate child will have the curses of both incest and the bastard. Furthermore, not only is the child conceived as illegitimate cursed, but also, the parents are cursed, and 10 generations of the parents' descendants are cursed. "Cursed shall be the fruit of thy body" (Deuteronomy 28:18). "A bastard shall not enter into the congregation of the Lord; even to his tenth generation shall he not enter into the congregation of the Lord" (Deuteronomy 23:2).

I had seven families of curses come out of me related to my being conceived illegitimately through the hooker raping my mother and my biological father being conceived through incest (his mother and father were brother and sister). Seventy-five thousand evil spirits with the name of Curse of Sexual Immorality; 100,000 evil spirits with the name of Curse of Rape; 50,000 evil spirits with the name of Curse of Sexual Abuse; 47,000 evil spirits with the name of Curse of Unloved Child; 75,000 evil spirits with the name of Curse of Incest; 25,000 evil spirits with the name of Curse of Ugliness and 45,000 evil spirits with the name of Curse of the Bastard were inside me. It is easy to see by my deliverance from these families of spirits who were cast out of me that the illegitimate child is conceived with curses. The child who has been forced into incest is cursed, and his or her descendants are cursed for 10 generations. My life is a living testimony that children who have been conceived through incest and who are bastards will never be content in any church and will possibly wander from church to church. As I did, they will possibly cause trouble in the churches they attend.

Further, there are families of evil spirits that follow in with and because of these curses. I had numerous families, with thousands of evil spirits to each family of sexual immorality and incest, all driving me into lustful debauchery. I had a degrading mind that was unclean. God has issued a three- to four-generation curse on the family line who worships other gods (Exodus 20:3–6), but God has issued a 10-generation curse on those who are conceived as bastards and practise incest (Deuteronomy 23:2). It seems to me that God is more concerned about what we do to our offspring than about our worship of other gods.

Because of my experience with my own deliverance, I am convinced that the result of this curse falls on those who conceived the bastard, on the illegitimate child and on all other children born to either of them. It also falls on all of their children conceived inside the legitimate marriage. The curse falls on 10 generations of descendants, beginning with the illegitimate child.

Because my own lifestyle was so corrupt, I have come to believe that all people who are born outside of marriage have a bad disadvantage. Through my own personal experience, I have come to believe that evil spirits of lust will follow all children of the illegitimately conceived person. Besides lust, other evil spirits, especially of a sexual nature, will follow this person and try to gain entrance. The Holy Spirit cast out of me with my second deliverance 801,400 evil spirits of a sexual nature. To top this off, I had a curse of rape on me, resulting in my experiencing spiritual rapes. I had been a victim of spiritual rape since my 23rd birthday, and I have been a victim of spiritual rape throughout most of my Christian walk with the Lord. These rapes only just recently stopped after I delivered myself from my curse of rape. I believe the curse of rape was coming down from both my mother's and my father's bloodlines. If you are a victim of spiritual rape, then it is easy to put a stop to your rapes. You just need to break, renounce and denounce the curse of rape and then cast out the spirits named Curse of Rape. You will find the prayers for your deliverance later in this book.

I believe that many babies conceived as illegitimate are not wanted by one or both of the parents. Of course my mother did not want a baby who was conceived through her being violently raped, and the hooker was in it for the money only. The only one I can assume might have wanted me at my birth would have been my dad, who paid the hooker to produce a child for him, but with the birth of his own blood children, he no longer wanted me either. On account of this, I was conceived with the curse of ugliness. This family of curses, as they came out, told the Holy Spirit and me that many children who are not wanted or loved at conception have the family of the curse of ugliness in them. I am therefore convinced that a child who was unwanted at conception could be conceived with the curse of ugliness.

As I looked back at the person I was before my spiritual deliverance, I came to understand that a child who is born illegitimately might experience rejection, and uncontrollable lust and anger, even to the point of committing unprovoked murder of people they don't know. I murdered the baby in my womb, and that child was innocent. When I first got saved, I harboured hatred, envy and jealousy. I was unsettled and irresponsible. I had a hard time sticking with a job, whether it be related to education, profession or marriage. Before I dedicated my life to Jesus, I did not trust myself; I could hear the evil spirits telling me to murder. Sometimes I felt a great urge to murder without any reason.

Because of the massive amount of evil spirits in me of a sexual nature, I often thought, even years after I had become a Christian, that some people were never meant to be married, and since I had a great urge to play around, I believed I was one of these people.

I knew there was something dreadfully wrong with me. I was helpless under the control of many negative spirits. I had a hard time keeping intimate relationships and had trouble with co-workers, sexual impurity and alcohol. Through my own personal weaknesses and sins, I came to believe that most people born outside of the marriage union have a fascination with crime, drugs, alcohol and the occult, which, as in my case, also distracts them from their success. I am grateful to the Holy Spirit for my freedom I received through my deliverances.

A co-operating chain of evil spirit families had worked together to destroy me in my family life, as I believe they do with all other illegitimately conceived people. These families of evil spirits will include families named Ahab, Jezebel, Asmodeus, Rejection, Bitterness, Rebellion, Automatic Failure, Self-Hatred and Obsessive-Compulsive Behaviour. The Holy Spirit assisted me in casting out of myself 100,000 evil spirits of the Rebellious family; 249,000 evil spirits of the Rejection family and 400,500 evil spirits of the Automatic Failure family. In total, 749,000 evil spirits of these families were cast out of me. Also, the Holy Spirit assisted me in casting out of myself the Jezebel family and the family of Bitterness.

I have mentioned that Satan's eyes looked as cold as steel, and I saw no life in them. When I was growing up and as an adult, my heart was as cold as steel; there was no life in it. What I mean is that as far as love went, I had no feelings. I could not feel love to give it or accept it. I could not feel compassion, sympathy or even empathy. My dad got injured in a car accident and spent several days in the hospital in bad condition. The family was concerned for him, but I could not feel anything—no compassion or concern. I felt nothing. I didn't even go to visit him in the hospital. I could not feel any emotional compassion, sympathy or empathy even for the man

I called Dad. Because of the rejection I had received in the womb, my heart was hardened without sensitivity of love. I believe this is what it is like for all children who were rejected in their mothers' wombs.

Only after I became a Christian could I feel love. Until I was 33 years old, I never knew what love actually felt like. When God gave me the ability to feel and give love, it was agape love that He gave me. I believe people of illegitimate birth will often not be able to give and receive love, and for this reason, they will choose for a mate someone who likewise has trouble expressing love, as I did.

I found it hard to trust people. If I made a good friend, it never failed that I would ruin everything with my sinful actions, which were mainly of a sexual nature. I couldn't keep friends. I believe it is the same with all people born illegitimately: they will find it difficult to maintain friendships, and they will develop a lot of hate and hurt relationships.

Knowing that since the 1970s, fornication has become widely accepted, and people have grown comfortably accustomed to children born out of wedlock, I have taken the liberty to check and see if there has been, in the last 40 years, a drop in church attendance. You will see in looking at the chart I have included that children born out of wedlock are certainly burdened with this 10-generation curse. The drop in church attendance is just dreadful.

The devil has this all worked out. Don't think for a moment that this rise in fornication, adultery and babies born out of wedlock is not a plan from the devil to, in these last days, do damage to the Christian church. This rise in sex outside of marriage and bastards being conceived is a hard-core attack against the church of God. Looking at this chart of church attendance, you will see a shocking drop in church attendance, which only started to occur since babies born outside of wedlock have become acceptable.

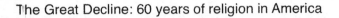

The Great Decline: 60 years of religion in America

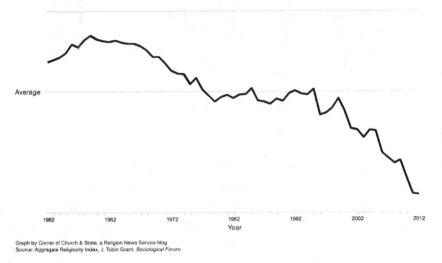

Average

| 1952 | 1962 | 1972 | 1982 | 1992 | 2002 | 2012 |

Year

Graph by Corner of Church & State, a Religion News Service blog
Source: Aggregate Religiosity Index, J. Tobin Grant. *Sociological Forum.*

The Religious Decline of 1952 to 2013

"A bastard shall not enter into the congregation of the Lord; even to his tenth generation shall he not enter into the congregation of the Lord" (Deuteronomy 23:2). It is obvious in looking at this chart that since sex outside of marriage and a rise in bastards being conceived have become the norms of the day, people's opinion of the value of religion has taken a downward drop and stayed there. I find in looking at this chart that it is obvious children born as bastards and their descendants are more likely not to attend church.

The suicide rise among teens has become only too familiar. Woodstock, Ontario, Canada, alone, a town of 37,754, had from January 2016 to July 2016, 25 high school students attempt suicide, of which five were successful in ending their lives. Rebellion is out of control. Adolescents are bringing weapons to school, and shootings have taken countless lives. It's shocking! When I attended school back in the 1960s and 1970s, outside of the bullies threatening to bop you one on the head, school was a safe place to be. The bullies did not bring loaded guns or knives to school. I was never popular; I was always bullied. Few kids liked me. I was a loner. I never had more than one friend at any given time. I was afraid of the other students and stayed clear of them, but the idea that any of these students would hold a loaded gun to my head never entered my thoughts. My present-day observation of society has shown clearly that with the acceptance of children born outside of the marriage union, child violence and suicides have taken an alarming leap.

Sexual disease is something that a promiscuous person can expect. Herpes, of which I received a divine healing, has no cure. Although it will not kill, it is embarrassing to have it spread over one's lips, when 99 percent of today's population know a cold sore is the herpes virus. AIDS, on the other hand, will kill, and as of right now, there is still no cure. These are just two of the many sexually transmitted diseases in circulation. It is my opinion that these diseases are a present-day plague attacking those who sin in a sexual manner.

When I was a youth, things greatly pressured me. I had a tendency toward perversion and violence, agitating passion, moral conflict and craving as well as covetousness. Crime fascinated me. I was excessively self-conscious. I felt ashamed when people looked at me, even when I could not understand why. I had an overblown desire to please peers and adults, a great fear of God not accepting me and no respect for myself. I could not trust God or my parents. I found myself drifting from God's moral code. I had no joy, and I was doubled-minded. I often sold myself short. If this describes you, then I have prayers later in this book that will help you find freedom. True joy comes from God. Only a pure heart can have true joy. This joy abides through thick and thin, through all of our troubles. All other joy is either partial or counterfeit. I speak this from my own experience.

Even after I became a Christian, as an adult, I had problems with the ability to love, guide and lead my children into a godly lifestyle. This was the curse of the bastard in me. I found this curse of the bastard to be a bondage that kept me as a prisoner. Each time a child is conceived outside of wedlock, whether the baby comes to birth or is aborted, through the conception of that child, 10 generations of this bondage start, and there is no way of calculating how many people will be affected by this sin.

I found that after engaging in immoral sex acts, it was difficult to give them up. Because of the families of spirits of a sexual nature dwelling in me, I found the sex drive incredibly powerful. Therefore, just as it is difficult for many people to leave their occult religions, I found it enormously hard to give up my immoral sex acts once I'd engaged in them. This was due to the spirits of a sexual nature that dwelt in me. Perhaps you can relate with what I have shared about myself. If so, I have prayers in this book that can set you free.

In order for me to receive my freedom, my repentance and forgiveness were absolutely necessary. I needed to see my sin as God sees it. For worshipping other gods, there is a three- to four-generation curse that follows; however, for conceiving a baby out of wedlock, there is a 10-generation curse that follows. A Bible generation adds up to 40 years; this curse will therefore last for 400 years if no one repeats it after the first occurrence. I had to break the curse of the bastard that was in me and then, through the aid of the Holy Spirit, call out my evil spirits. After this, I had to discipline my mind and body—in other words, sin no more.

Through Jesus becoming a curse for us, He has given us the privilege of breaking this curse as well as all other curses, obtaining our family freedom and living godly lives that will not profane God before the unsaved. We should be looking to obtain a harvest of righteousness (James 3:17–18), not a harvest of curses. Jesus, in becoming a curse for us, gave us the opportunity to break our curses. In doing this, Christ improved the Old Testament laws. Biblical curses no longer have to affect us. Jesus has given us this freedom.

Don't get me wrong: we only need to sincerely ask for the Lord's forgiveness, and we are forgiven. Our sins are forgotten as far as the east is from the west, and with this we will go to heaven. We can receive freedom from the chains that these spirits, although we are on our way to heaven, have bound us with. It is up to us to reach out and take what is ours—that is, our freedom in Christ Jesus. Christians are willing to accept a healing, knowing that it is through Christ's stripes that we are healed: "But he was wounded for our transgressions, he was bruised for our iniquities: the chastisement of our peace was upon him; and with his stripes we are healed" (Isaiah 53:5). When we become born-again saints, it is because Jesus sacrificed His life for us, making it possible for us to be forgiven of our sins and go to heaven: "For God so loved the world, that He gave His only begotten Son, that whosoever believeth in Him should not perish, but have everlasting life" (John 3:16). Is it that hard to accept the fact that through Christ becoming a curse for us by hanging on the cross, He has made it possible for us to break our curses and, in doing so, given us the ultimate freedom? "Christ hath redeemed us from the curse of the law, being made a curse for us: for it is written, cursed is everyone that hangeth on a tree: That the blessing of Abraham might come on the Gentiles through Jesus Christ;

that we might receive the promise of the Spirit through faith" (Galatians 3:13–14). The freedom from our curses has been paid for and promised to us. All we need to do is take what is ours.

Negative Consequences of Abortion

The Holy Spirit assisted me in casting out of myself the family of the curse of murder as well as the family of curse of abortion, which both had been following down my mother's family line. My mother tried to kill me while I was in her womb. She later murdered my baby brother. I then aborted my baby in my second month of pregnancy. Early in my pregnancies I could always feel a fluttering like a butterfly in my womb. The afternoon when I aborted my baby, I was alone in my mobile home. I could feel my baby fighting for it's life as he fluttered in a mad attempt to free himself from my effort to exterminate his life. Suddenly, the fluttering of the tiny child stopped, and I knew my baby was dead. There is no doubt in my mind that the fluttering I felt in the early stage of my pregnancy was the first stages of my tiny infant's movements.

Emotionally, I could not be set free from the dreaded choice I had made. Physically, I had done severe, irreversible damage to my womb. Therefore, it became clear to me that abortion affects both the physical health and the emotional health of the mother for the rest of her life. In the physical, in many cases there is long-term reproductive damage. Three to five percent of women who abort their babies are, as a result left sterile. They cannot ever again get pregnant. A woman who has an infection related to the abortion in addition to being sterile, is five to eight times more likely to have an ectopic pregnancy. An ectopic pregnancy is when the fetus develops outside of the uterus in the fallopian tube. The damage that is done to the mother's cervix during the abortion leaves 75 percent of women with a weakened cervix. This woman cannot carry a baby to full term, which means she'll continually miscarry her babies in the early stages of her wanted pregnancies as I did, or the baby will be born dreadfully premature, which will put the baby's life at risk. Also, should the mother be blessed to carry her baby to full term, a previous abortion can cause increased complications with labour while she gives birth. There is also a 58 percent greater chance that the mother could die during a later pregnancy.

For a short time after I had exterminated my baby I felt relief in knowing that the baby was no longer growing in my womb, but that feeling was short-lived. Therefore, I have come to believe that women who choose to abort their babies only experience one positive emotion—that is, relief—but in most cases, it is short-lived. It is understandable, as in my case, that a mother would feel this since her choice was to get rid of the baby, and she would have been feeling under pressure to get it over and done with, but later, the reality will set in. She will feel guilt and regret about her decision. I grew a dreadful hatred toward men; therefore, it has become my opinion that many women who abort their babies could become hateful toward men. Some might become promiscuous as I did. Emotionally, I desired to carry the baby I had aborted. It would not matter how many children I gave birth to; I would always long to carry and give birth to the baby I exterminated. Therefore, I believe a high percentage of women who, after aborting a baby, develop a deep desire to become pregnant again, and I believe for this reason, it is possible that some rush into hasty marriages.

On account of my abortion, my cervix was damaged. I could no longer carry a baby to full term. I was miscarrying my babies in the first month of pregnancy. I did finally, through a miracle, in 1977, give birth to my son, but in the sixth month of my pregnancy, I started running into difficulties in which my water bag would start springing leaks, and I spent the last three months of my pregnancy on total bed rest. My baby went full term, but it was touch-and-go all the way.

Early abortions affect menopause in a negative way. I found menopause difficult. On the emotional side, I never stopped longing for the child I had exterminated. I had an ongoing desire to be continually pregnant. I knew I would never be satisfied, no matter how many babies I gave birth to. The fact was, I was longing to carry and give birth to the baby I had killed. Later, after my two children had grown and left the nest, I bought a four-pound Chihuahua. I dressed her, fed her and cuddled her like a baby. When it comes to giving them attention, dogs are big sucks. She took it all in without any complaints. I needed her; she was the surrogate for the baby I had killed. At 13 years old, she died of cancer in my arms as I cuddled her. I took the lost as if she were my child. With my little dog's death, I lost the baby I'd aborted twice over.

It is true that the doctor and his assistant performed the abortion, but I believe the mother and anyone else who made the choice to end the pregnancy are just as guilty of this crime (James 2:10). The mother walked into the clinic and signed her John Hancock. Just as I was guilty for taking my baby's life, the mother and anyone else who wanted the baby aborted are just as guilty as the doctor who performs the murder of the unborn child. I found my freedom in repenting and asking God to forgive me. Any mother who has had a baby aborted will as well find her freedom in repenting, asking for forgiveness and forgiving the doctor, the doctor's assistant, herself, the father of the baby and any family members who pressured her to abort her baby. As I had to, she also has to renounce and denounce her sin and ask Jesus to forgive her. She also needs to forgive herself.

Can any one of us imagine the terror a baby goes through when it is murdered? I still recall the battle my unborn baby gave as I felt him fighting for his life in my womb. It is clear to me how shameful this world has become when the choice is made to murder those who are unable to do anything to defend themselves. I believe there will be a judgment for every nation that has chosen to shed innocent blood on their soil. Therefore, I believe it is important that everyone who has made this choice should repent of his or her act of murdering the innocent. I believe the one who gives consent for the abortion is just as guilty. "Cursed be he that taketh reward to slay an innocent person" (Deuteronomy 27:25). I learned through the many spirits that were cast out of me that abortion puts a curse on the mother, the doctor who performs the abortion, the doctor's assistant and the father. To murder an unborn child is an attempt to cover over other sins, and it only gets a person into more trouble than having the baby would have been.

I see it this way: if a couple does not want to have a child, then they should use birth control. This is much better than having an abortion of an unwanted baby. I also believe that single people should not be having babies. Through my deliverance from the many families of evil spirits of curses that were cast out of me, I have come to know that these innocent babies are cursed, and their descendants are cursed to the 10th generation (Deuteronomy 23:2). It is true that rape can lead to pregnancy. I was the result of rape. But rape does not give anyone the right to murder the innocent. Evil soul ties need to be broken with all partners outside of marriage, and this includes rape.

Prayer

Through Christ, my Lord, and through the power of the precious blood of Jesus Christ and the power of the Holy Spirit dwelling in me, Father, I come to you. There are curses that fall on individuals, families, races and nations for the sins of shedding innocent blood. For these curses that travel down my family line, I break, renounce, denounce and ask forgiveness for myself and those before me who have sinned against you and others by shedding innocent blood. We have greatly erred in shedding innocent blood in this nation. Lord, forgive us for this terrible sin, redeem us from all guilt and cleanse our nation. I repent of having become involved in acts that show worship and obedience to the devil and his demons. I repent, break, renounce and denounce all occult acts: worship, drugs, sex, thievery and murder. I break all evil soul ties with others I practise these acts with. You have given power over the power of the devil. I break the curse of shedding innocent blood off my family and my descendants in the name of Jesus Christ. I break all curses of idol worship, Satanism, the bastard, ugliness and illicit sex in Jesus Christ's name. You have said that if I call on the name of the Lord, I can be delivered. I call upon the name of the Lord, Jesus Christ, to set me free. I thank you, Lord Jesus, for all you have done for me. I commit my life to you in a greater way today than I have before. Please, Holy Spirit, instruct me, and help me to correct my life and bring it into subjection to Christ. I pray this in Jesus Christ's name and through the power of the Holy Spirit dwelling in me. Amen!

Prayer

In Jesus Christ's name, through the power of Christ's blood and the power of the Holy Ghost dwelling in me, I now break, renounce and denounce the curse of ugliness and the curse of the bastard in me. I confess Lord Jesus Christ as my Savior, and I renounce and denounce the kingdom of darkness and all of the works of the devil. I break, renounce and denounce all of the sins of my ancestors, back to Adam and Eve and everyone in between. I especially break, renounce and denounce all sexual sins of my ancestors and, in particular, the sins of adultery, fornication, rape and incest. If any of my ancestors committed these sins, I now declare their effects upon me null and void. If I have fathered an illegitimate child, I speak for that child and declare that the curse of ugliness and the curse of the bastard upon him or her are broken by the virtue of the power of Christ's blood and the authority in His name, and I do this through the power of the Holy Spirit dwelling in me. The curse of ugliness and the curse of the bastard are broken, renounced and denounced in perpetuity. This declaration is binding upon all demonic forces that have hitherto exercised any influence because of these curses. Every effect of the curse of the bastard is now broken, including all hindrances to worship, prayer, acts of charity, reading of God's Word, church attendance and any act of fellowship and Christian communion. I declare all the aforementioned are legal and binding on earth and in heaven. I and any illegitimate offspring of my own are free from the curse of the bastard and henceforth have every right to enter fully into a personal relationship with God and enjoy the full benefits of corporate worship, including receiving the body and blood of our Lord, Jesus Christ, through communion. The courts of heaven, the regions of hell and the agreement of my Christian brothers and sisters are all witness to this declaration and agreement in the name of the Father, the Son and the Holy Spirit that dwells in me. Amen!

In closing, here's some food for thought: Could the spirits grabbing my hand when I was worshipping in the church have been the evil spirits clinging to their legal right since I was a bastard freely worshipping Christ Jesus in the church? Interestingly, after my deliverance, this grabbing and holding of my hand never again occurred. Freedom is a wonderful thing!

TWENTY-THREE

National and Minority Group Curses

National and Minority Sins

Through my intense study and the devastating and extreme spiritual attacks I have had to struggle through, and because of my bloodline family sins, I have no doubt that curses come from our forefathers worshipping idols in the worship services and rites their tribes practised. These curses come from worshipping other gods and practising in the occult (Exodus 20:1–6). You will see that there is a great deal of demonic spirituality in the faith of these cults, and these curses need to be broken. Many nations were and still are demon worshippers. Therefore, we should become aware of the demonic activities rooted in our own national heritage.

Worldwide, many worship man-made gods. Every born-again saint of Christ needs to, in order to receive spiritual freedom from demonic influence, become aware of his or her ancestors' heritage of demon worship and then respond by doing everything needed to break the evil spirits' legal right to remain. Ask the Holy Spirit for discernment in this area of your life.

Many nations had and still have shamans. The term *shaman* has its origins in Siberia, and it is often used by anthropologists throughout the world to refer to Aboriginal healers. The shaman is the spiritual leader of each tribe. He is able to interpret the cause of a sickness or lack of hunting success. He can determine the individual or family responsible and isolate the broken taboo. He enters into a trance with the aid of drum beating and chanting. This allows his soul to leave his body, and he can soul-travel great distances to determine the causes of one's sickness and other community problems. The evil spirits are encouraged to occupy the shaman's body during public lodge ceremonies. Drum beating and chanting also aid this process. The spirits are then asked to depart from the shaman and perform the needed acts.

Many nations had people who were known as wise men. They were highly respected elders who were the ritual leaders of the masked ceremonies. As bearers of the cosmological truths, they were capable of communicating with the most powerful spirits as well as with the spirits of the animals. They were respected as more important than the shamans, and they were superior to the shamans.

In hunting ceremonies, many nations have been involved in the ritual of wearing a variety of amulets and charms believed to provide special powers from the animal spirits to enhance success in hunting.

Many cultures and nations used, and possibly still do, wooden masks in some ceremonial dances to conjure up powerful spirits. Dances to appease the evil spirits were a part of their ceremonies. An important practice was the bringing out of the elaborate masks that contained the spirit who was honoured by such representation. Masks representing animals and other spirits were an important part of the religious ceremony and dances. Soul-travel possibly was often part of this ceremony. Among many nations, boy babies were preferred over baby girls; therefore, girl babies were killed.

God is ready to forgive, endow with splendour, open doors to nations and make covenants and divine appointments for us. We are called to be warriors involved in spiritual warfare, frontiersmen, watchmen and trustworthy soldiers of the cross of Christ. We need to take whatever culture we have come from to the cross. We must act, proclaim, pray and cleanse our property of demonic spirits. Exercise prophetic proclamation, intercession, service, humility, repentance and gatekeeping. Listen, look and call on God.

Prayer

I forgive my ancestors and descendants. I ask you, Lord, to forgive me, and I forgive myself for sins that bring these curses on me: exotic and old diseases, new viruses, AIDS, Ebola and *E. coli*; killer bees, ants, locusts, mosquitoes, deer ticks and flies bringing devastation and disease; sin, trespass, disobedience and iniquity; cover-ups and secret and treacherous actions; moral, social, spiritual and land hardship; reverse-prejudice racism, division, rebellion and loneliness; pain, terror and defilement; attack of earthly leaders and demonic powers; anger, frustration, resentment, bitterness, revenge and pride; disease, domestic violence, hatred and broken relationships; and alcoholism and financial and substance abuse.

Prayer Continued (Religious)

I ask you, Lord, to forgive me, and I forgive myself for sins that bring these curses on me: religions and gods created by tribes and nations; mystical spiritism bound to carnal ceremony; a pseudo-apostolic spirit counterfeiting a true apostolic spirit; spiritual pacts, ceremonial altars and high places for worship; dances to worship demons, people, animals and objects; pagan rituals and non-Christian religions; native ceremonies cleansing the soul from sin; ceremonial laws bridging sin's barrier; folk Islam; and worship and fear of gods, deities, personalities and abstractions known and unknown.

Prayer Continued (Idolatry)

I ask you, Lord, to forgive me, and I forgive myself for sins that bring these curses on me: traditions involving icons and religious idolatry; tribal perversion of truth and idolatry; and ancient and New Age idolatry.

Prayer Continued (Curses)

I ask you, Lord, to forgive me, and I forgive myself for sins that bring these curses on me: generational curses of ethnic cleansing; root bondages; and superstition.

Prayer Continued (Shamanism)

I ask you, Lord, to forgive me, and I forgive myself for sins that bring these curses on me: shamanism, animism and totemism; shamanistic spirit; religious spirit; and false godhead.

Prayer Continued (Sexual Sins)

I ask you, Lord, to forgive me, and I forgive myself for sins that bring these curses on me: immorality, fornication, adultery, rape, incest, bestiality, homosexuality, pornography, perversion and prostitution.

Prayer Continued (Bloodshed)

I ask you, Lord, to forgive me, and I forgive myself for sins that bring these curses on me: unjust warfare, murder, suicide, infanticide, abortion, accidental deaths by bloodshed and ancient bloodshed defilement.

Prayer Continued (Sacred)

I ask you, Lord, to forgive me, and I forgive myself for sins that bring these curses on me: sacred objects, sites, valleys, caves, rivers, petroglyphs, mountains and ritual sites; worship of carved objects, totem poles, Buddhas and all other gods worshipped socially and nationally; and power, position and wealth.

Prayer Continued (Christian Services)

I ask you, Lord, to forgive me, and I forgive myself for sins that bring these curses on me: bongo drums used in Christian services; Christian syncretism of combining native religious beliefs, superstition, taboo, legalism and cults with historical Christian faith; cultural forms borrowed from pagan cultures used in Christian churches;

barriers to true Christian unity; spiritual warfare not taken seriously; and historical ties to the spirit world. (Note: Bongo drums summon evil spirits, are used in voodoo and should not be played in Christian church services.)

Prayer Continued (Attacks on Christianity)

I ask you, Lord, to forgive me, and I forgive myself for sins that bring these curses on me: public mockery of Christianity, physical persecution of Christians, militant secularism, philosophies and social groups, homosexuals, radical feminists, witches, shamans and ungodly alliances.

Prayer Continued (Ancient)

I ask you, Lord, to forgive me, and I forgive myself for sins that bring these curses on me: sins of ancestors; ancient cannibals; ancient and contemporary defilements; ancestral patterns of unforgiveness; addiction; lying; and ancient spiritual pacts and practices.

Prayer Continued (Slavery)

I ask you, Lord, to forgive me, and I forgive myself for sins that bring these curses on me: slavery and indentured service and broken agreements, treaties, contracts and covens.

Prayer Continued (Spirits)

I ask you, Lord, to forgive me, and I forgive myself for sins that bring these curses on me: evil, unclean indwelling and clinging spirits; spirits worshipped and consulted; drums used to conjure up evil spirits; and human voices and animal sounds coming from the drum.

Prayer Continued (Ungodly Spiritual Practices)

I ask you, Lord, to forgive me, and I forgive myself for sins that bring these curses on me: spiritual practices of liturgical use of mind-altering substances; blood sacrifices; participation in sexual immorality; physical torture; self-abuse; opposition to sound biblical doctrine; and sinful activities, attitudes, behaviours and practices.

Prayer Continued (Spiritual Mapping)

I ask you, Lord, to forgive me, and I forgive myself for sins that bring these curses on me: alcohol and drug abuse, designer drugs, injustice, poverty, discrimination and disease; divorce and spousal and child abuse; corruption and partisanship; layoffs; budget deficits; behavioural problems and low test scores; vices and legalized gambling; nature worship, spiritual darkness and militancy of sinners; dead influential human figures; spiritual and philosophical gurus; pornography, adult bookstores and clubs, phone sex and cybersex, child pornography, casual sex, homosexuality, abortion, teen sex, alternative lifestyles, AIDS, nightclubs and dance halls and movie theatres; Islam, Mormonism, Judaism, Buddhism, New Age movements, humanism, rationalism, materialism, pseudo-Christian cults, Jewish mystical kabbalah, African and Caribbean religions, voodoo and Santeria; secret societies, Masonic lodges, witchcraft covens, Christo-pagan celebrations, New Age meditation retreats and Native American vision quests; strongholds of idolatry, Hindu temples, ancestral sites, ambiguous centres of idolatry, territorial and regional deities, occultism, spiritual bondages and opposition spiritual stronghold backlash; inexplicable illnesses, financial reversals, accidents, depressions and haunted sites; traumas, pacts with spirits and deities, discernible designs and symbols, Freemasons and curses; invasions, natural disasters, migrations, alternative religions and influences, demonic master plans, famine and technological discontinuity. I pray this prayer and take authority over the kingdom of evil in the name of my Lord, Jesus Christ. I break all curses. Amen!

Place the names of organizations and nationalities in the spaces provided below. For instance, I am Italian and English; therefore, I would say, "I ask forgiveness for having Italian and English gods and artifacts in my home."

In Jesus Christ's Name and through the power of the Holy Spirit that dwells in me and the power of Christ's blood, I break, renounce, denounce and ask forgiveness for my ancestors' sins and for my sins involving [name of organization or nation] spiritual witchcraft. I ask forgiveness for having [name of nationality] gods and artifacts in my home. I forgive my ancestors for witchcraft against me and my relatives; for deeply hidden seething anger, bitterness, resentment and hatred of people of different nationalities; for cursing the land and the people; for eating and drinking flesh and blood; and for worshipping demons. I forgive the war women for their Jezebel-like matriarchal rule of the tribe. I forgive the witch doctors and shamans for cursing the descendants, dedicating them to Satan and causing physical problems and diseases. I forgive my ancestors. I ask forgiveness for myself for the sin of idol worship and disobedience as described in (Exodus 20); (Leviticus 26) and (Ezekiel 18). I ask you, Father, to forgive me for any sins associated with [name of organization and nation]. I will destroy all artifacts and man-made gods, and I will break, renounce and denounce all ungodly soul ties and break all ties I have with [name of organizations or nations]. I break, renounce and denounce the curses of incest, rape, immorality and the bastard. I break spiritual roots to any diseases brought about by curses. I break, renounce and denounce the [name of organization or nationality] curses that are on me and my descendants. I do this in the name of Jesus

Christ and through the power of the Holy Spirit dwelling within me. Thank you, Jesus, Father and Holy Spirit.

I forgive my ancestors, descendants and all others. I ask you to forgive me, and I forgive myself for worshipping traditions and idols; alcohol and drug abuse; rape; sexual abuse and perversion; murder; self-bitterness and hatred; the occult; [name of nation] and religions that suppress religious and cultural practices; dependence on welfare; reversal of gender roles; multiple spouses; false religions and demonic beliefs, ceremonies, dances and rituals; demonic paraphernalia, including talismans, amulets, charms, spirit poles, totem poles, objects of adornment and tattoos; sins of [name of nation]'s natives; mistreatment of my ancestors; those who brought alcoholism, drug addiction, heart disease, diabetes, fetal alcohol syndrome, serious abuse of both women and children, incarceration and suicide upon my people; warlike behaviour, slavery, barbarism, torture and cruelty; obedience to shamans and wise men; worship and following of demons; tribes, clans and groups with demonic beliefs; preferential female infanticide; myths and legends; transvestites, adultery, wife swapping and incest; seeking help from evil spirits; worship of animals and their spirits; reincarnation and ancestor worship; guardian spirits; seeking forbidden knowledge; demonic healing and divination; worship of nature and earth; transformation of people into animals and animals into people; fears of death and shamans; mistreatment and killing of slaves; cutting of the flesh; the use of human fat and mummies; magic and witchcraft; superstition and taboos; and insanity, severe sickness, early death and all diseases of [name of nation]. I do this in Jesus Christ's name through the power of Christ's blood and the power of the Holy Ghost living in me. Amen!

National and Minority Curses

Although my skin is ivory in colour, I see myself as transparent. Perhaps that is why it comes so naturally for me to speak openly and honestly about myself. As a child, I never fit in, not in my family or any other family. Growing up, I had three sisters and a baby brother, but I felt alone, as if I did not belong. I felt that to my mother, I was a burden that carried her memory of rape, and to my dad, I was the oddball, the child who was not of his flesh and blood. They had their favourite children. Cathy was Dad's favourite. Mom favoured Tammy and Sherry. Ricky died young. Then there was me.

I am not racist. Do I fit into a minority group? No, not really. Growing up, I did not feel love from my parents or, to a great degree, my siblings or from outsiders. I knew that my blood father's family were Italian, yet I would never meet or know them. This left me thinking, *Who am I? What am I? I don't belong—not here and not anywhere.* When I went to Chicago in my early teens and had a black family love me, I came home thinking, *My colour is transparent. I am not of the white race; I am not of the black race.* God's workmanship of the human race comes in the colours red, brown, yellow, black and white, but I have never felt like I fit into any of these categories. My skin is transparent.

It is my deepest desire that every one of God's children find the freedom I have found in Christ. No matter the colour of your skin, I love you! I am not red, brown, yellow, black or white. I am a saint in Christ Jesus, and you are a saint as well.

Placing a national, racial or minority group curse will affect many people, possibly, in some cases, up to millions of humans under the same curse. In this case, these will be spoken curses, which are often given through hate speeches. However, like any other curse, they can be broken.

A hate speech can be a play of words that attacks and places curses on ancestral races. Unfortunately, there is not enough room in any book to cover all of the curses that have followed down through ancestral sins, societal sins and hate speeches. It is my opinion that every nation and minority group worldwide will have national curses that follow down their people's bloodlines. It is also my opinion that in order to receive one's compete deliverance, a person must break the evil spirits' legal right to remain.

A gentleman once asked me, when I was placing various curses into this book, why I was only covering some curses and not all national curses spoken as hate speeches against groups of people. This particular man was sincerely concerned for his own nationwide curses that would need to be broken in order for people of his nationality to receive deliverance. I told him, "I could never place every nation of the earth into one book to cover every curse that lingers over the vast human race at large."

You will need to read up on the possible curses caused by historical hate speeches that have possibly been spoken against your nationality. For example, Adolf Hitler was a notorious World War II leader who murdered Jews, blacks and others in gas chambers. Willie Lynch was a heartless slave owner who wrote a book as well as a hate speech teaching slave owners how to mistreat their slaves. The hateful words they spoke in their speeches would have placed curses on whole nations at large. You can read more about these two topics on the Internet at https://enwikipedia. org/wiki/The_Holocaust   and   https://blog.archive.org/2016/10/23/ defining-web-pages-web-sites-and-web-captures/.

Remember, a curse is placed by speaking something negative about a person or a group of people. Willie Lynch was speaking negative words about a minority of people. In doing this, he was placing a curse.

Through our ancestral descendants' sins, they placed biblical curses on their grandchildren to the 3rd, 4th and 10th generations. When I was breaking my curses, because my blood father was Italian and my mother was English, I had to study Italian and British history for possible hate speeches that could have been spoken against the nation at large or people groups and possible sins that could be following down through my bloodline.

I highly suggest that no matter your nationality, you search and study all possible hate speeches that might have been spoken against your ancestral genealogical history. Leave no stone unturned. Even if you question the possibilities, still break the curse that might be following down your family line. For instance, if a person has two or more mixed races in his or her family line, then this person would need to study the nationalities of the many mixed races and break all of the curses he or she discovers. Search for possible hate speeches that could be giving demons the legal right to remain. Search also for possible nationwide sins that could be giving demons their legal right to remain. As I did, when you have discovered them, then break, renounce and denounce the evil spirits' legal rights and boot them out.

As I have repeatedly said, a curse can be verbally spoken. Spoken curses will follow down four generations. It takes few words to place a curse on an individual. Just a short play of words in a speech would be enough. It could be a person speaking negative words or speaking a curse against his or her enemy, which could be a minority group. This curse must be broken.

Our answer to powerful street drugs, such as crack cocaine; alcohol; unwed teenage mothers; and crimes, such as murder, is Jesus Christ made a curse for us (Galatians 3:13). Through Him, we must break the curses of our forefathers nationwide. The result of disobedience is death. God's rewards for our sin are iniquities, perversions and, for those who walk contrary to His Word, both natural and spiritual death (Romans 6:23).

Because of spoken curses against nations and minority groups, vast amounts of people are, instead of receiving blessings, receiving vexations that result in calamities overtaking them. It is from my own experience that I say this. I had to break my own curses. I found out about a curse placed on women to cause them to be unsuccessful or failures in their ministry and businesses. This curse would be against women as a minority group. I then broke that curse. I would like to add that breaking this curse has improved my outlook on myself, giving me more self-confidence. As a result, I have also seen a large improvement in my goals, with greater achievements. Did you know that if you are a woman, you are part of the female minority group, and if you are a man, you are a part of the male minority group?

If you feel that as a woman, your life achievements could be more rewarding, then pray this prayer, and then ask the Holy Spirit to assist you in casting out your evil spirits:

> Father, in Jesus Christ's name, through the power of Christ's blood and the power of the Holy Spirit dwelling in me, I break, renounce and denounce the power of the words spoken against me as a woman by men or anyone else that have caused me to be unsuccessful or a failure in my business, workplace, home and ministry. I ask you, Holy Spirit, to assist me in casting out my evil spirits. Thank you, Jesus, Holy Spirit and Father. Amen!

Blessings and curses rest upon families, communities and even entire nations worldwide. These curses provide for Satan a stronghold. If you are part of a minority group that has been under verbal attack, then I advise you to break all possible verbal curses that might have been spoken against you as a part of your minority group.

In the prayer below, place the name of the curses in the space provided. Ask the Holy Spirit to bring to your mind the names of the curses that need to be broken. If nothing comes to your mind, just the same, pray this prayer.

Prayer for Forgiveness

Father, in Jesus Christ's Name, I now confess that I have not loved but have resented certain people and groups who have hurt or disappointed me. I have unforgiveness in my heart. I call upon you, Father, to help me forgive. In the name of Jesus, I do now forgive [names, groups, institutions, etc., that the Holy Spirit brings to your mind]. Father, in the name of Jesus Christ, I also forgive myself. I claim and receive your forgiveness because I am your child. Amen!

Dear Father, I forgive people of all nationalities, races, colours and minorities for the way they have treated me and spoken against me. Forgive me for the way I have treated them and spoken against them. I ask you, Lord, to forgive them for how they have treated me and spoken against me. In Jesus Christ's name, I pray this. Amen!

In Jesus Christ's name and through the power of the Holy Spirit dwelling in me, Lord God, I forgive [name of hate speakers] and all others for the hateful words [name of curses] they have spoken against my ancestors and the bondage their words have placed my ancestors and their descendants, including myself, in. I forgive all who mistreat me as a minority or race, and I pray that you will forgive and bless them with spiritual blessings, good health and, especially, salvation. In Jesus Christ's name, I now renounce, denounce and break all curses spoken against me and my descendants as a minority group or as a nation. I release myself and my descendants from all of the negative words that have been spoken against us as a minority or nation. I command the demons to restore to me and my family everything they have stolen from us. I command this in Jesus Christ's name and through the power of the sweet Holy Spirit dwelling in me. I now ask you, Holy Spirit, to line up these spirits and help me in casting them out of myself by their family names and ranks. I thank you, Holy Spirit, Jesus and heavenly Father. Amen!

Prayer for Breaking the PTSD (Post-Traumatic Stress Disorder) Curse

Heavenly Father, in the name of Jesus Christ, I am truly your child. I have been purchased by the blood of Christ. I belong to you; I do not belong to the devil. The devil has no right to me and no power over me because of the precious Blood of Jesus. Father, you have known my sins. I confess them all. I repent of all of them now. I ask you to forgive me. Forgive me of every sin, and remove the stains from my heart and from my life, for your Word tells me that when I confess my sins, you will forgive me and will cleanse me of all unrighteousness. I confess the sins committed by my parents, grandparents and great-grandparents, which introduced curses into my family. I confess those sins to you that the power of the curse might be broken through the shed blood of Jesus—blood that was also shed for me. In the name of Jesus Christ, I now rebuke, break and loose myself and my family from my own sins and the sins of my ancestors or any other person. I am redeemed from the curse of the law. I break, renounce and denounce the power of every spoken curse and of every evil that came out of my mouth. I take back all of the ground I ever yielded to the devil and establish my faith in the Lord, Jesus Christ. I claim the blessing rather than the curse. I break, renounce and denounce the power of every evil word knowingly or unknowingly spoken against me by any person, cult or group. I cancel that spoken word, and I cancel the power of the curse in the authority of the Name of Jesus Christ. I believe in your power through the Holy Spirit, Lord Jesus. I believe in your redemption for me. I believe in my heart that you are my Savior and my Deliverer. I confess to you with my mouth, and I confess that the power of every curse is now broken in the authority of your Name. I command every evil spirit that has come in through the door of that curse to leave me now in the name of Jesus Christ. Through the power of Christ's blood and the power of the Holy Spirit dwelling in me, I pray this. Amen!

TWENTY-FOUR

Blessing and Being Blessed, Cursing and Being Cursed

Speaking a Blessing

It is easy to give a blessing in words. The Bible is packed full of information on how to bless others and how to be blessed. We hear a great deal taught about God blessing us and how we can bless others through our deeds, but we don't hear much about how we can bless others in our thoughts and words. I personally think an effective Christian would speak blessings into his or her follow believers' lives.

There is no blessing in the Bible that is unconditional. God's love is the only thing God gives us that is without conditions. For every blessing, there is a condition that we must fulfill before we can receive our blessing. *If* is one of the words in the Bible that holds the most power. I used to smoke up to two packs of cigarettes a day. All of my family, including my mom and dad, smoked as well; therefore, I can tell you how one little cigarette burn can deface an entire carpet. That one burn can look like an elephant in the room. When I read my Bible and come to the word *if*, for me, it stands out like that one cigarette burn defacing my carpet. Everything but God's unconditional love is established on the conditions of our good merits. Notice in this passage how the word *if* is presented as a promise for a blessing: "*If* thou shalt hearken diligently unto the voice of the Lord thy God, to observe and to do all his commandments which I command thee this day, that the Lord thy God will set thee on high above all nations of the earth: And all these blessings shall come on thee, and overtake thee, *If* thou shalt hearken unto the voice of the Lord thy God" (Deuteronomy 28:1–2, emphasis added). Now we move down to verse 15, which is a promise of a curse: "But it shall come to pass, *If* thou wilt not hearken unto the voice of the Lord thy God, to observe to do all His commandments and His statutes which I command thee this day; that all these curses shall come upon thee, and overtake thee" (Deuteronomy 28:15, emphasis added). *If* is a conditional word.

A blessing is the act of words that one blesses with. A blessing, like a curse, is a play of words. In the Bible, there are several words usually translated as "blessing" or "to bless." The Hebrew word most often used is *barak*, which is translated as "to bless." This means to praise, congratulate or salute. "God blessed them saying, Be fruitful and multiply, and fill the waters in the seas, and let fowl multiply in the earth" (Genesis 1:22). This was the first recorded blessing God issued out. He blessed the sea, creatures and birds, telling them to be fruitful and multiply. God gave a similar blessing to Adam and Eve as He gave them dominion over creation.

God blessed Abraham when He promised Abraham the promised land and told him that his seed would be as the sand on the seashore and that he would have a son in his old years:

> The Lord had said unto Abram, "get thee out of thy country, and from thy kindred, and from thy father's house unto a land that I will shew thee: And I will make of thee a great nation, and I will bless thee, and make thy name great, and thou shalt be a blessing: And I will bless them that bless thee, and curse him that curseth thee: and in thee shall all families of the earth be blessed." (Genesis 12:1–3)

By the way, God was not just talking about Abraham here; He was talking about the whole Jewish nation (all of Abraham's future descendants). This blessing and cursing of the nations and people on behalf of the Jewish nation still stands today. Be careful how you talk about the Jews, or your actions and words will place a curse on you.

> And said, "By Myself, have I sworn, saith the Lord, for because thou hast done this thing, and hast not withheld thy son, thine only son: That in blessing I will bless thee, and in multiplying I will multiply thy seed as the stars of the heaven, and as the sand which is upon the seashore;

and thy seed shall possess the gate of his enemies; And in thy seed shall all the nations of the earth be blessed; because thou hast obeyed my voice." (Genesis 22:16–18)

God is not the only one who blesses: "And they blessed Rebekah and said unto her, Thou art our sister, be thou the mother of thousands of millions, and let thy seed possess the gate of those which hate them" (Genesis 24:60). Rebekah's family sent her with a blessing when she became Isaac's wife. When Isaac was ready to die, he gave a verbal blessing to his son, Jacob: "Therefore God give thee of the dew of heaven and the fatness of the earth, and plenty of corn and wine: Let people serve thee, and nations bow down to thee. Be lord over thy brethren, and let thy mother's sons bow down to thee: cursed be everyone that curseth thee, and blessed be he that blesseth thee" (Genesis 27:28–29). The first time I gave a verbal blessing to a Christian believer, I used Genesis 27:28-29 as my example.

Another Hebrew word for blessing is *esher*, which is translated as "happiness." In (Job 5:17), Job declares that the man God corrects is blessed. (Psalm 1:1--3) carries on this theme, as it states that a man who remains faithful to God and does not sin as the wicked do is blessed.

In (Matthew 5:1–11 and Luke 6:20–26) is the blessing of being happy and fully at peace in the Lord. (Romans 4:6–8) ties this happy blessing to the person whose sins are forgiven and who is on the way to heaven. The greatest blessings a person receives from God is their new life in Christ Jesus, forgiveness and the promise of everlasting life.

Eulogy is another word for a blessing. It focuses more on the good word or good report that someone gives about a person. "Not rendering evil for evil, or railing for railing: but contrariwise blessing; knowing that ye are thereunto called, that ye should inherit a blessing" (1 Peter 3:9). This passage of scripture tells us that because we were called to receive blessings from God, we are to bless our enemies.

As you can see, a blessing is a statement of goodwill and happiness said about a person, as well as the condition that fulfills these good words. In the beginning—that is, before the fall of man in the garden—God originally planned that humankind would have peace, prosperity and fulfillment. However, that design was ruined with the sin in the Garden of Eden. Our statements of blessings are our wish for God to restore His favour on others or His declaration of His inherent goodness on them.

At one time, when our church always had with the evening service an altar call, the Holy Spirit would often send me to place blessings on everyone who stood at the altar. As I walked from one person to the next, I would place my hand on their shoulders and speak a blessing to them. People like it when you bless them. However, they don't like having a curse spoken on them. One husband and wife in the congregation were burdened with great despair when their pediatrician told them the tiny baby she carried in her womb was sick. I had the Holy Spirit tell me to place a blessing on the baby. I approached the mother and asked her permission to place my hand on her tummy and give her baby a blessing. Remember, don't place your hand on a pregnant mother's belly to give a blessing until you have her permission. She agreed to have me bless her baby, and I gave the baby a short blessing that he would be born healthy, live a long life in the Lord and die an old man, a Christian and wise in years. The boy was born healthy. I believe God healed that boy in his mother's womb. I also believe his blessing will be fully carried out as it was spoken.

It is easy to give a spoken blessing. For example, you can place your right hand on the shoulder of the person you are blessing, and say something like this: "May you be blessed with your coming in and going out. May you be blessed with prosperity. May you be blessed all of your days with good health. May your children and their children call you blessed. May you find comfort and joy in Christ all of your days. May you live a long and good life. And may you dwell with the Lord in His eternal blessings." Speaking a blessing is the opposite of speaking a curse.

Cursing Others

A psychic prayer is any prayer that does not line up with the Word of God. If you pray contrary to the Bible, then you are praying to Satan. This prayer does not go up to God but instead goes to Satan. This then gives Satan the right before God to attach his demons to the people you have prayed for, and furthermore, the devil also has the right to attach his demons to you. Your praying psychic prayers will definitely place curses on others and will, without fail, put a curse on yourself. Again, I tell you this from my own personal experience. I have prayed prayers that did not glorify God, and Satan took my prayer, and as a result, I was cursed.

There are two ways we can curse another person: with our thoughts and by speaking. You can pray a psychic prayer or speak negative words aloud, and you can do this in your thoughts as well. It is important that we are careful not only in what we do but also in what we think and speak. The words we think and speak go out into the air, and they have the power to do both good and evil. "Curse not the King, no not in thy thought; and curse not the rich in thy bedchamber: for a bird of the air shall carry the voice, and that which hath wings shall tell the matter" (Ecclesiastes 10:20).

As a small child, I saw that my mother had left an open book she had been reading on the kitchen table. I saw in the book a picture of frightful monsters, and I asked her what these strange winged creatures were. She quickly snatched the book from my hand and said, "You shouldn't be looking at that!" The creatures were black monkeys with wings, and they were dreadfully ugly. Their faces looked evil. I believe to this day that what I saw in this book were messengers of Satan.

In (Exodus 25:20), the cherubim have large wings that cover them. When the Holy Spirit opens my spiritual eyes to see the angels worshipping with us in the church, I see that they have wings lifted up. When I had my out-of-body experience, the angels I saw brushed me with their wings. Evil spirits that dwell in people are tiny, yet they can follow us as they watch to catch us slip up. (Ecclesiastes 10:20) is one of the mysteries in the Bible that will remain just that—a mystery. It is a guess on my part. I am assuming it's possible the tiny evil spirits are winged, and they carry the curse from the sender to the intended target and enter the victim along with the curse. Nevertheless, this Bible passage does declare that a curse follows through the air on wings to its target, and it tells us that this winged creature shall make mention of this curse. Evil spirits travel in large family groups. This spirit then has informed other spirits, and they have joined him on his quest.

Obey, and be blessed by God. Disobey, and be cursed. It is your choice. We will be blessed according to the amount of the Bible we follow. We are told to keep all of the words of God's Holy Bible.

Prayer

Through Christ, my Lord, heavenly Father, I come to you through the power of the Holy Spirit dwelling in me and through the power of Christ's precious blood. Father, I want to bless others and be blessed rather than curse others and be cursed. Please make me a blessing, and take away the curse. I ask that you, other people and my descendants forgive me for anything I have done to bring these curses. I forgive my ancestors and everyone else who has placed curses on me. Please forgive these people for their psychic prayers, spoken curses, ancestral curses, parental curses, curses by others, curses on me, curses of my descendants, disobedience, Ahab and Jezebel behaviour, charismatic witchcraft, conception of bastards, incest, Indian curses, cursed objects in the home and any other curses known and unknown found in your Holy Word.

I now break, renounce and denounce all curses placed on me or my descendants from uttering a wish of evil against anyone to cause evil, call for mischief or injury to fall upon, execrate, bring evil upon, blast, vex, harass or torment with great calamities. I break, renounce and denounce the curses back to 10 generations or even back to Adam and Eve on both sides of my family, and I destroy every legal ground that demons have to work in my life. I break, renounce and denounce curses that follow, in the name of Jesus Christ. Thank you, Father, Jesus and Holy Spirit. Amen!

This is a quick and simple prayer to use to break all verbal curses that you or someone else has spoken against you. Place the words spoken in the space provided. An example would be "I break the curse of 'I don't give that marriage six months.'"

1. I break the curse of (_____).
2. Please, dear Jesus, forgive me for having said or thought (_____).
3. I confess having said or thought (_____).
4. I renounce having said or thought (_____).
5. I denounce having said or thought (_____).
6. I forgive myself for having said or thought (_____).
7. Please, dear Jesus, forgive anyone who has said or thought (_____).
8. I confess anyone who has said or thought (_____).

9. I renounce that anyone has said or thought (_____).
10. I denounce that anyone has said or thought (_____).
11. I forgive anyone who has said or thought (_____).
12. Thank you, dear Jesus, for breaking the curse of (_____).

It's that simple. Through your reading this, your spoken curse of negative words is broken.

Biblical Curses

The question is this: Are you cursed? The answer is yes. Everyone has a curse on him or her. We are descendants of Adam and Eve. The first curses were handed down through Adam and Eve: the pain in childbearing, the weeds and the harvesting of our food by the sweat of our brow. These are curses. It's painful to give birth to a baby.

Many Christians don't know about curses and evil spirits. They have no clue what to do about their problems. It is important that we study the devil and his tactics enough to recognize him and know how to destroy his works in us. When I first started planning this book, the Holy Spirit started by leading me in studying the devil and all of the tricks he has up his sleeve. I learned quickly that unless we know his every plan of attack, we cannot stand up against our foe. We must see the enemy coming at us.

I have perceived that 90 percent of all Christians live in a fantasy world in which they have no idea what true hard-core spiritual warfare is. They are playing church; God is their Santa in a red suit, pouring down on them all of His riches in glory. Yet the Bible tells us that in order for us to receive His blessings, we must keep His commandments (James 1:25). There are no shortcuts to mature spirituality. We must follow the instructions.

Getting saved does not solve all of our problems; however, the Holy Spirit is our friend, and He does make our times when we walk through the valley much easier to bear. In reality, if we would start seeking spiritual deliverance from our problems, then getting saved would solve our problems. You see, realistically speaking, getting saved gives us the right to begin to untangle the mess we and our ancestors have made of our lives. If most Christians were to be perfectly honest with themselves as well as with God, then they would admit there are still problems in their lives that they cannot conquer. Many Christians become discouraged and give up. One of my problems was that I had an unrealistic expectation of the born-again believer's life. Most of our problems came from wanting an easy life. We are called to the battle line. There is nothing easy about a life on the battlefront. Jesus's disciples did not have easy lives. Most of them died as martyrs, yet each one of those men contributed to the success of every born-again Christian's life. Just the same, we should contribute to the lives of the generations of born-again believers to come.

It was a long time before I came to know that my problems were family and bloodline curses. I was frantically running from one Christian counsellor to another, and none of the counsellors mentioned anything to me about evil spirits travelling through our bloodlines and heading down through us to our 3rd, 4th and 10th generations. Beginning in the Old Testament, God gives us information on both blessings and curses. Whether you want to hear it or not, God is our boss, and He has the right to say how His kingdom will be run. In the book of Deuteronomy, blessings and curses are explained to the Israelite people.

These are some of the names of demons sent by biblical curses: Pestilence, Idol Worship, Graven Images, Consumption, Bastard, Pride, Fever, Wicked Balances, Catholic Prayers, Inflammation, Dislike, Hatred, Murder, Prince of Southern Curses, Extreme Burning, Curse of the Law, Prince of Occult, Blasting, Bless-You Spirits, Witchcraft Curses, Mildew, Incest, Voodoo Curses, Botch of Egypt, Lesbians, Occult Curses, Emeralds, Necromancers, Scab, Blasphemy, Charismatic Witchcraft, Itch, Sodomy, Horoscopes, Madness, Oral and Anal Sex, Rebellion, Blindness, Slackness, False Prophets, Astonishment of Heart, Deeper Teachings, Séances, Plagues, Irish Shamrock, Hex, Fortune-Telling, Sore Sickness, Fertility, Lack of Productivity, Diseases of Egypt, Deceiving, Personal Poverty, Trembling of Heart, Adultery, Misrepresentation, Failing Eyes, Disobedience, Perversion of Judgment, Sorrow of Mind, Cursed Objects, Doubt, Broken Vows, Thievery, Homosexual, Unicorn, False Swearing, Tulip, Twelve-Petal Rosette, Distelfink, Your Lucky Stars, Love and Romance, Eight-Pointed Star, Friendship Hex, Pentacle, Pentagram, Eastern Star, Hexagram, Star of David, Magen David, Cabalistic Magic Symbol, White Magic, Masonic Symbols, Italian Horn, Leprechaun's Staff, Unicorn's Horn, Egyptian Ankh, Egyptian Sun God, Ra, Zodiac, Mexican Sun God, Buddha, Crescent Moon and Star, Cursing, Vexation, Rebuke, Destroying, Perishing, Consuming, Groping, Lack of Prosperity, Oppressed, Spoiled, Failure, Crushed, Smite, Pursuing, Sore Botch of Knees, Legs and Whole Body, Overtaking,

Distress, Plucked, Chastisement, Removed, Not Healed, Astonishment, Proverb, Byword, Want, Besiege, Straightness, Evil, Adultery, Willing Deceivers, Harlotry and Prostitution, Mistreating God's Chosen People, Disobedience of the Bible, Idolatry, Keeping Cursed Objects, Refusing to Fight for God, House of Wicked, Not Giving to the Poor, Stealing, Swearing Falsely by God, Failing to Give Glory to God, Robbing God of Tithes, Dishonouring Parents, Hearkening to Wives Rather Than to God, Making Graven Images, Cheating People out of Property, Taking Advantage of the Blind, Oppressing Strangers, Oppressing Widows, Oppressing Orphans, Bestiality, Incest with Sister or Mother, Murder Secretly or for Hire, Putting Trust in Man, Doing the Work of God Deceitfully, Rewarding Evil for Good, Abortion or Causing the Unborn to Die, Having a Bastard, Murdering Indirectly, Striking Parents, Kidnapping, Cursing Parents, Not Preventing Death, Sacrificing to Gods, Witchcraft, Turning Someone away from God, Following Horoscopes, Rebelling against Pastors, Losing Virginity before Marriage, False Prophets, Rape, Not Disciplining Children, Teaching Rebellion against God, Cursing Rulers, Refusing to Warn Sinners, Defiling the Sabbath, Sacrificing Humans, Séances and Fortune-Tellers, Intercourse during Menstruation, Homosexuals and Lesbians, Blaspheming the Lord's Name, Being Carnally Minded, Children Rebelling, Lack of Productivity, Fugitive and Vagabond, Improper Family Structure, Destruction of Family Priesthood, Refusing to Do the Word of God, Family Disorder, Failure and Poverty, Any Sin Worthy of Death, Touching God's Anointed, Perversion of Gospel, Loving Cursing, Choosing That Which God Delights Not In, Looking to the World for Help, Stubbornness and Rebellion, Offending Children Who Believe in Christ and Adding To or Taking Away from the Bible. Not all biblical curses are listed above.

Prayers for Breaking Biblical Curses

I forgive my ancestors and anyone else who has cursed me. I ask you, God, to forgive me and them. I renounce, denounce and break any curses placed on me and my descendants from uttering a wish of evil against someone to cause evil, call for mischief or injury to fall upon, execrate, bring evil upon, blast, vex, harass or torment with great calamities. I break, renounce and denounce these curses in Jesus Christ's name. I break, renounce and denounce these curses back to 10 generations or even back to Adam and Eve on both sides of my family, and I destroy every legal hold and every legal ground that evil spirits have to work in my life. I break, renounce and denounce curses that follow, and I do this in the name of my Lord, Jesus Christ.

In the name of Jesus Christ, I now rebuke, break and loose myself and my children from any and all evil curses, charms, vexes, hexes, spells, jinxes, psychic powers, bewitchment, witchcraft and sorcery that have been put upon me and my family line from any persons or any occult or psychic sources. I cancel all connected or related spirits, and I command them to leave me. I thank you, Lord and Holy Spirit, for setting me free.

TWENTY-FIVE

Wizards, Witches and Sorcerers Casting Spells

Everything in this chapter is from my own learned experience. I have gone through this. Beware of wizards, witches and priests and priestesses of the Church of Satan in your home church. They come in as wolves in sheep's clothing. You could be sitting beside a wizard or witch every Sunday morning and be none the wiser. They make their way up as board members and church secretaries. They place spells on pastors and board members in order to take control. I knew of a high priest of the Church of Satan who was a pastor in a faith-believing Christian church. "Beware of false prophets, which come to you in sheep's clothing, but inwardly they are ravening wolves" (Matthew 7:15).

When the wizard casts his spell, a Christian's curses that haven't been dealt with let the wizard's soul fragments and the evil spirits he has called upon break through the born-again person's protective hedge. Unfortunately, everyone has curses; all are conceived in their mothers' wombs with the curses of Adam and Eve's fall from God's grace in the Garden of Eden.

Then we have all of our generational curses we are conceived with and curses our parents place on us in our mothers' wombs, and these occur before we are even birthed. Then there are all of the verbal curses we and others place on ourselves and all of the foolish sins we commit that place curses on us.

As I said, curses we haven't dealt with make it possible for the wizard (or witch) to place a spell on an otherwise protected Christian, but also, as he is casting his spell, he weakens the person's protective hedge enough to allow other families of evil spirits he has not called upon to enter his victim as well.

Something in the act of the sorcery allows the wizard's fragments and families of evil spirits to enter into a Christian whose curses have not been broken. To place a curse by the action of our sins or by speaking negative words is an act of witchcraft. Anyone uttering a curse on someone, even a Christian speaking something such as "You fool," can damage the receiver's protective hedge.

This is how a curse is placed on a person. Saying something negative about a person places a curse on him or her. The same stands for speaking negatively about a Christian. The damage the curse causes allows the evil spirits that represent the curse to come into the recipient, and there you go—the faith-believing Christian has a curse placed on him or her. In the case of a spell being cast or a curse being placed, 99 percent of the time, the evil spirits will enter the target as a family group. Evil spirits like to travel in families, and this is generally how they enter a person—in a family group.

By placing a spell on a person, the wizard makes the person into a human marionette. The wizard's soul fragments control his target. The fragments are the strings of the puppet. The wizard is a controller, and a wizard who places a spell on another person does so with the intention of controlling that person.

Your tongue is your worst enemy: "And the tongue is a fire, a world of iniquity: so is the tongue among our members, that it defileth the whole body, and setteth on fire the course of nature; and it is set on fire of hell" (James 3:6). You could have all curses broken back to Adam and Eve so that no witch or wizard could put a spell on you, and with as few as three words, you could put a curse on yourself and damage your protective hedge enough to let a wizard or witch place a spell on you. Your tongue will pollute your whole person—that is, place a curse powerful enough to open you up to a wizard's sorcery. The hedge of a Christian who is living a righteous life does protect him or her; however, when it comes to sorcery, we need the extra protection that breaking curses provides.

The families of evil spirits that came out of me kept exclaiming how afraid they were of the wizard who had sent them. They would plead with the Holy Spirit not to send them back to their sender. They kept saying as they came out, "His sorcery is very powerful, and this makes him a dangerous man."

The devil has given great power to wizards, and only Satan has charge over them. This power is what wizards are drawn to. Through this power, they can control whomever they choose. I was under a wizard's spell for four years before I became aware of the control he had over me. Wizards and witches communicate with demons. They talk back and forth with these spirits in the same way people talk back and forth with each other.

Wizards and witches are living, breathing human beings. When I first became aware that it was a wizard I was up against, I tried to battle him with spiritual warfare, but there was no beating him. In every direction I took, he had me outsmarted, and then the Holy Spirit told me, "Take your attention off of the human being who is targeting you, and place your sights on the demons and evil spirits he summons up. Start your spiritual battle against them."

I started by calling upon legions of angels who were prepared for war and battle and send them to stand guard around me and at night guard my bedroom so that demons and soul-travellers would not enter. However, I had not thought to send legions of God's powerful angels to the place my attacks were originating from. I then started sending angels prepared for battle to stand guard around the wizard as he cast his spells, so they would muck up the wizard's sorcery, rendering all of his efforts useless. Still, the wizard was outsmarting me, so I decided to take my battle to the second heaven, which is where Satan and his army battle against God's angels. This is where the demons are trying to battle against God's army of angels to prevent them from breaking through to our defence and protection (Daniel 10:10-14). It was, however, not until God placed His great wall around me that the wizard could no longer soul-travel within 20 feet of me.

Although the wizard could no longer come near me by soul-travel, he could still, through his sorcery, fill me with his fragments and evil spirits. That is when I discovered that our curses leave us defenceless. We are sitting targets for those who practice sorcery. This wizard continued to place his spells on me until I had all of my curses in my life broken, even back as far as Adam and Eve in the garden. One curse I hadn't dealt with in my life was all the wizard needed to place a spell on me. I had to break every curse I had over me. Once I'd broken all of my curses, my protective hedge took on a powerful strength like never before. When I had my final curse broken, he could no longer place his spells on me. Then I could with much joy and peace say, "He (God) delivered me from my strong enemy, and from them which hated me: for they were too strong for me" (Psalm 18:17).

Some of our curses go back as far as Adam and Eve. With the exception of Jesus Christ, all humans are born with these curses. I believe wizards and witches are controlling today's evangelistic churches, because 99 percent of Christians do not know enough to break their curses back to Adam and Eve.

Wizards, witches and even Satanists make their way into evangelistic churches and come across as favourable Christians. They quickly become so involved in many outstanding ways that it is practically impossible for the church body to function normally without them. All three practice sorcery. They place spells on pastors and on the congregation to gain their trust, so they can quickly make their way to the top as board members, church secretaries and others of outstanding high authority.

This makes it easier for these people to cause the pastors and other church leaders to falter in sin. Wizards, witches and Satanists place spells on the pastors and others in the church, such as board members, so they can control them by manipulating them into sinning and doing things they would not have naturally done.

Being controlled by a wizard's spell is like being pulled down into quicksand. The sand takes people down at a massive speed. They are going down fast, and they cannot help themselves. It means sure death for their spirits as their heads sink under. They are heading for a muddy end. If this is you, then through your finding your freedom, the Holy Spirit will reach out, take both of your hands and pull you out of the sand before your head goes under.

I have often heard it said that man is his own worst enemy. As odd as it might sound to a Christian, some people believe that Satan is their friend. Demons lie to wizards, witches, Satanists and sorcerers by telling them that Satan is their friend. These people are heavily loaded with spirits of wizardry and lying spirits. They are confused and caught in a powerful illusion of what Satan actually is. Evil spirits have taken these people by deception. Sadly, these people will not know how foolish they were to believe the devil's lies until the day when their silver cord is broken and they are in hell, where the great deceiver, Satan, will have no mercy as his fierce and ugly demons torment them for eternity.

I once had a wizard tell me, "Satan is my friend! He has promised me in hell my own office. I will have a mahogany desk and chair, and on my desk, I'll have my very own nameplate." I will tell you the truth: there is a lake of fire in hell. It is dreadfully hot there. Even if it were possible to have wood in hell, which it is not, in less than the blink of an eye, the heat of hell would consume it to less than ashes. There won't be handsomely carved mahogany desks and chairs or personalized nameplates. In the place of offices, there are prison cells in which three to four large, ugly spirits torment their victims both day and night for eternity. It is possible that the wizard might not be tormented in a cell. He might instead land in the lake of fire, where he will eternally burn. Nevertheless, hell is a place of torment.

I pray every day that the wizard who gave me a four-year battle will surrender his soul over to Christ.

> Ye have heard that it hath been said, Thou shalt love thy neighbour, and hate thine enemy. But I say unto you, Love your enemies, bless them that curse you, do good to them that hate you, and pray for them which despitefully use you, and persecute you; That ye may be the children of your Father which is in heaven: for he maketh his sun to rise on the evil and on the good, and sendeth rain on the just and on the unjust. For if ye love them which love you, what reward have ye? Do not even the publicans the same? And if ye salute your brethren only, what do ye more than others? Do not even the publicans so? Be ye therefore perfect, even as your Father which is in heaven is perfect. (Matthew 5:43–48)

Pray that your enemies will receive Christ and find salvation. Jesus suffered and died for wizards, witches, sorcerers and Satanists.

If you know the name of the person, then place his or her name in the prayer below.

Prayer

Almighty God, I break, renounce and denounce all evil soul ties I have with all wizards, witches, sorcerers, Satanists, [name of person] and all other people. Forgive me for developing these evil soul ties with wizards, witches, sorcerers, Satanists, [name of person] and all other people. I forgive all wizards, witches, sorcerers, Satanists, [name of person] and all other people for controlling me. I renounce and denounce these soul ties and break and wash these soul ties away with the shed blood of my Lord, Jesus Christ.

You will not know what spell this person has placed on you or to the extent of power that was used in the casting of the spell. Therefore, you will not know the names of the families of spirits that need to come out, and either will you know how many families has been cast into you, nor will you know the wizard or witches first and last name. In this case, your intimate relationship with the Holy Spirit will be important. You will be asking the Holy Spirit to help you receive the names of the families that has been cast into you and the name of the wizard or witch who cast this spell. You will be using (The Box) which is located in chapter 27, with the full explanatory how to use it. To get a full deliverance from the spell cast on you, it is important that the entire families of these spirits come out. Therefore, you will be calling them and casting them out in large groups of families. At this time you will also be calling out the wizard's or witch's soul fragments by full first and last names. In doing this, you will find out the name and identity of the person who cast the spell on you. If you already know the name of the wizard or witch who cast the spell on you, then place his or her name in the spaces provided below. To receive your freedom and send fragments back to wizards and witches who have cast spells on you, follow this command:

Using the manual provided (The Box in chapter 27), put the spokesman for these spirits into the box with the command that he gives you the names of the families that has been cast into you, and the full first and last name of the witch or wizard that cast this spell. Even should this spirit beg you to let him out, don't let him out. You will be depending on the Holy Spirit to let you know when this spokesman has given you all the names. This is because often this spirit will quit speaking to you to abstain you from receiving your freedom. It is important that you write down every name of the families and the full first and last name of the person's soul fragments. You will know when the evil spirits are leaving for you will vomit them out as if you are vomiting and yet nothing comes out.

To break spells pray

I break, renounce and denounce all evil soul ties I have with [name of wizard, witch or satanist]. Please forgive me for developing this soul tie with [name of wizard, witch or satanist]. I forgive [name of wizard, witch or satanist] for controlling me. I renounce and denounce this evil soul tie, and I break and wash away this soul tie with the shed blood of Jesus Christ.

Lord God, I break all curses of witchcraft, sorcery and spells that [name of wizard, witch or satanist] has placed on me. I return the witchcraft sorcery and spells back to their sender, [name of wizard, witch or satanist], sevenfold, and I seal them up in Jesus Christ's Name.

Holy Spirit, please line up these spirits by their names including all fragments of the soul of [name of wizard, witch or satanist] that has been placed in me through witchcraft, sorcery and spells. Now you individually tell each family of spirits and the soul fragments to come out of you by speaking with a loud commanding voice, "In the Name of Jesus Christ I tell you spirit of (name of family) come out of me now", repeat this with every family on your list. Command that the spirits gives their family names as they come out and then once they have given it check their name off the list. In this way you will know when they are all out. The Spokesman will be released from the box when he comes out with the families of spirits.

[After the spirits are cast out, continue with], I send the soul fragments back to [name of wizard, witch or satanist], and I bind them to the sender. I cast the evil spirits that have come out of me into the abyss and bind them there. I ask you, Holy Spirit, to fill these rooms left vacant with yourself so that no other spirits can enter. I do this in Christ Jesus Name, through Christ Blood and by the power of the Holy Spirit dwelling in me. Thank you, Holy Spirit, Jesus and heavenly Father. Amen!

TWENTY-SIX

Sins in General

Breaking Evil Soul Ties

An evil soul tie, also known as an unholy covenant, is caused when a person develops a spiritually unhealthy relationship with another person. This relationship is one of unholiness. It is evil because of the demonic influence involved. Because of the penetrating deceit in that relationship, the devil gets a foothold, which is a stronghold. This unholy relationship opens the door for many more families of evil spirits to enter.

Although I have chosen to use sin of a sexual nature as an example, there are other ways in which we can develop an evil soul tie with another person. Evil soul ties can be established between friends and between family members. Also, when wizards, witches and sorcerers cast spells or perform witchcraft and sorcery, they develop evil soul ties with their targets. A person seeking his or her future from a fortune-teller will develop an evil soul tie with the one who is telling the future. Not forgiving a person will develop an evil soul tie between the offended and the offender. The fact is, all morally unhealthy relationships create in us evil soul ties. To receive your total deliverance, you will need to break all of your evil soul ties that have developed.

One way of developing an unhealthy soul tie would be through fornication and adultery. For instance, you have an evil soul tie with every sexual partner you have had outside of the person you are now married to. If this is you, then you need to break soul ties with every person outside of your legal spouse you are now with. This includes if you have been married before; you must break soul ties with all previous spouses. You need to make a clean slate from all previous sexual partners. This includes rape and astral sex as well. They say you will never forget your first sexual partner. That is because you are bound to him or her by an evil soul tie.

Earlier in this book, I discussed how, with sexual intercourse, a couple becomes one in their spirit form. In God's perfect plan, this is consummated on their wedding night through intercourse; thus, their oneness in their marital union is holy by nature. This then is a holy soul tie. When a person has sex with someone he or she is not married to, this same spiritual bond occurs, making the two into one in spirit. This develops an unholy bond that is an evil soul tie between the two. Although asking forgiveness for our sins will definitely get us into heaven, this does not free us from spiritual bondage. We need also to break the bondage that Satan has on our life. If the evil spirits' legal right to stay is not annulled, then this person will not receive deliverance. Part of annulling the spirits' legal right is breaking our evil soul ties. When I became a Christian, I was careful to ask for forgiveness for all of my past sins. I was, according to the Word of God, on my way to heaven; however, I was still bound to these evil spirits within me. The truth was, to find complete freedom, I still had to break the evil soul ties I had from my past lovers.

If not dealt with, these evil soul ties from our previous sexual relations before we got married will be brought into our marriage and will cause evil soul ties, or unhealthy covenants, between our spouses and ourselves. Again, I speak from my own experience. I brought bad baggage into my second marriage, and I had to deal with it and correct it.

If you were at one time in the habit of masturbating, it is possible you have developed with another person an evil soul tie you are not aware of. The Bible tells us that if you have thought a lustful thought in your head, you have already committed the sexual crime: "But I say unto you, that whosoever looketh on a woman to lust after her hath committed adultery with her already in his heart" (Matthew 5:28). The spiritual part of the sexual act is so powerful that when a person thinks about a particular person while masturbating, the person he or she is thinking about can actually feel it and get the strong urge to masturbate as well. If this person then masturbates, he or she has then developed an evil soul tie with that person. Two people can be hundreds of miles apart, and one person can still feel the other person's lustful thoughts aimed at him or her.

I mentioned sex as a way of developing evil soul ties, but there are other ways of developing evil soul ties as well. A person placing a curse on you by the play of a few words will cause you to have an evil soul tie with that person. A wizard or witch, by casting a spell on a person, will create an evil soul tie with his or her target. The fact is, all unhealthy relationships create evil soul ties.

To find spiritual freedom, we must break all evil soul ties with ancestors, family, past lovers, fortune-tellers, etc. Ask the Holy Spirit to bring to your mind anyone you need to break soul ties with. Then pray the following:

> Lord God, I break, renounce and denounce the evil soul tie I have with [name of person]. Forgive me for developing this evil soul tie with [name of person]. I forgive [name of person] for controlling me. I renounce and denounce this evil soul tie, and I break and wash away this evil soul tie with the shed blood of my Lord, Jesus Christ. Thank you, Father, Jesus and Holy Spirit. Amen!

Should the Holy Spirit bring the name of more than one person to your mind, then repeat this prayer with the name of each person.

Abominable Behaviours

An abominable behaviour is any action that is a detestable offence against God's perfect law. It can be watching TV programs or movies, listening to music, looking at something on the Internet, reading something, watching or looking at pornography or saying or doing something. Anything that is against God's good and perfect law is an abominable behaviour.

All movies and programs featuring sexuality, the supernatural, cursing, cussing and swearing are detestable for a Christian believer to watch and listen to. The same rule goes for the Internet. The lyrics of most secular music are inappropriate, and Christian believers should not be listening to it. We are sanctified and set aside; we are to be holy just as Christ is holy: "But ye are a chosen generation, a royal priesthood, an holy nation, a peculiar people; that ye should shew forth the praises of him who hath called you out of darkness into his marvellous light" (1 Peter 2:9). Ask the Holy Spirit to bring to your mind any movies, programs or music that you need to renounce, denounce and repent of having listened to or watched, and ask Christ's forgiveness for watching and listening to them.

Pray the prayer below to break all bondage, and if possible, mention the name of the movie or TV program you watched or the music or musician you listened to. Also mention in this prayer any sins you have committed that come to your mind. Ask the Holy Spirit to bring to your mind any sins you need to repent and ask forgiveness of.

> Almighty God, in the name of my Lord, Jesus Christ, your Son, through the power of the precious blood of Jesus Christ and the power of the Holy Spirit dwelling in me, I renounce and denounce having watched (_____), having listened to (_____) and having said or done anything that is an abomination before you. Please forgive me for having watched (_____), having listened to (_____) and having said or done anything that is an abomination before you. I forgive myself for having watched (_____), listened to (_____) and said or done anything that is an abomination before you. I ask you, dear Father, to now break all holds that Satan has on my life because I watched (_____), listened to (_____) and said or did anything that is an abomination before you. I confess my sin, and I ask you to forgive me. I know you forgive me, and I forgive myself. I believe you died on the cross, took all of my iniquities and threw them into the sea of forgetfulness to never be remembered. I declare that I am forgiven, and I proclaim that I am a holy vessel and will serve you as my Lord and Savior in Jesus Christ's name. Please, Holy Spirit, assist me in casting out of myself the evil spirits that have entered me because I watched (_____), listened to (_____) and said or did anything that is an abomination before you. Thank you, Jesus, Father and Holy Spirit. Amen!

Should you need to confess a sin and ask forgiveness, this is a prayer you can always repeat at a later date.

In summary, you will need to break the spirits' legal right to remain in you. To break these spirits' legal right and curses, consider the following:

1. You need to break, renounce, denounce and confess all sins down your family line. Give the names of the sins and, if possible, the names of the people (grandparents, ancestors, etc.) all the way back to Adam and Eve. You need to forgive them. You need to ask the Lord to forgive you, and you need to forgive yourself. You need to confess your sins and the sins of your ancestors. Ask the Holy Spirit to bring to your mind the names of the sins and the names of the people.

2. You need to break, renounce and denounce all curses as far back as Adam and Eve. You need to break all curses that others have placed on you, and you need to break all curses you have placed on yourself. Ask the Holy Spirit to bring to your mind the names of the curses and the names of the people who have placed the curses on you.

3. You need to break, renounce and denounce all evil soul ties. You need to forgive each person you have an evil soul tie with. You need to forgive yourself for developing these evil soul ties with these people, ask Jesus to forgive you for developing these evil soul ties and forgive those who developed these soul ties with you.

4. Now you can ask the Holy Spirit to help you in casting out from within yourself fragments of souls of the people you have had evil soul ties with and your evil spirits. After the spirits' legal rights are broken, you can command the spirits by their names to come out of you. You have authority over these spirits, and they must listen and come out as you command them to. After you have cast out these fragments and spirits, ask the Holy Spirit to fill the rooms the spirits have left vacant with Himself. It is important that these rooms are filled with the Holy Spirit; otherwise, evil spirits can enter the vacant rooms and take up lodging. The spirits who came out need to be placed into the abyss, or they will return and try to regain entry.

5. You now need to sin no more: "Afterward Jesus findeth him in the temple, and said unto him, Behold, thou art made whole: sin no more, lest a worse thing come unto thee" (John 5:14). If you continue sinning in the way that represents a spirit's name, spirits of the same sort and name then gain the legal right to enter. Live a lifestyle that will not allow the spirits of this name and nature to come back in.

TWENTY-SEVEN

Warfare Deliverance Prayers

Note that first, before your physical deliverance, you must do your spiritual house cleaning.

> The graven images of their gods shall ye burn with fire: thou shalt not desire the silver or gold that is on them, nor take it unto thee, lest thou be snared therin: for it is an abomination to the Lord thy God. Neither shalt thou bring an abomination into thine house, lest thou be a cursed thing like it: but thou shalt utterly detest it, and thou shalt utterly abhor it; for it is a cursed thing. (Deuteronomy 7:25–26)

All artifacts, Buddhas and other gods—anything that will give demons the legal right to remain in your home—will interfere with the success of your deliverance. It is important that you first spiritually clean your home and car, and then, after that, do your physical deliverance.

I was baptized full immersion, baptized in the Spirit with the evidence of speaking in tongues, washed in the blood and on my way to heaven, but I was in a spiritual mess. I put myself in debt while searching for help from numerous Christian counsellors only to come out no further ahead. It seemed no one could help me. Often, Christians are born again, baptized in water and baptized in the Spirit with evidence of speaking in tongues, but it is not enough. Some Christians struggle their whole lives; they need deliverance, and there are few deliverance ministries out there.

If you have been at some time involved in witchcraft and sorcery or if you were at one time a practising witch, wizard or Satanist and you have not received your deliverance, then you need help. Perhaps like I was, you are a victim of wizardry, witchcraft, sorcery or Satanism, or you were conceived out of wedlock. If so, then as I had, you too need deliverance and freedom. Perhaps you struggle with drug addiction, alcoholism or sexual sin. These prayers are designed to set the captive free. As I verbally spoke these prayers while I was placing them in this section, I went through an amazing deliverance in which I cancelled many spirits' legal right to remain in me, and many spirits came out. Some came out by my singing continually "O the Blood of Jesus." These prayers do work. I suggest that even if you have never practised in the occult, still, just the same, pray these prayers.

Even if your life has not been so dramatic, since you have read this far, it is clear you are seeking help, and praying these prayers I have included will lead you to deliverance and to your freedom in Christ Jesus.

When receiving a deliverance, it is important that you break, renounce, denounce, claim and proclaim. When you renounce, you make a proclamation, confession and declaration. I have personally found these prayers to aid in my own deliverance. After I prayed these prayers, many evil spirits came out of me. Remember that if you smoke cigarettes, this habitual sin will hinder you from receiving your deliverance. Bitterness and lack of forgiveness will also hinder our deliverance. Remember, God forgives us as we forgive those who sin against us. It is important that you hold no grievance with anyone. Just as we need to forgive those who sin against us in order to be forgiven, we need to forgive in order to receive our deliverance. Also remember with respect that it is the Holy Spirit that will be guiding you through your deliverance. Give Him the honour He deserves for taking you through your deliverance. All Christians should pray these prayers.

Warfare Deliverance Prayers

If it is possible, pray these prayers in your private prayer room. Note that there should not be anything in this room that would give evil spirits the legal right to be in there.

Ask the Holy Spirit to bring to your mind your sins, and then pray as you verbally announce them out loud:

Through Christ, my Lord, dear Father in heaven, I break, renounce and denounce any ungodly acts I have committed either knowingly, such as [name sins], or unknowingly upon myself and others. I confess my sins [name sins] and ask you to forgive me. I know I am forgiven, and I forgive myself. Dear Jesus, I believe you died on the cross and took all of my iniquities and all of my sicknesses and sorrows and threw them into the sea of forgetfulness never to be remembered again. I declare that I am forgiven, and I proclaim that I am a holy vessel and will serve you as my Lord and Savior in Jesus Christ's name. Amen!

Through the power of the Holy Ghost dwelling in me and the name of my Lord, Jesus Christ, and through the power of the precious blood of Jesus Christ, I bind the strongman over this temple. I plead the blood of Jesus Christ against or on anything I have touched, am touching or will touch. I bind all outside demonic activities and all the forces of evil in, around, about, beneath and outside myself that would try to interfere, including principalities, powers and rulers of darkness; forces of spiritual wickedness; spirits of distraction, deception, confusion and repression; witchcraft; and strife, stress and competition.

I bind the carnal and passive mind of myself, and I command it to cease and be shut down in Jesus Christ's name. I refuse the carnal and passive mind from interfering in any way. I command these voices of evil spirits to be silenced. I bind the forces of evil from this room and from having any knowledge of what is or what will take place in this room. I bind, renounce, denounce and break the powers and effects of all doorkeepers and gatekeepers. In Jesus Christ's name, be gone. In the name of Jesus Christ, I claim absolution for myself from all negative schemes that have heretofore been set in perpetual motion, such as bottomless holes, endless needs, repeated conditions, problems without end and mazes.

I command that Satan's legal right over me be broken and that all backup systems be destroyed. I command there to be a purging and a healing of my spiritual being and a purging and healing of my physical being. I direct the healing lights of the Holy Spirit to the source of each physical problem. I command a purging and a healing of all relationships, of my personal ministry and of my material being. In Jesus Christ's name, Father, sever any demonic links between my soul and my spirit, and I ask you to completely cleanse, purify and sanctify my spirit.

Father in heaven, I actively will my soul to you. All evil human spirits be bound and cast out. All human occult evil spirits be bound; your power and effects on my life are broken. I forbid the forces of evil to use any human spirits against me. I take authority over the bloodline and bind, break, renounce and denounce any negative transfers from my ancestors and all spirits of iniquity passed down from the 3rd and 4th to the 20th generation since the time of conception within the womb. I break the lines on inheritance in my life. I come against all inherited demons in Jesus Christ's name, "Be gone out of my life." In the name of Jesus Christ, I destroy every legal hold, and I break, renounce, denounce and withdraw all legal grounds that Satan and his demons and evil spirits feel they have in my life. I bind, break, renounce and denounce the power and effects of all demonic curses, spells, incantations, blessings of evil, bewitchments, enchantments, hexes and cult and occult transfers; all evil effects of sins; all physical transfers; all spirits passed down; and all soul ties, evil oaths, commitments and vows put upon myself and my children because of disobedience of my ancestors and family. I do this back to Adam and Eve. I do this in the name of Jesus Christ.

Father, in the name of my Lord, Jesus Christ, I come against all former marriages and previous negative unions, and I break the influence of the present effects they have on my life. Father, in Jesus Christ's name and through the power of the Holy Ghost dwelling within me, I erase all negative suggestions and attitudes recorded in my subconscious mind.

I deprogram and break every evil, negative program, tendency and pattern in myself. I destroy all support and supply of spirits and evil networks and past effects in Jesus Christ's Name, including hypnotic trances, damnations, grinders, puppet strings, evil seedpods, pressures, contracts, hindrances, blockages, frogs, jinxes, false burdens, pulsators and auras into the abyss. In Jesus Christ's name, I loose my bands of wickedness, undo heavy burdens and let my oppressions go free, and I break my every yoke.

I break, renounce and denounce the core of evil, and I break, renounce and denounce, in Jesus Christ's name, my fleshly carnal will and every evil desire over, about, on or within myself. I command the carnal mind to be silenced in Jesus Christ's name. I command all evil claws, oppressions, barriers, bondages, strings, grudges, stumbling blocks, evil alliances, evil eyes, camouflages, moulds, stigmas, bands, yokes, traps, walls, entrapments, mood swings, binders, masks and plagues in Jesus Christ's name to be broken and thrown into the abyss. I pray over my spirit, soul, body, mind, will, emotions, memories and heart in the name of Jesus Christ. I come against words, predictions and the power of words, and I bind, break, renounce and denounce the words, the fear and the results of hearing the words.

In the name of Jesus Christ and through the power of the Holy Ghost dwelling in me, I close all cult and psychic doors and seal them with the blood of Jesus Christ. I cut myself free from all commitments previously made to Satan or to cult or occult societies, knowingly or unknowingly. In the name of Jesus Christ and by the power of the Holy Ghost dwelling in me, I bind, break, renounce and denounce the powers and effects of every evil, unpleasant memory and every evil word spoken to or over me since my conception. I bind and break the power and effects of every evil prayer to or over me since my conception.

I ask you, Lord Jesus, to begin to heal all hurts and wounds caused by my own sins, by others, by ancestral transfers, by spiritual warfare, by idolatry, and by decisions and wicked works in the spirit, soul, body, mind, will, emotions, heart and memories by the blood of Jesus Christ, the name of Jesus Christ and the healing balm of Gilead (Jeremiah 8:22). I command myself to be sutured and healed in Jesus Christ's name. Now, Father, I ask you to send your Holy Spirit and angels to gather and restore to their proper places all the pieces of my fragmented mind, fragmented will, fragmented emotions and fragmented memories and soul. Bring them into their proper original and perfect positions, as you planned them to be. Thank you, Jesus, for all that has taken place and will be taking place because of your love and grace for me. In the name of and by the blood of Jesus Christ. Amen! (Note: If you have committed adultery or fornication or practised witchcraft or wizardry, then you will need your pieces of your fragmented soul returned.)

When it comes to breaking satanic dedications and covenants, remember that any prayer you pray to God that is not according to the Word of God is a witchcraft prayer and is actually prayed to Satan. Ask the Holy Spirit to bring to your mind anytime that you might have prayed a prayer that was against God's good and perfect will. One prayer I should not have prayed came to my memory while I was placing this information in this book, and I broke, renounced and denounced it in this next paragraph. In doing so, I broke several evil spirit families' legal right to remain in me.

I break, renounce and denounce ever signing my name over to Satan or having my name signed over to Satan. I break, renounce and denounce having signed my soul over to Satan or ever having my soul signed over to Satan. I announce that my name is written in the Lamb's Book of Life. I break, renounce and denounce any ceremony in which I might have been wed to Satan, and I announce that I am a bride of Christ. I break, renounce and denounce all satanic assignments, covenants, packs and dedications that I made with Satan or that were made for me. I announce that I am a partaker of the new covenant with Christ. I reject, break, renounce and denounce all curses and assignments made for me or by me for the service of Satan. [Stop here, and break, renounce and denounce any specific pacts you can remember, including any prayers you have prayed that don't line up with the gospel (i.e., witchcraft prayers).] I ask you, dear Jesus, to forgive me for every sin pertaining to this. I trust only in the blood of my Lord, Jesus Christ, and what He accomplished on the cross. I look to the Holy Spirit for guidance. I break, renounce and denounce all guardians and surrogate parents assigned to me by Satanists. I break, renounce and denounce all baptisms, rituals or teachings by Satanists. I announce that I have been baptized into Christ Jesus, and my identity is now in Christ. I break, renounce, denounce and reject all demons and familiar spirits attached to any part of me by Satanists. I reject all spirit guides assigned to me. I announce that God is my heavenly Father, and the Holy Spirit is my guardian. By this, I am sealed until the day of my redemption. I accept only God's assignments for me. In Jesus Christ's name, amen!

Cancelling Assignments

Father, I come to you covered in the Name and Blood of my Lord, Jesus Christ. I acknowledge that you are the ruler far above all principalities, mights, powers and dominions. In the name of Jesus Christ, I ask that you break all assignments, spells, curses, incantations, vows and other forms of harm set against me and [name of system or insiders affected] by [name or entity if you know it]. In Jesus Christ's name, I ask that you cancel any such assignments and prevent all influence by forces of darkness. All evil spirits and forces of darkness allowed access through this assignment, I break, renounce and denounce you, all of your works and all of your ways in the name of Jesus Christ. I am a child of God, and you are a trespasser here. In Jesus Christ's name, you are commanded to depart, never to return. Father, I ask that you fill me with your presence and bring light fully, setting darkness under your feet. Thank you. It is in Jesus Christ's name that I ask, and it is in faith that I do receive. Amen!

Prayer against Sin

Say the names of sins as the Holy Spirit brings them to your mind.

In the name of my Lord, Jesus Christ, and by the power of the Word, the shed blood of Jesus Christ and the Holy Spirit that dwells within me, I bind the evil spirits of pride, ignorance, unforgiveness, gossip, envy, competitiveness, criticism, impatience, resentment, haughtiness, rebellion, stubbornness, deceitfulness, defiance, disobedience, strife, violence, divorce, laziness, accusation, confusion, procrastination, self-hatred, suicide, shame, depression, oppression, rejection, poor self-image, anger, schizophrenia, manipulation, anxiety, timidity, jealousy, greed, revenge, covetousness, fear, possessiveness, control, division, retaliation, distrust, selfishness, loneliness, isolation, ostracism, lack, paranoia, nervousness, passivity, indecision, doubt, deception, dishonesty, unbelief, withdrawal, betrayal, escape, infirmity, nerve disorders, lung disorders, brain disorders or dysfunction, AIDS, cancer, hypochondria, fatigue, anorexia, bulimia, addictions, sexual impurities and sexual perversion, seduction, lust, incest, pedophilia, pedophile, lesbianism, homosexuality, pornography, adultery, masturbation, homophobia, frigidity, impotency, immorality, witchcraft, enticing spirits, deafness, dumbness, blindness, muteness, sleeping spirits, hyperactivity, New Age spirits, occult spirits, religious spirits, Antichrist spirits and any other spirits of death and darkness, all in the name of the risen Lord Jesus Christ. In the name of Jesus Christ, I call forth and ask you, Holy Spirit, to fill me with the gifts of peace, patience, love, joy, charity, humility, forgiveness, kindness, generosity, faithfulness, gentleness, goodness, discipline, relinquishment, freedom from shame, good self-image, prosperity, obedience, a sound mind, order, fulfillment in Christ, truth, acceptance of self, acceptance of others, trust, self-control, freedom in Christ's name and unconditional love. Amen!

Prayer for Inner Healing

Lord Jesus, please come heal my wounded and troubled heart. I ask you to heal the torments that cause anxiety in my heart; I ask you, in a particular way, to heal all who are the causes of my sinfulness. I ask you to come into my life and heal me of the psychological harms that struck me in my childhood and the injuries that they caused throughout my life.

Lord Jesus, you know my burdens. I lay them all on your Good Shepherd's heart. I beseech you by the merits of the great open wound in my heart to heal the small wounds that are in me. Heal the pain of my memories so that nothing that has happened to me will cause me to remain filled with pain, anguish and anxiety.

Heal, O Lord, all of the wounds that have been the cause of the evil rooted in my life. I want to forgive all those who have offended me. Look to those inner sores that make me unable to forgive. You who came to forgive the afflicted of heart, please heal my heart.

Heal, my Lord, Jesus Christ, those intimate wounds that cause me physical illness. I offer you my heart. Accept it, Lord. Purify it, and give me the sentiments of your divine heart. Help me to be meek and humble. .

Heal me, O Lord, from the pain caused by the deaths of my loved ones that is oppressing me. Help me to regain peace and joy in the knowledge that you are the resurrection and the life. Make me an authentic witness to your resurrection, your victory over sin and death and your living presence among all men. Amen!

Thank you, Lord Jesus Christ, for awakening my sleeping spirit and bringing me into your light. Thank you, Lord, for transforming me by the renewing of my mind. Thank you, Lord, for pouring out your Holy Spirit on me and revealing your Word to me. Thank you, Lord, for giving your angels charge over me in all my ways. Thank you, Lord, for my faith in you, and I pray that from my innermost being shall flow rivers of living water. Thank you, Lord, for directing my mind and heart into the love of the Father and steadfastness of your ways. Fill me to overflowing with your life and your love, my Lord and King, Jesus Christ.

Regarding breaking soul ties, sexual sin is one way of causing an evil soul tie. There are many more ways of causing evil soul ties. Any kind of an unholy relationship sin that we commit causes evil soul ties. Ask the Holy Spirit to bring to your mind all sins and ungodly relationships you need to confess and repent of. This can include all sorority groups.

Heavenly Father, I confess and repent of the sin of [name the sin that caused the evil soul tie, such as adultery, fornication or any other sin that comes to your thought; if you are unaware of the sin that caused the evil soul tie, then ask the Holy Spirit to reveal it to your heart and mind], and I ask that you forgive me of this sin. Thank you, Jesus, Father and Holy Spirit. It is in Jesus's name that I pray. Amen!

Now is a good time to destroy or get rid of any physical gifts or other objects that could hold the soul tie together, such as a gift given in an adulterous relationship. Anything that could hold the bond together between you and that person needs to go.

> In the name of my Lord, Jesus Christ, and by the power of Christ's blood and the power of the Holy Ghost dwelling in me, I now renounce, denounce, break and sever all unholy soul ties formed between [name of person] and me through the sin of [name of the sin that caused the evil soul tie]. I command any evil spirits that have taken advantage of this unholy soul tie to leave me now in the name of Jesus Christ. (Repeat this prayer if you have more than one evil soul tie to break.)

Renouncing and Denouncing
Ungodly Vows

Heavenly Father, I repent of, break, renounce and denounce the vow I made to [Satan, or name of person, even God, whom you made the vow to] to perform [description of what the vow entailed]. I realize this was foolish and rash on my part, and I ask that you forgive me and release me from the bondage this vow has brought me under.

In the name of my Lord, Jesus Christ, and by the power of Christ's blood and the power of the Holy Ghost dwelling in me, I now renounce, denounce, break and nullify the vow to [Satan or name of person, even God] to perform [name of the vow] and confess that I am released from this vow and its bondage in Jesus Christ's name.

I now command any evil spirits and fragments of souls that have taken advantage of this unholy vow to leave me in the name of Jesus Christ. Amen! (Repeat this prayer if you have more than one unholy vow to break.)

Denounce and Renounce
Involvement with Unhealthy (Demonic) Music

Heavenly Father, I confess that I used to listen to unhealthy, demonic music. I ask that you forgive and cleanse me from this sin.

In the name of my Lord, Jesus Christ, and through the power of Christ's blood and the power of the Holy Ghost dwelling in me, I now renounce, denounce, break and sever all evil soul ties that have been formed between myself and the unhealthy music [names of specific songs and artists or groups if possible] I used to listen to and enjoy, as well as evil soul ties formed between myself and artists and groups [specific names if possible] and demonic influence that have been produced by these unhealthy songs and music. In Jesus Christ's name, I also renounce, denounce, break and nullify any curses I might have come under as a result of listening to the unhealthy music I used to listen to and enjoy.

In the name of my Lord, Jesus Christ, I now command all evil spirits that have taken advantage of these soul ties I have just broken, renounced and denounced to leave me. In the name of Jesus Christ and through the power of the Holy Ghost dwelling in me, I also renounce, denounce and command any spirits that have taken advantage of any curses I have come under as a result of listening to unhealthy music to leave me now in Jesus Christ's name. I also renounce and denounce any evil spirits who have entered me through my listening to this unhealthy music. I command these spirits to leave me, and I ask you, Holy Spirit, to help me by assisting me in casting these spirits out of myself. I ask this in Jesus Christ's name!

Breaking Generational Curses

Ask the Holy Spirit to bring to your mind any sins.

In the name of my Lord, Jesus Christ, I confess the sins and iniquities of my parents, such as [names of specific sins if known]; my grandparents, such as [names of specific sins if known]; and all other ancestors.

In the name of my Lord, Jesus Christ, and by the power of Christ's blood and the power of the Holy Ghost dwelling in me, I now renounce, denounce, break and sever all cords of iniquity and generational curses I have inherited from my parents, my grandparents and all other ancestors, and I break and sever all unholy soul ties formed between myself and my parents, my grandparents and all generations back to Adam and Eve.

In the name of my Lord, Jesus Christ, and through the power of the Holy Ghost dwelling within me, I now loose myself and my future generations from any bondages passed down to me from my ancestors, and I command all soul fragments and any evil spirits that have taken advantage of these cords of iniquity, generational curses and unholy soul ties to leave me now in the name of Jesus Christ. Amen!

Prayer against Mental Attacks

I come to you, Lord, my Deliverer. You know all my problems—all the things that bind, blind, torment, defile and harass me. I refuse to accept anything that comes from Satan, and I loose myself from every dark spirit, every spirit in me that is not the spirit of God, every evil influence and every satanic bondage. I command all such soul fragments and spirits to leave me now. I confess that my body is the temple for the Holy Spirit, redeemed, cleansed, sanctified and justified by the blood of Jesus

Christ. Therefore, Satan has no place in me and no power over me through the blood of Jesus Christ.

In the name of my Lord, Jesus Christ, and through the power of the Holy Ghost dwelling within me, I now break, renounce, denounce and loose myself from all psychic heredity; demonic holds; psychic powers; bondage and bonds of physical or mental illness; and curses upon me or my family line as a result of sin, transgression, iniquities, occult or psychic involvements of myself, my parents, my ancestors, my spouse, ex-spouses, their parents or any of their ancestors. I thank you, Lord, for setting me free. In the name of Jesus Christ!

In the name of my Lord, Jesus Christ, and through the power of Christ's blood and the power of the Holy Ghost dwelling within me, I now rebuke, break and loose myself, my spouse and my children from any and all evil curses, charms, vexes, spells, jinxes, psychic powers, bewitchments, witchcraft or sorcery—and all demons that come with them—that have been put upon me or my family lines by any person or persons or any occult source. Thank you, Jesus, for setting me free. Devils, witches, wizards and cohorts, I see that you are attempting to harass and embarrass God's ministry in my life, attempting to smear and discredit so as to discourage others who would receive this ministry. I'm not ignorant of your tricks, wiles or strategies (2 Corinthians 2:11). Now I command you to stop your operations, and I command that all of your psychic commands, incantations, prayers and desires against my home be turned against whoever sent them out. Demons that come with them, I command you to retreat and flee in defeat at this moment. I also command that the mouths of all who help spread lies against me be stopped (Psalm 63:11). The Lord rebuke you and all who help you. In Jesus Christ's name.

Prayer for Protection

Father, I thank you for your hand of protection upon my family, my friends and myself. In the name of my Lord, Jesus Christ, I thank you that you watched over your Word to perform it. I thank you that my family, my friends and I dwell in the secret place of the Most High and that we remain stable and fixed under the shadow of the Almighty, whose power no foe can withstand. Through the power of the Holy Ghost dwelling within me, I cover my family, my friends and myself with the precious blood of my Lord, Jesus Christ, your Son, thus keeping us safe from the hideous snares of Satan and all of his cohorts. Father, you are our refuge and our fortress. No evil shall befall us; no accident shall overtake us, nor shall any plague or calamity come near my home. I release ministering angels to go forth and envelop my family, my friends and myself. Accompany, defend and preserve us in all of our ways of obedience and service. The angels are encamped around us. I bind the devil from trying to influence them in any way. Shelter us in the palm of your hand, and save our homes from all storms. Keep us close to your heart.

Father, you are our confidence, firm and strong. You keep our feet from being caught in a trap or hidden danger. When we lie down, you will give my family, my friends and me a peaceful night's sleep. Father, you give this family safety and ease us. Jesus is our safety! In Jesus Christ's name, amen!

Dear heavenly Father, I come before you to break, renounce and denounce all sinful occult practices and idolatry, including seeking information, knowledge, healing, comfort, identity or power from any occult, psychic or secret source.

Should the Holy Spirit bring to your mind anything else to break, renounce and denounce, then fit it into the following list:

I break, renounce and denounce ever playing with decks of playing cards or reading books about the black arts, parapsychology, magic and satanic rituals, including the Sixth and Seventh Books of Moses, the Satanic Bible, books on false religions and other satanic books and writings. I break, renounce and denounce all sins of divination: palm reading, fortune-telling, tarot card reading, tea leaf reading, crystal ball or crystal gazing, candle gazing, Ouija boards, ESP, telepathy, horoscopes, automatic handwriting or spirit writing, water divining and the rod and pendulum. I break, renounce and denounce trace channeling; consultation of familiar spirits; clairvoyance; communication with the dead; séances; consultation of counsellors from the spirit realm; and consultation of wizards, ascended masters, spirit guides, wise masters, fortune-tellers, witches, shamans, mediums or spiritists. I break, renounce and denounce all demonic, occult or psychic healing practices, including powwow healing, charming to heal, pendulum healing, magic healing, psychic healing, magnetism and mesmerism. I break, renounce and denounce all use of occult power, including the casting of spells or witchcraft; voodoo; black, grey and white magic; Santeria and other forms of witchcraft. I break, renounce and denounce magical or occult hypnosis, metaphysics, mind science, yoga, transcendental meditation, sorcery, astral projection, astral sex and soul travel, table lifting or levitation, pyramid power, mind control, amulets and charms, power crystals and religious medals. I break, renounce and denounce movies and TV programs. I break, renounce and denounce all secret oaths to pagan gods as part of initiation ceremonies into organizations, fraternities, sororities and other organizations that practice these ceremonies. I break, renounce and denounce being involved in or in contact with secret lodges or societies and their organizations, including the Eastern Star, Rosicrucians, Edgar Cayce's teachings and reading, Erhard Seminars Training (EST), Scientology, Eastern mysticism, Christian Science,

Unitarians, The Way, the Unification Church, the New Age and its practices and any religion or organization of an occult nature. I break, renounce, denounce and repent of ever taking part in any of these practices or organizations. I ask you, Father, to forgive and restore me. In Jesus Christ's name, amen!

Casting Out Evil Spirits

By praying these prayers, you have now cancelled your evil spirits' legal right to remain in you. Now that you have prayed these prayers, you are ready to start casting these spirits out. Through my own personal experiences, I have come to believe that most evangelistic pastors, laypersons, board members and elders have not been properly schooled in how to perform a spiritual deliverance. When the correct procedure is not properly followed, the person who has received the spiritual deliverance remains in danger of each evil spirit coming back in with seven more much worse than himself.

> When the unclean spirit is gone out of a man, he walketh through dry places, seeking rest, and findeth none. Then he saith, I will return into my house from whence I came out; and when he is come, he findeth it empty, swept, and garnished. Then goeth he, and taketh with himself seven other spirits more wicked than himself, and they enter in and dwell there: and the last state of that man is worse than the first. Even so shall it be also unto this wicked generation. (Matthew 12:43–45)

Because of the lack of education in spiritual warfare, Jesus said today's generation will experience this calamity of the spirit coming back in and the person's condition worsening. You see in this passage of scripture that the room was clean, but you also see that when the spirit returned, he saw that the room he had left was empty, which gave him the opportunity to come back in. In addition, evil spirits like to travel with their buddies; therefore, the evil spirit came back in with his bad crowd. It is important that the Holy Spirit enter the room the evil spirit has left vacant, and the Holy Spirit can only dwell in a Christian. Therefore, do not try to cast evil spirits out of unsaved people. Also, the person who is casting the evil spirit out of the Christian needs to make certain he or she asks the Holy Spirit to enter the vacant room the spirit has been cast out of.

Remember that you need to break, renounce and denounce all evil soul ties and all curses. By this, I mean cancelling all of the evil spirits' legal rights to remain in you. You must do this before you can receive your deliverance.

I mentioned that evil spirits are mainly tiny. Some are larger. A witch once placed a spirit in me that was the size of a rat. I could feel it crawling in my stomach. I could hear it growl like a wild beast. When it came out through my mouth, it was huge. When it came out, it told me it was my guardian angel, David. I also had two-foot snakes come out. I also had a snake wrapped around my spine that held back my healing of scoliosis. The spirit of diabetes is large; he looks like a squid and has 10 arms. His main body is centred in the pancreas, where insulin is developed. His arms work with him as they reach out and touch the brain, kidneys, eyes, liver, feet, bladder, skin, lungs, ears and reproductive organs.

Evil spirits and soul fragments come out through an open passage. When an evil spirit or soul fragment comes out, it comes out through your mouth, and you barf up as when you vomit but nothing comes out. Don't fight against the spirit; hold your mouth open, and let it come out. There is nothing to be afraid of. Fear comes from the devil. God has given us a heart not of fear but of faith and courage: "For God hath not given us the spirit of fear; but of power, and of love and of a sound mind" (2 Timothy 1:7). Once the evil spirits' legal right to stay is cancelled, then it is easy to cast them out. You only need to command them to leave. I have often cast my evil spirits out by saying with a strong, commanding voice, "In the name of Jesus Christ and through the power of Christ's blood and the power of the Holy Spirit within me, I tell you, evil spirit, to come out of me." Then I let my mouth hang loosely open. They come out just as I have commanded them to. This type of deliverance works well with procedure B below. However, if you are uncertain about casting out your own evil spirits, then it might be better to do procedure A below.

Note first that you should have a private prayer room. If possible, your prayer room should have no more than one or two chairs, a small table or nightstand, a Bible and specific prayers and Bible verses tacked on the wall. It is a prayer room, not a rec room. In many homes, there might not be enough room for a private prayer room, so in that case, the room you use for prayer should be kept spiritually clean and should not have a TV in it. In my case, we don't have a spare room, so my prayer room is a bedroom, sewing room and prayer room combined. Here are a few suggestions of Bible verses you could pin on the wall of your prayer room: (Luke 10:18–19); (James 4:7); (Hebrews 4:12); (John 8:32) and (Ephesians 6:11). These should be enough scripture suggestions to give you an idea. I should also mention that a large walk-in closet can be used as a prayer room. Note also that when casting spirits out of yourself, you should have a box of tissues and a small pail close by.

There are two different ways to do your deliverance. One is to sing continually "O the Blood of Jesus," and the second is to sit in your prayer room and command the spirits to come out. For your deliverance to work, you need to have an enriched one-on-one relationship with the Holy Spirit. Remember always to thank Jesus, the Father and the Holy Spirit!

Procedure A

You will need at the least two hours of private prayer time with no interference, and that includes no phone. As you would with spiritual house cleaning, in your private prayer room, anoint the walls, doors and windows with Christ's blood and olive oil, and place a hedge of protection around the walls, doors and windows. Cast all demons and evil spirits out of the room. Say, "Holy Spirit, you are welcome in this place; fill this place with your glory and grace." Sit in a comfortable chair. Ask the Holy Spirit to start lining up the evil spirits to come out of you. Then start repeatedly singing the below four lines of "O the Blood of Jesus." Don't put the Holy Spirit in a box—that is, don't give Him a short time limit. Sometimes if the demons are really stubborn, it takes longer to start them moving. I have seen it take 30 minutes for the evil spirits to start coming out. Demons and evil spirits don't like to hear about Jesus's blood, and they don't like to hear Jesus's name. They will flee at the mention of Christ's name. Sing loudly and clearly so the demons can hear you. Keep repeating the following:

O the blood of Jesus,
O the blood of Jesus,
O the blood of Jesus,
That washes over me!

Procedure B

With this procedure, deliverance moves along much more quickly.

Make sure you have at least two free hours without any interference. Shut off the phone. In your private prayer room, anoint the walls, windows and doors with Christ's blood and olive oil, and place a hedge of protection around them. Cast all demons and evil spirits out of the room. Say, "Holy Spirit, you are welcome in this place; fill this room with your glory and grace." Ask the Holy Spirit to start lining up the evil spirits to start coming out. You now have the legal right to take liberty on your own and command the evil spirit to come out of you. Sit in a comfortable chair, and say with a strong, commanding voice, "I tell you spirit of [name of spirit] to come out of me now." And he will come out.

Many times, when you get a stubborn evil spirit that will not come out and you ask him why he won't come out, he will tell you that he has the legal right to be there and does not have to leave. Sometimes he will tell you what his legal right is. Should he tell you what his legal right is, then this makes your work much easier. Then you need to go through the procedure to annul his legal right to stay. I have found often that putting him in the box will drive the evil spirit to tell what his legal right is. The box is not a pleasant place to be. Note that evil spirits speak to us through the voices we hear in our head. Therefore, when the spirit is answering you, you will hear his voice in your head. Remember, if you break, renounce and denounce the evil spirits' legal right, they will come out.

The Box

If you have a spirit that will not leave, then say, "*Do you want to go in the box?*" In most cases, the evil spirit will say no or shake the person's head back and forth, meaning no. Then say, "*If you don't want to go in the box, then I command you to leave now in the name of Jesus Christ.*" If he does not leave, then say, "*I am going to count to ten, and then I am going to put you in the box."* Then count to 10. Most times, the spirit will wait until you get to 10 and then go.

If the evil spirit still won't leave, then say:

> *"Father, in the name of Jesus Christ, I put this spirit in the box. I tie the box up with iron chains and fetters. I fill the box with the blood of Jesus Christ. I ask for two angels to go into the box to read to the spirit the Word of God day and night. Evil spirit, you will get no peace and no rest. I fill the box with the glory of God to blind you. I put a gag in your mouth so you cannot communicate with any other demons or the devil himself."*

Then say, *"Do you like it in there? Are you ready to leave now?"* If he still won't leave, then say, *"In the name of Jesus Christ, I shrink the box to fit like a body glove. I ask you, Lord, to boil the blood in the box."* Now give him a chance to leave. If he refuses, then say, *"I am going to leave you in the box until you beg to come out."* Note that you can also use the box procedure to force an evil spirit to tell you his name and what his legal right is. As well when you need to know the names of more than one family use the box to place the spokesman over various families in.

After the demons are cast out, it is important that they are not left free to wander about the earth. You must now say, "In Jesus Christ's name and through the power of the Holy Spirit dwelling in me, I cast this evil spirit into the abyss and bind him there; what has been done on earth has been done in heaven through Jesus Christ's name and the Holy Spirit who dwells in me."

> When the unclean spirit is gone out of a man, he walketh through dry places, seeking rest; and finding none, he saith, I will return unto my house whence I came out. And when he cometh, he findeth it swept and garnished. Then goeth he, and taketh to him seven other spirits more wicked than himself; and they enter in, and dwell there: and the last state of that man is worse than the first. (Luke 11:24–26)

The evil spirit that came out needs to immediately be placed into the abyss. Send the fragments of souls that came out of you back to the proprietors, or if that is not possible, then send them to the dry place.

If the room the evil spirit has been cast out of is left vacant, then it and other spirits can enter the room. For this reason, you need to ask the Holy Spirit to fill the vacant room with Himself.

Once you ask the Holy Spirit to fill the room your evil spirit was cast out of, His presence will ensure that no other evil spirits can enter the empty room. To ask the Holy Spirit to enter the empty room the demon left, pray, "*Holy Spirit, fill this vacant room that this demon was cast out of with your presence so that there is not even an air pocket left. Thank you, Holy Spirit. Amen!*"

Prayers to Pray Daily

As you now know, our nations and government leaders worldwide are all under the influence of Satan's massive rulership. It's easy to condemn, mock and ridicule Donald Trump, Barack Obama, George W. Bush, Justin Trudeau and Stephen Harper, but what they really need is our daily prayer. (First Timothy 2:1–3) says that Christians should all pray for their authoritative leaders. This means that we should pray not only for our church leaders but also for our government leaders. If all Christians would daily lift up their government leaders in spiritual warfare, I believe we would see a massive change.

I pray the prayer below every morning for my pastors, board members, church leadership and government leadership. You can also put in the names of family members and anyone else who comes to mind. Place the name of the person you are praying for in the blanks provided.

> I bind for 26 hours the kingdom of evil. I bind principalities, powers, rulers of darkness of this world, spiritual wickedness in high places and the kingdom of Satan. I bind the demonic spirits of the air, earth and seas that are binding the lives of [name of person]. I command evil spirits that have their wills bound to loose their wills. You cannot bind and control their minds. I loose their minds from your grip. I loose their minds to the gospel of grace. I bind powers over their spirits, souls and bodies.

I command the demons driving the sins of lust, drugs, alcohol, spiritual blindness, greed, the Antichrist and all other sins to cease their activity.

I bind for the next 26 hours all demonic efforts to control, spiritually blind, kill, steal and destroy through curses, hexes, vexes, spells, charms, fetishes, psychic prayers, psychic thoughts, witchcraft, sorcery, magic, voodoo, mind control, jinxes, potions, bewitchments, death, destruction, sickness, pain, torment, psychic power, psychic warfare, prayer chains, incense and candle burning, incantations, chanting, ungodly blessings, hoodoo, crystals, root works and everything else being sent my way and [person's name]'s way. I bind all fragments, evil spirits, evil powers, strongmen and families of evil spirits within [person's name] so [he or she] can think and see clearly.

In Jesus Christ's name, I cut and burn all ungodly silver cords and ley lines. As your war club and weapon of war, I break down, undam and blow up walls of protection around all curses, hexes, vexes, spells, charms, fetishes, psychic prayers, psychic thoughts, witchcraft, sorcery, magic, voodoo, mind control, jinxes, potions, bewitchments, death, destruction, sickness, pain, torment, psychic power, psychic warfare, prayer chains, incense and candle burning, incantations, chanting, ungodly blessings, hoodoo, crystals, root works and everything else being sent my way or the way of my family members, all deliverance ministries, the [name of your church] family and [person's name]. I return it all and the demons to the sender, [name of wizard, witch or sorcerer], sevenfold and bind it to the sender by the blood of Jesus Christ. I pray this in Jesus Christ's name and through the power of Christ's blood. I thank you, Jesus, Father and Holy Spirit. Amen!

When you are practising spiritual warfare as a daily routine, you will become more of a target. To return all witchcraft curses, I pray the prayer below several times a day. Again, if you know the name of your sender, then place his or her name in the blank. If you don't know the sender's name, then pray this just the same.

> In Jesus Christ's name and through the power of the blood of Jesus Christ and the power of the Holy Spirit dwelling within me, I cut and burn all ungodly silver cords and ley lines. As your war club and weapon of war, I break down, undam and blow up walls of protection around all curses, hexes, vexes, spells, charms, fetishes, psychic prayers, psychic thoughts, witchcraft, sorcery, magic, voodoo, mind control, jinxes, potions, bewitchments, death, destruction, sickness, pain, torment, psychic powers, psychic warfare, prayer chains, incense and candle burning, incantations, chanting, ungodly blessings, hoodoo, crystals, root works and everything else being sent my way. I return it all and the demons to the sender, [name of sender], sevenfold, and I bind them to the sender by the blood of Jesus Christ. Amen!

Prayer if You Are Under a Lot of Outer Attacks from Wizards, Witches or Demons

If you know the name of the wizard or witch, then place his or her name in the space provided below. For instance, "Father, please direct these angels to destroy all of [name of wizard, witch or sorcerer]'s attempts to prevent sleep." If you know of someone who is under attack, then you can also place his or her name in: "Father, I ask you to send millions and millions of angels to directly attack the place from which these attacks against me, [person's name] and your church are originating."

> In the name of Jesus Christ and through the power of the blood of Jesus Christ and the power of the Holy Spirit dwelling in me, Father, I ask you to send millions and millions of angels to directly attack the place from which these attacks against me, [person's name] and your church are originating. Father, place direct these angels to destroy all of [name of wizard, witch or sorcerer]'s attempts to prevent sleep, control, spiritually blind, kill, steal and

destroy through curses, hexes, vexes, spells, charms, fetishes, psychic prayers, psychic thoughts, witchcraft, sorcery, magic, voodoo, mind control, jinxes, potions, bewitchments, death, destruction, sickness, pain, torment, psychic power, psychic warfare, prayer chains, incense and candle burning, incantations, chanting, ungodly blessings, hoodoo, crystals, root works and everything else that [name of wizard, witch or sorcerer] is using for these attacks against myself, [person's name] and your church. I ask that these angels will attack and confuse the demons and all other spirits that [name of wizard, witch or sorcerer] has called upon and is using for these attacks against myself, [person's name] and your church, rendering their attacks against myself, [person's name] and your church completely useless.

In Jesus Christ's name and through the power of Christ's blood and the power of the Holy Spirit dwelling in me, I set myself and my family free. I break curses, soul ties and demonic holds; I return these to the senders. I break ley lines and silver cords. I reverse weapons formed against me. If a person has deliberately spiritually attacked me, I command the demons to go back and attack the sender. The condemnation, falsehood, mischief, sleepless nights and violence shall return upon him or her sevenfold, and he or she shall fall into his or her own pit. Thank you, Father, Jesus and Holy Spirit. Amen!

Our dreams are an open playground for evil spirits. When we sleep, we cannot protect ourselves. Before you go to bed, pray according to the following steps:

1. Say, "*I plead the blood of Jesus Christ over my body, mind, spirit and soul.*" Stand in the middle of your bedroom, stretch your arm out at full length while pointing your finger and turn in a full circle as you say, "*I draw a blood line around my bedroom with the blood of Jesus Christ. I do this with faith in my words.*"

2. Say, "*I ask you, Lord God, to protect me, and I declare that I abide under the shadow of the Almighty. Under your wings shall I take my refuge.*"

3. Say, "*I declare out loud that all of the intruders are trespassers, and they are not allowed to touch me.*"

4. Say, "*I ask you, Lord God, to strengthen my spirit so I can push my intruder away with my spirit and not with my flesh.*" If you sense a spirit touching you or on top of you, then, with your physical body, use your arms and hands to push the spirit away as you say to him, "*I push you away with my spirit and not with my flesh.*" When I did this, as I was pushing the spirit, I could feel his body against the palms of my hands. By the way, soul-travellers and demons don't like this! They are there to manipulate and control you. When you push them away, you are showing them you are strong.

5. Say, "*I ask you, Lord God, for the grace not to give in to the attackers.*"

6. Say, "*In the name of my Lord, Jesus Christ of Nazareth, I take the sword of the Spirit and cut and burn all ungodly silver cords and ley lines. I close all portals into my house and bedroom by the shed blood of Christ, the Lamb of God. Amen.*" I have had soul-travellers travel into my bedroom while I slept. If the soul-traveller is inexperienced, then sometimes you can threaten to cut his or her silver cord, and the traveller might possibly leave.

In a case that you are finding it very difficult to sleep this will be families of spirits with the names, *Insomnia,* and *Sleeplessness.* You can break renounce and denounce these spirits legal rights and bind them for multiple hours at a time or cast them out of yourself. This will help to provide you your sleep.

TWENTY-EIGHT

Maintenance of Your Deliverance

First of all, I can't express strongly enough the importance of reading your Bible and praying daily. Set aside a time of day to do this, and make it a habit, preferably in the morning before your first coffee of the day. Praying and reading the Bible first thing in the morning will balance your whole day in a positive way. You will need the Word of God to overcome the temptations coming your way. Read your Bible every day.

God has given you your freedom. Now your moral and spiritual progress will depend upon the use you make of that freedom. Satan is determined to have his way with you. You have been kept captive for a long time by the bondages these families of spirits have had over you, so be prepared to go through conditions that will prove to be severe.

These evil spirits will be striking at the areas in your life that represent the names of the spirits that came out of you. You will need to resist temptation. These spirits who were once inside of you are now on the outside, and that is where you want them to stay. To overcome, you will need to depend upon the Holy Spirit and the Word of God.

Remember (James 4:7): resist the devil, and he will flee. Perhaps in your experience until now, when you tried to resist him, he did not flee, but now the spirit trying to tempt you is no longer inside of you. He has no choice but to flee.

Jesus gave us the greatest example to follow. After His baptism, Jesus was led up onto the mount. He had fasted for 40 days. That was when Satan chose to strike, as he thought Jesus would be at His weakest point. After Jesus had fasted, the Tempter thought, *Jesus will now be hungry, so I will tempt Him with food.*

Only 40 days before that, Satan had heard the Father say, "Thou art my beloved Son." The devil said to Jesus (likely with a sarcastic tone and maybe even a smirk on his face), "If thou be the Son of God, command that these stones be made bread." Now, take notice of this. Jesus answered him with the Word of God: "Man shall not live by bread alone, but by every word that proceedeth out of the mouth of God" (Matthew 4:3–4). The devil tempted Jesus two more times, and every time, Jesus answered the devil with the Word of God. This made the devil flee.

Many of these spirits have been in you for a long time. They know your weaknesses. They will go after your weakest point to try to gain their way in. When you resist these spirits and the temptation they bring at you, you will gain strength, and they will weaken in their strength.

As you become stronger, no matter what your surroundings might be, you will be able to say with great victory, "Get thee behind me, Satan: for it is written, Thou shalt worship the Lord thy God, and Him only shalt thou serve" (Luke 4:8).

You are in the midst of temptation, but as Christ on the Mount of Temptation rose above and triumphant over the devil, you too will rise over the temptations these spirits bring across your path. You too will be triumphant. This triumph will not only keep you free but also give you the peace and joy that surpass all understanding. Remember these words spoken by Christ: "Whosoever will save his life shall lose it: and whosoever will lose his life for my sake shall find it" (Matthew 16:25). Remember, all good things require our effort. You are now free. Remain free!

After the Holy Spirit assisted me in casting the last of these spirits out, He told me that from that day forward, I would be a Nazarite, set aside totally for God's use. He then gave me strict rules to follow. The consequence for not staying within these guidelines would be the evil spirits coming back in, bringing in with them seven more even worse than themselves. "This is the law of the Nazarite who hath vowed, and of his offering unto the Lord for his separation, besides that that his hand shall get: according to the vow which he vowed, so he must do after the law of his separation" (Numbers 6:21). So I became a Nazarite, set aside for God, with strict rules I was to follow to ensure my protection from these spirits reentering me. With this, I knew I could never again go back to indulging in the things that represented these spirits' names.

As the final spirit to leave me was coming out, he said, "We know your weakness. You will fall into temptation, and then we will reenter you."

The first year was difficult, but I remained strong, and I did not give in to pressure. My first deliverance was in March of 1999, and not one of those original spirits ever reentered me. In order to maintain your freedom, it is important that you do not indulge in the things that represent the names of the spirits who came out of you. Evil spirits will be watching you, waiting for you to make mistakes. They are sneaky. It is important that you never again indulge in the sins that represented the spirits that came out of you. Even with your spirits cast into the abyss, there will always be evil spirits watching, ready to enter you with one slip-up.

Again, I want to remind you of two Bible verses. The first is this:

> When the unclean spirit is gone out of a man, he walketh through dry places, seeking rest, and findeth none. Then he saith, I will return into my house from whence I came out; and when he is come, he findeth it empty, swept, and garnished. Then goeth he, and taketh with himself seven other spirits more wicked than himself, and they enter in and dwell there: and the last state of that man is worse than the first. Even so shall it be also unto this wicked generation. (Matthew 12:43–45)

The spirits you cast out of yourself need to always be immediately cast into the abyss so they cannot return to you. The second verse is this: "Afterward Jesus findeth him in the temple, and said unto him, Behold, thou art made whole: sin no more, lest a worse thing come unto thee" (John 5:14). You are delivered; you are well. Don't go back to the sin that a cast-out spirit represented, or you will give spirits of that sort freedom to enter you.

There will be in most cases lingering evil spirits that are still within the delivered person. Remember, once you have the knowledge to break evil spirits' legal rights to remain in you, then it is easy to cast spirits out of yourself. If a spirit from within should try to tempt you, you will know the spirit's name by the sin the spirit is using to make you slip up. If you are tempted to commit adultery, then say, *"Spirit of adultery, I break, renounce and denounce your legal right to stay in me."* Then, with a loud, strong and forceful voice, say, *"I command you, spirit of adultery, to come out of me now!"* Make sure you cast the spirit into the abyss, and ask the Holy Spirit to enter the empty room.

Epilogue

God's Love Letter to You

In closing this book, I intend this final chapter to be God's love letter to you, His dear child. When my children were still living at home, the last thing I would do at night before I went to bed was quietly slip into the room where they slept, get down close to them and watch them sleep. I could, in the silence of the room, hear the beats of their hearts. I could feel every breath they took. I cherished that peaceful moment with my children as a rose takes in the sweet dew on its petals. I would kiss them on their foreheads and then just as silently leave the room and make my way to my own bed.

For me, this was a moment of soft motherhood, my time of tranquility—a tenderness that could never be equalled. It was priceless. Although my childhood had left my heart badly damaged and scarred, still, there was a tender warmth I felt for my precious children.

Just think how much more God loves His little children. I have often felt in my spirit a receiving blanket wrapped around me as I was being cuddled in my Father's arms. God loves you so much more than you will ever understand—much more than you could ever love your own children or ever love Him. Not only does Jesus lift you up and carry you through the tough times, but also, God wraps you up in a baby blanket and cuddles you in His arms. We never go through our hard times alone.

Next time you are in the valley of despair, take some time to read the poem "Footprints in the Sand," and remember this: when life is at its toughest, you will never walk it alone. You can access the poem at http://s7.addthis.com/js/250/addthis_widget.js#pubid=pearls.

(Romans 5:8) tells us, "God shows his love for you in that while you were still a sinner, Christ died for you." According to (Galatians 2:20), "You have been crucified with Christ. It is no longer you who live, but it is Christ who lives in you. And the life you now live in the flesh you live by faith in the Son of God who loves you and gave himself for you."

(Jeremiah 29:11) says, "For I know the thoughts that I think toward you, saith the Lord, thoughts of peace, and not of evil." (John 13:34–35) tells us, "A new commandment I give unto you, that ye love one another: as I have loved you, that ye also love one another."

Because the meaning of its words are so sadly misunderstood, (Psalm 23) is read mainly at funerals. Yet I have found it to be one of God's most beautiful love letters to His church. His love is poured out to us in every word of this Psalm.

> "The Lord is my shepherd." This involves a one-on-one relationship—you are not just a number in the flock. After reading *Good Morning, Holy Spirit* by Benny Hinn, I took a chance on getting to know the Holy Spirit in a one-on-one relationship. I started talking with the Holy Spirit as one would talk with a friend, and He set me free in ways I never would have imagined. Just think of this: a one-on-one relationship with the Spirit of God. How exciting!

> "I shall not want." Jesus is the source of our needs. Jesus, our Shepherd, supplies the way, the truth and the life.

> "He maketh me to lie down in green pastures." The Lord blesses His children with contentment and peaceful rest.

> "He leadeth me beside the still waters." The waters are cool, peaceful and refreshing.

> "He restoreth my soul." God's provision heals and revitalizes my burdened soul. My burdened soul finds liberty.

> "He leadeth me in the paths of righteousness." Through the Holy Spirit's guidance and leadership, we follow God's will.

"For His Name sake." Christ's Name gives a higher purpose for our lives.

"Yea, though I walk through the valley of the shadow of death." Our times of testing are our lowest times. These are the times when I find myself leaning on the Father's comforting arms. When it seems you can't see the sky for the trees as you go through the darkest valley, even should you go through the death of a close family member, He is there with you.

"I will fear no evil." We are protected even in our lowest hours. There is nothing to fear. During all the attacks I had to endure while writing this book, I knew all along who my Redeemer was, and I was never afraid.

"For thou art with me." This line speaks of the continual faithfulness of our Shepherd. He never leaves us. The Holy Spirit is the Spirit of God; He dwells within us. We can't go anywhere where His Spirit is not with us.

"Thy rod and thy staff they comfort me." This line speaks of the protection God gives us against our enemies.

"Thou preparest a table before me in the presence of mine enemies." This is our assurance of God's support and our hope in times of danger.

"Thou anointest my head with oil." This line speaks of God's care for us, dedication to us and consecration. This is His anointing on us.

"My cup runneth over." This is God's abundance flowing out to you, me and other Christians.

"Surely goodness and mercy shall follow me all the days of my life." This is the blessing and power of God's grace through our faith as we remember that God is love, not just words.

"And I will dwell in the house of the Lord." This is our security and promise of eternal life in God's paradise (heaven).

"For ever." God's love and promise are now, always, forevermore and for eternity! What marvellous love He has for us!

Psalm 23

The Lord is my shepherd; I shall not want.
He maketh me to lie down in green pastures:
He leadeth me beside the still waters.
He restoreth my soul:
He leadeth me in paths of righteousness for his name's sake.
Yea, though I walk through the valley of the shadow of death,
I will fear no evil: for thou art with me;
Thy rod and thy staff they comfort me.
Thou preparest a table before me in the presence of mine enemies:
Thou anointest my head with oil; my cup runneth over.
Surely goodness and mercy shall follow me all the days of my life:
And I will dwell in the house of the Lord for ever.

As I struggled through my early days as a Christian, seeking one counsellor after another, after seeing one particular counsellor, I left his office thinking, *How on earth did you ever get your credentials?* Because of the nature of my spiritual attacks, he accused me of not being a born-again Christian.

I was being raped by a spirit, and I was searching for someone who could help me find deliverance. This counsellor accused me of wanting the rapes. Anger flared up in me as I sharply said to him, "I've been washed in the blood of Christ. I am sanctified and made new in Christ Jesus. I am baptized in the Holy Spirit of God with the evidence of speaking in tongues, and I am on my way to heaven. Since I am here in your office, it should be obvious to you that I don't want the rapes."

With that, I convinced him I was a Christian and wholeheartedly searching for help, although ultimately, there was not a thing he could do to help me. However, he did do this: as I was on my way out the door, he placed in my hand an envelope, and in it were three other envelopes, each envelope inside the last.

Written on the first envelope was "I am in Christ." The next envelope tucked inside said, "Christ is in me." The next envelope tucked inside of that one said, "Christ is in God." The final envelope read, "And I am in God." I'd never before realized that, I was tucked safely and securely inside of God. In reading those little envelopes, I knew that when I'd asked Jesus to come into my heart many years before, the Holy Spirit had entered my spiritual heart and brought me back into my first home. I was back in the heart of God, where my tiny spirit had begun.

When you accepted Jesus and the Holy Spirit of God entered you, you went back to your beginning. You were back in the heart of God. Today you are safely tucked in the Father's heart, where your little spirit began.

I've mentioned wizards, witches and Satanists making their way into Christian churches. This is not an excuse for you not to attend church. Fear comes not from God but from the devil (2 Timothy 1:7). Christians should not avoid gathering together in one accord. All Christians should attend a church that practises all the gifts of the Holy Spirit and the fivefold ministry. We are blessed when we tithe our 10 percent to God. When we don't tithe to God, we receive the opposite of a blessing. All Christians should attend church and tithe to their home churches that which is God's.

About the Author

Patricia L. Loranger is also the author of Child of Woe, Child of Sorrow. She currently lives in Ingersoll, Ontario, Canada.

Printed in the United States
By Bookmasters